Mark Twain on Religion

Mark Twain on Religion

What is Man, The War Prayer, Thou Shalt Not Kill, The Fly, Letters from the Earth

By

Mark Twain

First published 1906

Republished 2007 by Forgotten Books

www.forgottenbooks.org

DID YOU KNOW...?

You can read any and all of our _thousands_ of books online for

<u>FREE</u>

Just visit:

www.forgottenbooks.org

PUBLISHER'S PREFACE

About the Book

Mark Twain talks about his personal views on religion, the Bible and God, in these five writings.

About the Author

Mark Twain (1835 - 1910)

"Samuel Langhorne Clemens... better known by the pen name Mark Twain, was an American humorist, satirist, lecturer and writer. Twain is most noted for his novels Adventures of Huckleberry Finn, which has since been called the Great American Novel, and The Adventures of Tom Sawyer. He is also known for his quotations. During his lifetime, Clemens became a friend to presidents, artists, leading industrialists and European royalty.

Clemens enjoyed immense public popularity, and his keen wit and incisive satire earned him praise from both critics and peers. American author William Faulkner called Twain 'the father of American literature.'"

(Quote from wikipedia.org)

CONTENTS

WHAT IS MAN? AND OTHER ESSAYS OF MARK TWAIN

WHAT IS MAN?

I

a. Man the Machine. b. Personal Merit

[The Old Man and the Young Man had been conversing. The Old Man had asserted that the human being is merely a machine, and nothing more. The Young Man objected, and asked him to go into particulars and furnish his reasons for his position.]

Old Man. What are the materials of which a steam-engine is made?

Young Man. Iron, steel, brass, white-metal, and so on.

O.M. Where are these found?

Y.M. In the rocks.

O.M. In a pure state?

Y.M. No--in ores.

O.M. Are the metals suddenly deposited in the ores?

Y.M. No--it is the patient work of countless ages.

O.M. You could make the engine out of the rocks themselves?

Y.M. Yes, a brittle one and not valuable.

O.M. You would not require much, of such an engine as that?

Y.M. No--substantially nothing.

O.M. To make a fine and capable engine, how would you proceed?

Y.M. Drive tunnels and shafts into the hills; blast out the iron ore; crush it, smelt it, reduce it to pig-iron; put some of it through the Bessemer process and make steel of it. Mine and treat and combine several metals of which brass is made.

O.M. Then?

Y.M. Out of the perfected result, build the fine engine.

O.M. You would require much of this one?

Y.M. Oh, indeed yes.

O.M. It could drive lathes, drills, planers, punches, polishers, in a word all the cunning machines of a great factory?

Y.M. It could.

O.M. What could the stone engine do?

Y.M. Drive a sewing-machine, possibly--nothing more, perhaps.

O.M. Men would admire the other engine and rapturously praise it?

Y.M. Yes.

O.M. But not the stone one?

Y.M. No.

O.M. The merits of the metal machine would be far above those of the stone one?

Y.M. Of course.

O.M. Personal merits?

Y.M. PERSONAL merits? How do you mean?

O.M. It would be personally entitled to the credit of its own performance?

Y.M. The engine? Certainly not.

O.M. Why not?

Y.M. Because its performance is not personal. It is the result of the law of construction. It is not a MERIT that it does the things which it is set to do--it can't HELP doing them.

O.M. And it is not a personal demerit in the stone machine that it does so little?

Y.M. Certainly not. It does no more and no less than the law of its make permits and compels it to do. There is nothing PERSONAL about it; it cannot choose. In this process of "working up to the matter" is it your idea to work up to the proposition that man and a machine are about the same thing, and that there is no personal merit in the performance of either?

O.M. Yes--but do not be offended; I am meaning no offense. What makes the grand difference between the stone engine and the steel one? Shall we call it training, education? Shall we call the stone engine a savage and the steel one a civilized man? The original rock contained the stuff of which the steel one was built--but along with a lot of sulphur and stone and other obstructing inborn heredities, brought down from the old geologic ages--prejudices, let us call them. Prejudices which nothing within the rock itself had either POWER to remove or any DESIRE to remove. Will you take note of that phrase?

Y.M. Yes. I have written it down; "Prejudices which nothing within the rock itself had either power to remove or any desire to remove." Go on.

O.M. Prejudices must be removed by OUTSIDE INFLUENCES or not at all. Put that down.

Y.M. Very well; "Must be removed by outside influences or not at all." Go on.

O.M. The iron's prejudice against ridding itself of the cumbering rock. To make it more exact, the iron's absolute INDIFFERENCE as to whether the rock be removed or not. Then comes the OUTSIDE INFLUENCE and grinds the rock to powder and sets the ore free. The IRON in the ore is still captive. An OUTSIDE INFLUENCE smelts it free of the clogging ore. The iron is emancipated iron, now, but indifferent to further progress. An OUTSIDE INFLUENCE beguiles it into the Bessemer furnace and refines it into steel of the first quality. It is educated, now --its training is complete. And it has reached its limit. By no possible process can it be educated into GOLD. Will you set that down?

Y.M. Yes. "Everything has its limit--iron ore cannot be educated into gold."

O.M. There are gold men, and tin men, and copper men, and leaden mean, and steel men, and so on--and each has the limitations of his nature, his heredities, his training, and his environment. You can build engines out of each of these metals, and they will all perform, but you must not require the weak ones to do equal work with the strong ones. In each case, to get the best results, you must free the metal from its obstructing prejudicial ones by education--smelting, refining, and so forth.

Y.M. You have arrived at man, now?

O.M. Yes. Man the machine--man the impersonal engine. Whatsoever a man is, is due to his MAKE, and to the INFLU-ENCES brought to bear upon it by his heredities, his habitat, his associations. He is moved, directed, COMMANDED, by EXTERIOR influences--SOLELY. He ORIGINATES nothing, not even a thought.

Y.M. Oh, come! Where did I get my opinion that this which you are talking is all foolishness?

O.M. It is a quite natural opinion--indeed an inevitable opinion--but YOU did not create the materials out of which it is formed. They are odds and ends of thoughts, impressions, feelings, gathered unconsciously from a thousand books, a thousand conversations, and from streams of thought and feeling which have flowed down into your heart and brain out of the hearts and brains of centuries of ancestors. PERSONALLY you did not create even the smallest microscopic fragment of the materials out of which your opinion is made; and personally you cannot claim even the slender merit of PUTTING THE BORROWED MATERIALS TOGETHER. That was done AUTOMATICALLY--by your mental machinery, in strict accordance with the law of that machinery's construction. And you not only did not make that machinery yourself, but you have NOT EVEN ANY COMMAND OVER IT.

Y.M. This is too much. You think I could have formed no opinion but that one?

O.M. Spontaneously? No. And YOU DID NOT FORM THAT ONE; your machinery did it for you--automatically and instantly, without reflection or the need of it.

Y.M. Suppose I had reflected? How then?

O.M. Suppose you try?

Y.M. (AFTER A QUARTER OF AN HOUR.) I have reflected.

O.M. You mean you have tried to change your opinion--as an experiment?

Y.M. Yes.

O.M. With success?

Y.M. No. It remains the same; it is impossible to change it.

O.M. I am sorry, but you see, yourself, that your mind is merely a machine, nothing more. You have no command over it, it has no command over itself--it is worked SOLELY FROM THE

OUTSIDE. That is the law of its make; it is the law of all machines.

Y.M. Can't I EVER change one of these automatic opinions?

O.M. No. You can't yourself, but EXTERIOR INFLUENCES can do it.

Y.M. And exterior ones ONLY?

O.M. Yes--exterior ones only.

Y.M. That position is untenable--I may say ludicrously untenable.

O.M. What makes you think so?

Y.M. I don't merely think it, I know it. Suppose I resolve to enter upon a course of thought, and study, and reading, with the deliberate purpose of changing that opinion; and suppose I succeed. THAT is not the work of an exterior impulse, the whole of it is mine and personal; for I originated the project.

O.M. Not a shred of it. IT GREW OUT OF THIS TALK WITH ME. But for that it would not have occurred to you. No man ever originates anything. All his thoughts, all his impulses, come FROM THE OUTSIDE.

Y.M. It's an exasperating subject. The FIRST man had original thoughts, anyway; there was nobody to draw from.

O.M. It is a mistake. Adam's thoughts came to him from the outside. YOU have a fear of death. You did not invent that— you got it from outside, from talking and teaching. Adam had no fear of death--none in the world.

Y.M. Yes, he had.

O.M. When he was created?

Y.M. No.

O.M. When, then?

Y.M. When he was threatened with it.

O.M. Then it came from OUTSIDE. Adam is quite big enough; let us not try to make a god of him. NONE BUT GODS HAVE EVER HAD A THOUGHT WHICH DID NOT COME FROM THE OUTSIDE. Adam probably had a good head, but it was of no sort of use to him until it was filled up FROM THE OUTSIDE. He was not able to invent the triflingest little thing with it. He had not a shadow of a notion of the difference between good and evil--he had to get the idea FROM THE OUTSIDE. Neither he nor Eve was able to originate the idea that it was immodest to go naked; the knowledge came in with the apple FROM THE OUTSIDE. A man's brain is so constructed that IT CAN ORIGINATE NOTHING WHATSOEVER. It can only use material obtained OUTSIDE. It is merely a machine; and it works automatically, not by will-power. IT HAS NO COMMAND OVER ITSELF, ITS OWNER HAS NO COMMAND OVER IT.

Y.M. Well, never mind Adam: but certainly Shakespeare's creations--

O.M. No, you mean Shakespeare's IMITATIONS. Shakespeare created nothing. He correctly observed, and he marvelously painted. He exactly portrayed people whom GOD had created; but he created none himself. Let us spare him the slander of charging him with trying. Shakespeare could not create. HE WAS A MACHINE, AND MACHINES DO NOT CREATE.

Y.M. Where WAS his excellence, then?

O.M. In this. He was not a sewing-machine, like you and me; he was a Gobelin loom. The threads and the colors came into him FROM THE OUTSIDE; outside influences, suggestions, EXPE-RIENCES (reading, seeing plays, playing plays, borrowing ideas, and so on), framed the patterns in his mind and started up his complex and admirable machinery, and IT AUTOMATICALLY turned out that pictured and gorgeous fabric which still compels the astonishment of the world. If Shakespeare had been born and bred on a barren and unvisited rock in the ocean his mighty intellect would have had no OUTSIDE MATERIAL to work with, and could have invented none; and NO OUTSIDE INFLUENCES, teachings, moldings, persuasions, inspirations, of a valuable sort, and could have invented none; and so Shakespeare would have produced nothing. In Turkey he would have produced something--something up to the highest limit of Turkish influences, associations, and training. In France he would have produced something better--something up to the highest limit of the French influences and training. In England he rose to the highest limit attainable through the OUTSIDE HELPS AFFORDED BY THAT LAND'S IDEALS, INFLUENCES, AND TRAINING. You and I are but sewing-machines. We must turn out what we can; we must do our endeavor and care nothing at all when the unthinking reproach us for not turning out Gobelins.

Y.M. And so we are mere machines! And machines may not boast, nor feel proud of their performance, nor claim personal merit for it, nor applause and praise. It is an infamous doctrine.

O.M. It isn't a doctrine, it is merely a fact.

Y.M. I suppose, then, there is no more merit in being brave than in being a coward?

O.M. PERSONAL merit? No. A brave man does not CREATE his bravery. He is entitled to no personal credit for possessing it. It is born to him. A baby born with a billion dollars--where is the personal merit in that? A baby born with nothing--where is the personal demerit in that? The one is fawned upon, admired, worshiped, by sycophants, the other is neglected and despised-- where is the sense in it?

Y.M. Sometimes a timid man sets himself the task of conquer- ing his cowardice and becoming brave--and succeeds. What do you say to that? O.M. That it shows the value of TRAINING IN RIGHT

DIRECTIONS OVER TRAINING IN WRONG ONES. Inestimably valuable is training, influence, education, in right directions— TRAINING ONE'S SELF-APPROBATION TO ELEVATE ITS IDEALS.

Y.M. But as to merit--the personal merit of the victorious coward's project and achievement?

O.M. There isn't any. In the world's view he is a worthier man than he was before, but HE didn't achieve the change—the merit of it is not his.

Y.M. Whose, then?

O.M. His MAKE, and the influences which wrought upon it from the outside.

Y.M. His make?

O.M. To start with, he was NOT utterly and completely a coward, or the influences would have had nothing to work upon. He was not afraid of a cow, though perhaps of a bull: not afraid of a woman, but afraid of a man. There was something to build upon. There was a SEED. No seed, no plant. Did he make that seed himself, or was it born in him? It was no merit of HIS that the seed was there.

Y.M. Well, anyway, the idea of CULTIVATING it, the resolution to cultivate it, was meritorious, and he originated that.

O.M. He did nothing of the kind. It came whence ALL impulses, good or bad, come--from OUTSIDE. If that timid man had lived all his life in a community of human rabbits, had never read of brave deeds, had never heard speak of them, had never heard any one praise them nor express envy of the heroes that had done them, he would have had no more idea of bravery than Adam had of modesty, and it could never by any possibility have occurred to him to RESOLVE to become brave. He COULD NOT ORIGINATE THE IDEA--it had to come to him from the OUTSIDE. And so, when he heard bravery extolled and cowardice derided, it woke him up. He was ashamed. Perhaps his sweetheart turned up her nose and said, "I am told that you are a coward!" It was not HE that turned over the new leaf--she did it for him. HE must not strut around in the merit of it--it is not his.

Y.M. But, anyway, he reared the plant after she watered the seed.

O.M. No. OUTSIDE INFLUENCES reared it. At the command-- and trembling--he marched out into the field--with other soldiers and in the daytime, not alone and in the dark. He had the INFLUENCE OF EXAMPLE, he drew courage from his comrades' courage; he was afraid, and wanted to run, but he did not dare; he was AFRAID to run, with all those soldiers looking on. He was progressing, you see--the moral fear of shame had risen superior to the physical fear of harm. By the end of the campaign experience will have taught him that not ALL who go into battle get hurt--an outside influence which will be helpful to him; and he will also have learned how sweet it is to be praised for courage and be huzza'd at with tear-choked voices as the war-worn regiment marches past the worshiping multitude with flags flying and the drums beating. After that he will be as securely brave as any veteran in the army--and there will not be a shade nor suggestion of PERSONAL MERIT in it anywhere; it will all have come from the OUTSIDE. The Victoria Cross breeds more heroes than--

Y.M. Hang it, where is the sense in his becoming brave if he is to get no credit for it?

O.M. Your question will answer itself presently. It involves an important detail of man's make which we have not yet touched upon.

Y.M. What detail is that?

O.M. The impulse which moves a person to do things—the only impulse that ever moves a person to do a thing.

Y.M. The ONLY one! Is there but one?

O.M. That is all. There is only one.

Y.M. Well, certainly that is a strange enough doctrine. What is the sole impulse that ever moves a person to do a thing?

O.M. The impulse to CONTENT HIS OWN SPIRIT--the NECESSITY of contenting his own spirit and WINNING ITS APPROVAL.

Y.M. Oh, come, that won't do!

O.M. Why won't it?

Y.M. Because it puts him in the attitude of always looking out for his own comfort and advantage; whereas an unselfish man often does a thing solely for another person's good when it is a positive disadvantage to himself.

O.M. It is a mistake. The act must do HIM good, FIRST; otherwise he will not do it. He may THINK he is doing it solely for the other person's sake, but it is not so; he is contenting his own spirit first--the other's person's benefit has to always take SECOND place.

Y.M. What a fantastic idea! What becomes of self- sacrifice? Please answer me that.

O.M. What is self-sacrifice?

Y.M. The doing good to another person where no shadow nor suggestion of benefit to one's self can result from it.

II

Man's Sole Impulse--the Securing of His Own Approval

Old Man. There have been instances of it--you think?

Young Man. INSTANCES? Millions of them!

O.M. You have not jumped to conclusions? You have examined them--critically?

Y.M. They don't need it: the acts themselves reveal the golden impulse back of them.

O.M. For instance?

Y.M. Well, then, for instance. Take the case in the book here. The man lives three miles up-town. It is bitter cold, snowing hard, midnight. He is about to enter the horse-car when a gray and ragged old woman, a touching picture of misery, puts out her lean hand and begs for rescue from hunger and death. The man finds that he has a quarter in his pocket, but he does not hesitate: he gives it her and trudges home through the storm. There--it is noble, it is beautiful; its grace is marred by no fleck or blemish or suggestion of self-interest.

O.M. What makes you think that?

Y.M. Pray what else could I think? Do you imagine that there is some other way of looking at it?

O.M. Can you put yourself in the man's place and tell me what he felt and what he thought?

Y.M. Easily. The sight of that suffering old face pierced his generous heart with a sharp pain. He could not bear it. He could endure the three-mile walk in the storm, but he could not endure the tortures his conscience would suffer if he turned his back and left that poor old creature to perish. He would not have been able to sleep, for thinking of it.

O.M. What was his state of mind on his way home?

Y.M. It was a state of joy which only the self-sacrificer knows. His heart sang, he was unconscious of the storm.

O.M. He felt well?

Y.M. One cannot doubt it.

O.M. Very well. Now let us add up the details and see how much he got for his twenty-five cents. Let us try to find out the REAL why of his making the investment. In the first place HE couldn't bear the pain which the old suffering face gave him. So he was thinking of HIS pain--this good man. He must buy a salve for it. If he did not succor the old woman HIS conscience would torture him all the way home. Thinking of HIS pain again. He must buy relief for that. If he didn't relieve the old woman HE would not get any sleep. He must buy some sleep--still thinking of HIMSELF, you see. Thus, to sum up, he bought himself free of a sharp pain in his heart, he bought himself free of the tortures of a waiting conscience, he bought a whole night's sleep--all for twenty-five cents! It should make Wall Street ashamed of itself. On his way home his heart was joyful, and it sang--profit on top of profit! The impulse which moved the man to succor the old woman was--FIRST--to CONTENT HIS OWN SPIRIT; secondly to relieve HER sufferings. Is it your opinion that men's acts proceed from one central and unchanging and inalterable impulse, or from a variety of impulses?

Y.M. From a variety, of course--some high and fine and noble, others not. What is your opinion?

O.M. Then there is but ONE law, one source.

Y.M. That both the noblest impulses and the basest proceed from that one source?

O.M. Yes.

Y.M. Will you put that law into words?

O.M. Yes. This is the law, keep it in your mind. FROM HIS CRADLE TO HIS GRAVE A MAN NEVER DOES A SINGLE THING WHICH HAS ANY FIRST AND FOREMOST OBJECT BUT ONE--TO SECURE PEACE OF MIND, SPIRITUAL COMFORT, FOR HIMSELF.

Y.M. Come! He never does anything for any one else's comfort, spiritual or physical?

O.M. No. EXCEPT ON THOSE DISTINCT TERMS--that it shall FIRST secure HIS OWN spiritual comfort. Otherwise he will not do it.

Y.M. It will be easy to expose the falsity of that proposition.

O.M. For instance?

Y.M. Take that noble passion, love of country, patriotism. A man who loves peace and dreads pain, leaves his pleasant home and his weeping family and marches out to manfully expose himself to hunger, cold, wounds, and death. Is that seeking spiritual comfort?

O.M. He loves peace and dreads pain?

Y.M. Yes.

O.M. Then perhaps there is something that he loves MORE than he loves peace--THE APPROVAL OF HIS NEIGHBORS AND THE PUBLIC. And perhaps there is something which he dreads more than he dreads pain--the DISAPPROVAL of his neighbors and the public. If he is sensitive to shame he will go to the field--not because his spirit will be ENTIRELY comfortable there, but because it will be more comfortable there than it would be if he remained at home. He will always do the thing which will bring him the MOST mental comfort--for that is THE SOLE LAW OF HIS LIFE. He leaves the weeping family behind; he is sorry to make them uncomfortable, but not sorry enough to sacrifice his OWN comfort to secure theirs.

Y.M. Do you really believe that mere public opinion could force a timid and peaceful man to--

O.M. Go to war? Yes--public opinion can force some men to do ANYTHING.

Y.M. ANYTHING?

O.M. Yes--anything.

Y.M. I don't believe that. Can it force a right-principled man to do a wrong thing?

O.M. Yes.

Y.M. Can it force a kind man to do a cruel thing?

O.M. Yes.

Y.M. Give an instance.

O.M. Alexander Hamilton was a conspicuously high-principled man. He regarded dueling as wrong, and as opposed to the teachings of religion--but in deference to PUBLIC OPINION he fought a duel. He deeply loved his family, but to buy public approval he treacherously deserted them and threw his life away, ungenerously leaving them to lifelong sorrow in order that he might stand well with a foolish world. In the then condition of the public standards of honor he could not have been comfortable with the stigma upon him of having refused to fight. The teachings of religion, his devotion to his family, his kindness of heart, his high principles, all went for nothing when they stood in the way of his spiritual comfort. A man will do ANYTHING, no matter what it is, TO SECURE HIS SPIRITUAL COMFORT; and he can neither be forced nor persuaded to any act which has not that goal for its object. Hamilton's act was compelled by the inborn necessity of contenting his own spirit; in this it was like all the other acts of his life, and like all the acts of all men's lives. Do you see where the kernel of the matter lies? A man cannot be comfortable without HIS OWN approval. He will secure the largest share possible of that, at all costs, all sacrifices.

Y.M. A minute ago you said Hamilton fought that duel to get PUBLIC approval.

O.M. I did. By refusing to fight the duel he would have secured his family's approval and a large share of his own; but the public approval was more valuable in his eyes than all other approvals put together--in the earth or above it; to secure that would furnish him the MOST comfort of mind, the most SELF-approval; so he sacrificed all other values to get it.

Y.M. Some noble souls have refused to fight duels, and have manfully braved the public contempt.

O.M. They acted ACCORDING TO THEIR MAKE. They valued their principles and the approval of their families ABOVE the public approval. They took the thing they valued MOST and let the rest go. They took what would give them the LARGEST share of PERSONAL CONTENTMENT AND APPROVAL--a man ALWAYS does. Public opinion cannot force that kind of men to go to the wars. When they go it is for other reasons. Other spirit-contenting reasons.

Y.M. Always spirit-contenting reasons?

O.M. There are no others.

Y.M. When a man sacrifices his life to save a little child from a burning building, what do you call that?

O.M. When he does it, it is the law of HIS make. HE can't bear to see the child in that peril (a man of a different make COULD), and so he tries to save the child, and loses his life. But he has got what he was after--HIS OWN APPROVAL.

Y.M. What do you call Love, Hate, Charity, Revenge, Humanity, Magnanimity, Forgiveness?

O.M. Different results of the one Master Impulse: the necessity of securing one's self approval. They wear diverse clothes and are subject to diverse moods, but in whatsoever ways they masquerade they are the SAME PERSON all the time. To change the figure, the COMPULSION that moves a man--and there is but the one--is the necessity of securing the contentment of his own spirit. When it stops, the man is dead.

Y.M. That is foolishness. Love--

O.M. Why, love is that impulse, that law, in its most uncom-promising form. It will squander life and everything else on its object. Not PRIMARILY for the object's sake, but for ITS OWN. When its object is happy IT is happy--and that is what it is unconsciously after.

Y.M. You do not even except the lofty and gracious passion of mother-love?

O.M. No, IT is the absolute slave of that law. The mother will go naked to lothe her child; she will starve that it may have food; suffer torture to save it from pain; die that it may live. She takes a living PLEASURE in making these sacrifices. SHE DOES IT FOR THAT REWARD--that self-approval, that contentment, that peace, that comfort. SHE WOULD DO IT FOR YOUR CHILD IF SHE COULD GET THE SAME PAY.

Y.M. This is an infernal philosophy of yours.

O.M. It isn't a philosophy, it is a fact.

Y.M. Of course you must admit that there are some acts which-

O.M. No. There is NO act, large or small, fine or mean, which springs from any motive but the one--the necessity of appeasing and contenting one's own spirit.

Y.M. The world's philanthropists--

O.M. I honor them, I uncover my head to them--from habit and training; and THEY could not know comfort or happiness or self-approval if they did not work and spend for the unfortunate. It makes THEM happy to see others happy; and so with money and labor they buy what they are after--HAPPINESS, SELF-APPROVAL. Why don't miners do the same thing? Because they can get a thousandfold more happiness by NOT doing it. There is no other reason. They follow the law of their make.

Y.M. What do you say of duty for duty's sake?

O.M. That IS DOES NOT EXIST. Duties are not performed for duty's SAKE, but because their NEGLECT would make the man UNCOMFORTABLE. A man performs but ONE duty--the duty of contenting his spirit, the duty of making himself agreeable to himself. If he can most satisfyingly perform this sole and only duty by HELPING his neighbor, he will do it; if he can most satisfyingly perform it by SWINDLING his neighbor, he will do it. But he always looks out for Number One--FIRST; the effects upon others are a SECONDARY matter. Men pretend to self-sacrifices, but this is a thing which, in the ordinary value of the phrase, DOES NOT EXIST AND HAS NOT EXISTED. A man often honestly THINKS he is sacrificing himself merely and solely for some one else, but he is deceived; his bottom impulse is to content a requirement of his nature and training, and thus acquire peace for his soul.

Y.M. Apparently, then, all men, both good and bad ones, devote their lives to contenting their consciences.

O.M. Yes. That is a good enough name for it: Conscience-- that independent Sovereign, that insolent absolute Monarch inside of a man who is the man's Master. There are all kinds of consciences, because there are all kinds of men. You satisfy an assassin's conscience in one way, a philanthropist's in another, a miser's in another, a burglar's in still another. As a GUIDE or INCENTIVE to any authoritatively prescribed line of morals or conduct (leaving TRAINING out of the account), a man's conscience is totally valueless. I know a kind-hearted Kentuck-ian whose self-approval was lacking--whose conscience was troubling him, to phrase it with exactness--BECAUSE HE HAD NEGLECTED TO KILL A CERTAIN MAN--a man whom he had never seen. The stranger had killed this man's friend in a fight, this man's Kentucky training made it a duty to kill the stranger for it. He neglected his duty--kept dodging it, shirking it, putting it off, and his unrelenting conscience kept persecuting him for this conduct. At last, to get ease of mind, comfort, self-approval, he hunted up the stranger and took his life. It was an immense act of SELF- SACRIFICE (as per the usual definition), for he did not want to do it, and he never would have done it if he could have bought a contented spirit and an unworried mind at smaller cost. But we are so made that we will pay ANYTHING for that contentment--even another man's life.

Y.M. You spoke a moment ago of TRAINED consciences. You mean that we are not BORN with consciences competent to guide us aright?

O.M. If we were, children and savages would know right from wrong, and not have to be taught it.

Y.M. But consciences can be TRAINED?

O.M. Yes.

Y.M. Of course by parents, teachers, the pulpit, and books.

O.M. Yes--they do their share; they do what they can.

Y.M. And the rest is done by--

O.M. Oh, a million unnoticed influences--for good or bad: influences which work without rest during every waking moment of a man's life, from cradle to grave.

Y.M. You have tabulated these?

O.M. Many of them--yes.

Y.M. Will you read me the result?

O.M. Another time, yes. It would take an hour.

Y.M. A conscience can be trained to shun evil and prefer good?

O.M. Yes.

Y.M. But will it for spirit-contenting reasons only?

O.M. It CAN'T be trained to do a thing for any OTHER reason. The thing is impossible.

Y.M. There MUST be a genuinely and utterly self-sacrificing act recorded in human history somewhere.

O.M. You are young. You have many years before you. Search one out.

Y.M. It does seem to me that when a man sees a fellow-being struggling in the water and jumps in at the risk of his life to save him--

O.M. Wait. Describe the MAN. Describe the FELLOW-BEING. State if there is an AUDIENCE present; or if they are ALONE.

Y.M. What have these things to do with the splendid act?

O.M. Very much. Shall we suppose, as a beginning, that the two are alone, in a solitary place, at midnight?

Y.M. If you choose.

O.M. And that the fellow-being is the man's daughter?

Y.M. Well, n-no--make it someone else.

O.M. A filthy, drunken ruffian, then?

Y.M. I see. Circumstances alter cases. I suppose that if there was no audience to observe the act, the man wouldn't perform it.

O.M. But there is here and there a man who WOULD. People, for instance, like the man who lost his life trying to save the child from the fire; and the man who gave the needy old woman his twenty-five cents and walked home in the storm--there are here and there men like that who would do it. And why? Because they couldn't BEAR to see a fellow-being struggling in the water and not jump in and help. It would give THEM pain. They would save the fellow-being on that account. THEY WOULDN'T DO IT OTHERWISE. They strictly obey the law which I have been insisting upon. You must remember and always distinguish the people who CAN'T BEAR things from people who CAN. It will throw light upon a number of apparently "self-sacrificing" cases.

Y.M. Oh, dear, it's all so disgusting.

O.M. Yes. And so true.

Y.M. Come--take the good boy who does things he doesn't want to do, in order to gratify his mother.

O.M. He does seven-tenths of the act because it gratifies HIM to gratify his mother. Throw the bulk of advantage the other way and the good boy would not do the act. He MUST obey the iron law. None can escape it.

Y.M. Well, take the case of a bad boy who--

O.M. You needn't mention it, it is a waste of time. It is no matter about the bad boy's act. Whatever it was, he had a spirit-contenting reason for it. Otherwise you have been misinformed, and he didn't do it.

Y.M. It is very exasperating. A while ago you said that man's conscience is not a born judge of morals and conduct, but has to be taught and trained. Now I think a conscience can get drowsy and lazy, but I don't think it can go wrong; if you wake it up--

A Little Story

O.M. I will tell you a little story:

Once upon a time an Infidel was guest in the house of a Christian widow whose little boy was ill and near to death. The Infidel often watched by the bedside and entertained the boy with talk, and he used these opportunities to satisfy a strong longing in his nature--that desire which is in us all to better other people's condition by having them think as we think. He was successful.   But the dying boy, in his last moments, reproached him and said:

"I BELIEVED, AND WAS HAPPY IN IT; YOU HAVE TAKEN MY BELIEF AWAY, AND MY COMFORT. NOW I HAVE NOTHING LEFT, AND I DIE MISERABLE; FOR THE THINGS WHICH YOU HAVE TOLD ME DO NOT TAKE THE PLACE OF THAT WHICH I HAVE LOST."

And the mother, also, reproached the Infidel, and said:

"MY CHILD IS FOREVER LOST, AND MY HEART IS BROKEN. HOW COULD YOU DO THIS CRUEL THING? WE HAVE DONE YOU NO HARM, BUT ONLY KINDNESS; WE MADE OUR HOUSE YOUR

HOME, YOU WERE WELCOME TO ALL WE HAD, AND THIS IS OUR REWARD."

The heart of the Infidel was filled with remorse for what he had done, and he said:

"IT WAS WRONG--I SEE IT NOW; BUT I WAS ONLY TRYING TO DO HIM GOOD. IN MY VIEW HE WAS IN ERROR; IT SEEMED MY DUTY TO TEACH HIM THE TRUTH."

Then the mother said:

"I HAD TAUGHT HIM, ALL HIS LITTLE LIFE, WHAT I BELIEVED TO BE THE TRUTH, AND IN HIS BELIEVING FAITH BOTH OF US WERE HAPPY. NOW HE IS DEAD,--AND LOST; AND I AM MISERABLE. OUR FAITH CAME DOWN TO US THROUGH CENTURIES OF BELIEVING ANCESTORS; WHAT RIGHT HAD YOU, OR ANY ONE, TO DISTURB IT? WHERE WAS YOUR HONOR, WHERE WAS YOUR SHAME?"

Y.M. He was a miscreant, and deserved death!

O.M. He thought so himself, and said so.

Y.M. Ah--you see, HIS CONSCIENCE WAS AWAKENED1!

O.M. Yes, his Self-Disapproval was. It PAINED him to see the mother suffer. He was sorry he had done a thing which brought HIM pain. It did not occur to him to think of the mother when he was misteaching the boy, for he was absorbed in providing PLEASURE for himself, then. Providing it by satisfying what he believed to be a call of duty.

Y.M. Call it what you please, it is to me a case of AWAKENED CONSCIENCE. That awakened conscience could never get itself into that species of trouble again. A cure like that is a PERMANENT cure.

O.M. Pardon--I had not finished the story. We are creatures of OUTSIDE INFLUENCES--we originate NOTHING within. Whenever we take a new line of thought and drift into a new line of belief and action, the impulse is ALWAYS suggested from the OUTSIDE. Remorse so preyed upon the Infidel that it dissolved his harshness toward the boy's religion and made him come to regard it with tolerance, next with kindness, for the boy's sake and the mother's. Finally he found himself examining it. From that moment his progress in his new trend was steady and rapid. He became a believing Christian. And now his remorse for having robbed the dying boy of his faith and his salvation was bitterer than ever. It gave him no rest, no peace. He MUST have rest and peace--it is the law of nature. There seemed but one way to get it; he must devote himself to saving imperiled souls. He became a missionary. He landed in a pagan country ill and helpless. A native widow took him into her humble home and nursed him back to convalescence. Then her young boy was taken hopelessly ill, and the grateful missionary helped her tend him. Here was his first opportunity to repair a part of the wrong done to the other boy by doing a precious service for this one by undermining his foolish faith in his false gods. He was successful. But the dying boy in his last moments reproached him and said:

"I BELIEVED, AND WAS HAPPY IN IT; YOU HAVE TAKEN MY BELIEF AWAY, AND MY COMFORT. NOW I HAVE NOTHING LEFT, AND I DIE MISERABLE; FOR THE THINGS WHICH YOU HAVE TOLD ME DO NOT TAKE THE PLACE OF THAT WHICH I HAVE LOST."

And the mother, also, reproached the missionary, and said:

"MY CHILD IS FOREVER LOST, AND MY HEART IS BROKEN. HOW COULD YOU DO THIS CRUEL THING? WE HAD DONE YOU NO HARM, BUT ONLY KINDNESS; WE MADE OUR HOUSE YOUR HOME, YOU WERE WELCOME TO ALL WE HAD, AND THIS IS OUR REWARD."

The heart of the missionary was filled with remorse for what he had done, and he said:

"IT WAS WRONG--I SEE IT NOW; BUT I WAS ONLY TRYING TO DO HIM GOOD. IN MY VIEW HE WAS IN ERROR; IT SEEMED MY DUTY TO TEACH HIM THE TRUTH."

Then the mother said:

"I HAD TAUGHT HIM, ALL HIS LITTLE LIFE, WHAT I BELIEVED TO BE THE TRUTH, AND IN HIS BELIEVING FAITH BOTH OF US WERE HAPPY. NOW HE IS DEAD--AND LOST; AND I AM MISERABLE. OUR FAITH CAME DOWN TO US THROUGH CENTURIES OF BELIEVING ANCESTORS; WHAT RIGHT HAD YOU, OR ANY ONE, TO DISTURB IT? WHERE WAS YOUR HONOR, WHERE WAS YOUR SHAME?"

The missionary's anguish of remorse and sense of treachery were as bitter and persecuting and unappeasable, now, as they had been in the former case. The story is finished. What is your comment?

Y.M. The man's conscience is a fool! It was morbid. It didn't know right from wrong.

O.M. I am not sorry to hear you say that. If you grant that ONE man's conscience doesn't know right from wrong, it is an admission that there are others like it. This single admission pulls down the whole doctrine of infallibility of judgment in consciences. Meantime there is one thing which I ask you to notice.

Y.M. What is that?

O.M. That in both cases the man's ACT gave him no spiritual discomfort, and that he was quite satisfied with it and got pleasure out of it. But afterward when it resulted in PAIN to HIM, he was sorry. Sorry it had inflicted pain upon the others, BUT FOR NO REASON UNDER THE SUN EXCEPT THAT THEIR PAIN GAVE HIM PAIN. Our consciences take NO notice of pain inflicted upon others until it reaches a point where it gives pain to US. In ALL cases without exception we are absolutely indifferent to another person's pain until his sufferings make us uncomfortable. Many an infidel would not have been troubled by that Christian mother's distress. Don't you believe that?

Y.M. Yes. You might almost say it of the AVERAGE infidel, I think.

O.M. And many a missionary, sternly fortified by his sense of duty, would not have been troubled by the pagan mother's distress--Jesuit missionaries in Canada in the early French times, for instance; see episodes quoted by Parkman.

Y.M. Well, let us adjourn. Where have we arrived?

O.M. At this. That we (mankind) have ticketed ourselves with a number of qualities to which we have given misleading names. Love, Hate, Charity, Compassion, Avarice, Benevolence, and so on. I mean we attach misleading MEANINGS to the names. They are all forms of self-contentment, self-gratification, but the names so disguise them that they distract our attention from the fact. Also we have smuggled a word into the dictionary which ought not to be there at all--Self-Sacrifice. It describes a thing which does not exist. But worst of all, we ignore and never mention the Sole Impulse which dictates and compels a man's every act: the imperious necessity of securing his own approval, in every emergency and at all costs. To it we owe all that we are. It is our breath, our heart, our blood. It is our only spur, our whip, our goad, our only impelling power; we have no other. Without it we should be mere inert images, corpses; no one would do anything, there would be no progress, the world would stand still. We ought to stand reverently uncovered when the name of that stupendous power is uttered.

Y.M. I am not convinced.

O.M. You will be when you think.

III

Instances in Point

Old Man. Have you given thought to the Gospel of Self-Approval since we talked?

Young Man. I have.

O.M. It was I that moved you to it. That is to say an OUTSIDE INFLUENCE moved you to it--not one that originated in your head. Will you try to keep that in mind and not forget it?

Y.M. Yes. Why?

O.M. Because by and by in one of our talks, I wish to further impress upon you that neither you, nor I, nor any man ever originates a thought in his own head. THE UTTERER OF A THOUGHT ALWAYS UTTERS A SECOND-HAND ONE.

Y.M. Oh, now--

O.M. Wait. Reserve your remark till we get to that part of our discussion--tomorrow or next day, say. Now, then, have you been considering the proposition that no act is ever born of any but a self-contenting impulse--(primarily). You have sought. What have you found?

Y.M. I have not been very fortunate. I have examined many fine and apparently self-sacrificing deeds in romances and biographies, but--

O.M. Under searching analysis the ostensible self-sacrifice disappeared? It naturally would.

Y.M. But here in this novel is one which seems to promise. In the Adirondack woods is a wage-earner and lay preacher in the lumber-camps who is of noble character and deeply religious. An earnest and practical laborer in the New York slums comes up there on vacation--he is leader of a section of the University Settlement. Holme, the lumberman, is fired with a desire to throw away his excellent worldly prospects and go down and save souls on the East Side. He counts it happiness to make this sacrifice for the glory of God and for the cause of Christ. He resigns his place, makes the sacrifice cheerfully, and goes to the East Side and preaches Christ and Him crucified every day and every night to little groups of half-civilized foreign paupers who scoff at him. But he rejoices in the scoffings, since he is suffering them in the great cause of Christ. You have so filled my mind with suspicions that I was constantly expecting to find a hidden questionable impulse back of all this, but I am thankful to say I have failed. This man saw his duty, and for DUTY'S SAKE he sacrificed self and assumed the burden it imposed.

O.M. Is that as far as you have read?

Y.M. Yes.

O.M. Let us read further, presently. Meantime, in sacrificing himself--NOT for the glory of God, PRIMARILY, as HE imagined, but FIRST to content that exacting and inflexible master within him--DID HE SACRIFICE ANYBODY ELSE?

Y.M. How do you mean?

O.M. He relinquished a lucrative post and got mere food and lodging in place of it. Had he dependents?

Y.M. Well--yes.

O.M. In what way and to what extend did his self-sacrifice affect THEM?

Y.M. He was the support of a superannuated father. He had a young sister with a remarkable voice--he was giving her a musical education, so that her longing to be self-supporting might be gratified. He was furnishing the money to put a young brother through a polytechnic school and satisfy his desire to become a civil engineer.

O.M. The old father's comforts were now curtailed?

Y.M. Quite seriously. Yes.

O.M. The sister's music-lessens had to stop?

Y.M. Yes.

O.M. The young brother's education--well, an extinguishing blight fell upon that happy dream, and he had to go to sawing wood to support the old father, or something like that?

Y.M. It is about what happened. Yes.

O.M. What a handsome job of self-sacrificing he did do! It seems to me that he sacrificed everybody EXCEPT himself. Haven't I told you that no man EVER sacrifices himself; that there is no instance of it upon record anywhere; and that when a man's Interior Monarch requires a thing of its slave for either its MOMENTARY or its PERMANENT contentment, that thing must and will be furnished and that command obeyed, no matter who may stand in the way and suffer disaster by it? That man RUINED HIS FAMILY to please and content his Interior Monarch--

Y.M. And help Christ's cause.

O.M. Yes--SECONDLY. Not firstly. HE thought it was firstly.

Y.M. Very well, have it so, if you will. But it could be that he argued that if he saved a hundred souls in New York--

O.M. The sacrifice of the FAMILY would be justified by that great profit upon the--the--what shall we call it?

Y.M. Investment?

O.M. Hardly. How would SPECULATION do? How would GAMBLE do? Not a solitary soul-capture was sure. He played for a possible thirty-three-hundred-per-cent profit. It was

GAMBLING-- with his family for "chips." However let us see how the game came out. Maybe we can get on the track of the secret original impulse, the REAL impulse, that moved him to so nobly self- sacrifice his family in the Savior's cause under the superstition that he was sacrificing himself. I will read a chapter or so. . . . Here we have it! It was bound to expose itself sooner or later. He preached to the East-Side rabble a season, then went back to his old dull, obscure life in the lumber-camps "HURT TO THE HEART, HIS PRIDE HUMBLED." Why? Were not his efforts acceptable to the Savior, for Whom alone they were made? Dear me, that detail is LOST SIGHT OF, is not even referred to, the fact that it started out as a motive is entirely forgotten! Then what is the trouble? The authoress quite innocently and unconsciously gives the whole business away. The trouble was this: this man merely PREACHED to the poor; that is not the University Settlement's way; it deals in larger and better things than that, and it did not enthuse over that crude Salvation-Army eloquence. It was courteous to Holme--but cool. It did not pet him, did not take him to its bosom. "PERISHED WERE ALL HIS DREAMS OF DISTINCTION, THE PRAISE AND GRATEFUL APPROVAL--" Of whom? The Savior? No; the Savior is not mentioned. Of whom, then? Of "His FELLOW-WORKERS." Why did he want that? Because the Master inside of him wanted it, and would not be content without it. That emphasized sentence quoted above, reveals the secret we have been seeking, the original impulse, the REAL impulse, which moved the obscure and unappreciated Adirondack lumberman to sacrifice his family and go on that crusade to the East Side-- which said original impulse was this, to wit: without knowing it HE WENT THERE TO SHOW A NEGLECTED WORLD THE LARGE TALENT THAT WAS IN HIM, AND RISE TO DISTINCTION. As I have warned you before, NO act springs from any but the one law, the one motive. But I pray you, do not accept this law upon my say- so; but diligently examine for yourself. Whenever you read of a self-sacrificing act or hear of one, or of a duty done for DUTY'S SAKE, take it to pieces and look for the REAL motive. It is always there.

Y.M. I do it every day. I cannot help it, now that I have gotten started upon the degrading and exasperating quest. For it is hatefully interesting!--in fact, fascinating is the word. As soon as I come across a golden deed in a book I have to stop and take it apart and examine it, I cannot help myself.

O.M. Have you ever found one that defeated the rule?

Y.M. No--at least, not yet. But take the case of servant- tipping in Europe. You pay the HOTEL for service; you owe the servants NOTHING, yet you pay them besides. Doesn't that defeat it?

O.M. In what way?

Y.M. You are not OBLIGED to do it, therefore its source is compassion for their ill-paid condition, and--

O.M. Has that custom ever vexed you, annoyed you, irritated you?

Y.M. Well, yes.

O.M. Still you succumbed to it?

Y.M. Of course.

O.M. Why of course?

Y.M. Well, custom is law, in a way, and laws must be submitted to--everybody recognizes it as a DUTY.

O.M. Then you pay for the irritating tax for DUTY'S sake?

Y.M. I suppose it amounts to that.

O.M. Then the impulse which moves you to submit to the tax is not ALL compassion, charity, benevolence?

Y.M. Well--perhaps not.

O.M. Is ANY of it?

Y.M. I--perhaps I was too hasty in locating its source.

O.M. Perhaps so. In case you ignored the custom would you get prompt and effective service from the servants?

Y.M. Oh, hear yourself talk! Those European servants? Why, you wouldn't get any of all, to speak of.

O.M. Couldn't THAT work as an impulse to move you to pay the tax?

Y.M. I am not denying it.

O.M. Apparently, then, it is a case of for-duty's-sake with a little self-interest added?

Y.M. Yes, it has the look of it. But here is a point: we pay that tax knowing it to be unjust and an extortion; yet we go away with a pain at the heart if we think we have been stingy with the poor fellows; and we heartily wish we were back again, so that we could do the right thing, and MORE than the right thing, the GENEROUS thing. I think it will be difficult for you to find any thought of self in that impulse.

O.M. I wonder why you should think so. When you find service charged in the HOTEL bill does it annoy you?

Y.M. No.

O.M. Do you ever complain of the amount of it?

Y.M. No, it would not occur to me.

O.M. The EXPENSE, then, is not the annoying detail. It is a fixed charge, and you pay it cheerfully, you pay it without a murmur. When you came to pay the servants, how would you like it if each of the men and maids had a fixed charge?

Y.M. Like it? I should rejoice!

O.M. Even if the fixed tax were a shade MORE than you had been in the habit of paying in the form of tips?

Y.M. Indeed, yes!

O.M. Very well, then. As I understand it, it isn't really compassion nor yet duty that moves you to pay the tax, and it isn't the AMOUNT of the tax that annoys you. Yet SOMETHING annoys you. What is it?

Y.M. Well, the trouble is, you never know WHAT to pay, the tax varies so, all over Europe.

O.M. So you have to guess?

Y.M. There is no other way. So you go on thinking and thinking, and calculating and guessing, and consulting with other people and getting their views; and it spoils your sleep nights, and makes you distraught in the daytime, and while you are pretending to look at the sights you are only guessing and guessing and guessing all the time, and being worried and miserable.

O.M. And all about a debt which you don't owe and don't have to pay unless you want to! Strange. What is the purpose of the guessing?

Y.M. To guess out what is right to give them, and not be unfair to any of them.

O.M. It has quite a noble look--taking so much pains and using up so much valuable time in order to be just and fair to a poor servant to whom you owe nothing, but who needs money and is ill paid.

Y.M. I think, myself, that if there is any ungracious motive back of it it will be hard to find.

O.M. How do you know when you have not paid a servant fairly?

Y.M. Why, he is silent; does not thank you. Sometimes he gives you a look that makes you ashamed. You are too proud to rectify your mistake there, with people looking, but afterward you keep on wishing and wishing you HAD done it. My, the shame and the pain of it! Sometimes you see, by the signs, that you have it JUST RIGHT, and you go away mightily satisfied. Sometimes the man is so effusively thankful that you know you have given him a good deal MORE than was necessary.

O.M. NECESSARY? Necessary for what?

Y.M. To content him.

O.M. How do you feel THEN?

Y.M. Repentant.

O.M. It is my belief that you have NOT been concerning yourself in guessing out his just dues, but only in ciphering out what would CONTENT him. And I think you have a self-deluding reason for that.

Y.M. What was it?

O.M. If you fell short of what he was expecting and wanting, you would get a look which would SHAME YOU BEFORE FOLK. That would give you PAIN. YOU--for you are only working for yourself, not HIM. If you gave him too much you would be ASHAMED OF YOURSELF for it, and that would give YOU pain--another case of thinking of YOURSELF, protecting yourself, SAVING YOURSELF FROM DISCOMFORT. You never think of the servant once--except to guess out how to get HIS APPROVAL. If you get that, you get your OWN approval, and that is the sole and only thing you are after. The Master inside of you is then satisfied, contented, comfortable; there was NO OTHER thing at stake, as a matter of FIRST interest, anywhere in the transaction.

Further Instances

Y.M. Well, to think of it; Self-Sacrifice for others, the grandest thing in man, ruled out! non-existent!

O.M. Are you accusing me of saying that?

Y.M. Why, certainly.

O.M. I haven't said it.

Y.M. What did you say, then?

O.M. That no man has ever sacrificed himself in the common meaning of that phrase--which is, self-sacrifice for another ALONE. Men make daily sacrifices for others, but it is for their own sake FIRST. The act must content their own spirit FIRST. The other beneficiaries come second.

Y.M. And the same with duty for duty's sake?

O.M. Yes. No man performs a duty for mere duty's sake; the act must content his spirit FIRST. He must feel better for DOING the duty than he would for shirking it. Otherwise he will not do it.

Y.M. Take the case of the BERKELEY CASTLE.

O.M. It was a noble duty, greatly performed. Take it to pieces and examine it, if you like.

Y.M. A British troop-ship crowded with soldiers and their wives and children. She struck a rock and began to sink. There was room in the boats for the women and children only. The colonel lined up his regiment on the deck and said "it is our duty to die, that they may be saved." There was no murmur, no protest. The boats carried away the women and children. When the death-moment was come, the colonel and his officers took their several posts, the men stood at shoulder-arms, and so, as on dress-parade, with their flag flying and the drums beating, they went down, a sacrifice to duty for duty's sake. Can you view it as other than that?

O.M. It was something as fine as that, as exalted as that. Could you have remained in those ranks and gone down to your death in that unflinching way?

Y.M. Could I? No, I could not.

O.M. Think. Imagine yourself there, with that watery doom creeping higher and higher around you.

Y.M. I can imagine it. I feel all the horror of it. I could not have endured it, I could not have remained in my place. I know it.

O.M. Why?

Y.M. There is no why about it: I know myself, and I know I couldn't DO it.

O.M. But it would be your DUTY to do it.

Y.M. Yes, I know--but I couldn't.

O.M. It was more than thousand men, yet not one of them flinched. Some of them must have been born with your temperament; if they could do that great duty for duty's SAKE, why not you? Don't you know that you could go out and gather together a thousand clerks and mechanics and put them on that deck and ask them to die for duty's sake, and not two dozen of them would stay in the ranks to the end?

Y.M. Yes, I know that.

O.M. But your TRAIN them, and put them through a campaign or two; then they would be soldiers; soldiers, with a soldier's pride, a soldier's self-respect, a soldier's ideals. They would have to content a SOLDIER'S spirit then, not a clerk's, not a mechanic's. They could not content that spirit by shirking a soldier's duty, could they?

Y.M. I suppose not.

O.M. Then they would do the duty not for the DUTY'S sake, but for their OWN sake--primarily. The DUTY was JUST THE SAME, and just as imperative, when they were clerks, mechanics, raw recruits, but they wouldn't perform it for that. As clerks and mechanics they had other ideals, another spirit to satisfy, and they satisfied it. They HAD to; it is the law. TRAINING is potent. Training toward higher and higher, and ever higher ideals is worth any man's thought and labor and diligence.

Y.M. Consider the man who stands by his duty and goes to the stake rather than be recreant to it.

O.M. It is his make and his training. He has to content the spirit that is in him, though it cost him his life. Another man, just as sincerely religious, but of different temperament, will fail of that duty, though recognizing it as a duty, and grieving to be unequal to it: but he must content the spirit that is in him--he cannot help it. He could not perform that duty for duty's SAKE, for that would not content his spirit, and the contenting of his spirit must be looked to FIRST. It takes precedence of all other duties.

Y.M. Take the case of a clergyman of stainless private morals who votes for a thief for public office, on his own party's ticket, and against an honest man on the other ticket.

O.M. He has to content his spirit. He has no public morals; he has no private ones, where his party's prosperity is at stake. He will always be true to his make and training.

IV

Training

Young Man. You keep using that word--training. By it do you particularly mean--

Old Man. Study, instruction, lectures, sermons? That is a part of it--but not a large part. I mean ALL the outside influences. There are a million of them. From the cradle to the grave, during all his waking hours, the human being is under training. In the very first rank of his trainers stands ASSOCIATION. It is his human environment which influences his mind and his feelings, furnishes him his ideals, and sets him on his road and keeps him in it. If he leave that road he will find himself shunned by the people whom he most loves and esteems, and whose approval he most values. He is a chameleon; by the law of his nature he takes the color of his place of resort. The influences about him create his preferences, his aversions, his politics, his tastes, his morals, his religion. He creates none of these things for himself. He THINKS he does, but that is because he has not examined into the matter. You have seen Presbyterians?

Y.M. Many.

O.M. How did they happen to be Presbyterians and not Congregationalists? And why were the Congregationalists not Baptists, and the Baptists Roman Catholics, and the Roman Catholics Buddhists, and the Buddhists Quakers, and the Quakers Episcopalians, and the Episcopalians Millerites and the Millerites Hindus, and the Hindus Atheists, and the Atheists Spiritualists, and the Spiritualists Agnostics, and the Agnostics Methodists, and the Methodists Confucians, and the Confucians

Unitarians, and the Unitarians Mohammedans, and the Mohammedans Salvation Warriors, and the Salvation Warriors Zoroastrians, and the Zoroastrians Christian Scientists, and the Christian Scientists Mormons--and so on?

Y.M. You may answer your question yourself.

O.M. That list of sects is not a record of STUDIES, searchings, seekings after light; it mainly (and sarcastically) indicates what ASSOCIATION can do. If you know a man's nationality you can come within a split hair of guessing the complexion of his religion: English--Protestant; American-- ditto; Spaniard, Frenchman, Irishman, Italian, South American-- Roman Catholic; Russian--Greek Catholic; Turk--Mohammedan; and so on. And when you know the man's religious complexion, you know what sort of religious books he reads when he wants some more light, and what sort of books he avoids, lest by accident he get more light than he wants. In America if you know which party-collar a voter wears, you know what his associations are, and how he came by his politics, and which breed of newspaper he reads to get light, and which breed he diligently avoids, and which breed of mass-meetings he attends in order to broaden his political knowledge, and which breed of mass-meetings he doesn't attend, except to refute its doctrines with brickbats. We are always hearing of people who are around SEEKING AFTER TRUTH. I have never seen a (permanent) specimen. I think he had never lived. But I have seen several entirely sincere people who THOUGHT they were (permanent) Seekers after Truth. They sought diligently, persistently, carefully, cautiously, profoundly, with perfect honesty and nicely adjusted judgment--until they believed that without doubt or question they had found the Truth. THAT WAS THE END OF THE SEARCH. The man spent the rest of his life hunting up shingles wherewith to protect his Truth from the weather. If he was seeking after political Truth he found it in one or another of the hundred political gospels which govern men in the earth; if he was seeking after the Only True Religion he found it in one or another of the three thousand that are on the market. In any case, when he found the Truth HE SOUGHT NO FURTHER; but from that day forth, with his soldering-iron in one hand and his bludgeon in the other he tinkered its leaks and reasoned with objectors. There have been innumerable Temporary Seekers of Truth--have you ever heard of a permanent one? In the very nature of man such a person is impossible. However, to drop back to the text-- training: all training is one from or another of OUTSIDE INFLUENCE, and ASSOCIATION is the largest part of it. A man is never anything but what his outside influences have made him. They train him downward or they train him upward-- but they TRAIN him; they are at work upon him all the time.

Y.M. Then if he happen by the accidents of life to be evilly placed there is no help for him, according to your notions--he must train downward.

O.M. No help for him? No help for this chameleon? It is a mistake. It is in his chameleonship that his greatest good fortune lies. He has only to change his habitat--his ASSOCIA- TIONS. But the impulse to do it must come from the OUTSIDE-- he cannot originate it himself, with that purpose in view. Sometimes a very small and accidental thing can furnish him the initiatory impulse and start him on a new road, with a new idea. The chance remark of a sweetheart, "I hear that you are a coward," may water a seed that shall sprout and bloom and flourish, and ended in producing a surprising fruitage--in the fields of war. The history of man is full of such accidents. The accident of a broken leg brought a profane and ribald soldier under religious influences and furnished him a new ideal. From that accident sprang the Order of the Jesuits, and it has been shaking thrones, changing policies, and doing other tremendous work for two hundred years--and will go on. The chance reading of a book or of a paragraph in a newspaper can start a man on a new track and make him renounce his old associations and seek new ones that are IN SYMPATHY WITH HIS NEW IDEAL: and the result, for that man, can be an entire change of his way of life.

Y.M. Are you hinting at a scheme of procedure?

O.M. Not a new one--an old one. One as mankind.

Y.M. What is it?

O.M. Merely the laying of traps for people. Traps baited with INITIATORY IMPULSES TOWARD HIGH IDEALS. It is what the tract-distributor does. It is what the missionary does. It is what governments ought to do.

Y.M. Don't they?

O.M. In one way they do, in another they don't. They separate the smallpox patients from the healthy people, but in dealing with crime they put the healthy into the pest-house along with the sick. That is to say, they put the beginners in with the confirmed criminals. This would be well if man were naturally inclined to good, but he isn't, and so ASSOCIATION makes the beginners worse than they were when they went into captivity. It is putting a very severe punishment upon the comparatively innocent at times. They hang a man--which is a trifling punishment; this breaks the hearts of his family--which is a heavy one. They comfortably jail and feed a wife-beater, and leave his innocent wife and family to starve.

Y.M. Do you believe in the doctrine that man is equipped with an intuitive perception of good and evil?

O.M. Adam hadn't it.

Y.M. But has man acquired it since?

O.M. No. I think he has no intuitions of any kind. He gets ALL his ideas, all his impressions, from the outside. I keep repeating this, in the hope that I may impress it upon you that you will be interested to observe and examine for yourself and see whether it is true or false. Y.M. Where did you get your own aggravating notions?

O.M. From the OUTSIDE. I did not invent them. They are gathered from a thousand unknown sources. Mainly UNCONS-CIOUSLY gathered.

Y.M. Don't you believe that God could make an inherently honest man?

O.M. Yes, I know He could. I also know that He never did make one.

Y.M. A wiser observer than you has recorded the fact that "an honest man's the noblest work of God."

O.M. He didn't record a fact, he recorded a falsity. It is windy, and sounds well, but it is not true. God makes a man with honest and dishonest POSSIBILITIES in him and stops there. The man's ASSOCIATIONS develop the possibilities--the one set or the other. The result is accordingly an honest man or a dishonest one.

Y.M. And the honest one is not entitled to--

O.M. Praise? No. How often must I tell you that? HE is not the architect of his honesty.

Y.M. Now then, I will ask you where there is any sense in training people to lead virtuous lives. What is gained by it?

O.M. The man himself gets large advantages out of it, and that is the main thing--to HIM. He is not a peril to his neighbors, he is not a damage to them--and so THEY get an advantage out of his virtues. That is the main thing to THEM. It can make this life comparatively comfortable to the parties concerned; the NEGLECT of this training can make this life a constant peril and distress to the parties concerned.

Y.M. You have said that training is everything; that training is the man HIMSELF, for it makes him what he is.

O.M. I said training and ANOTHER thing. Let that other thing pass, for the moment. What were you going to say?

Y.M. We have an old servant. She has been with us twenty-two years. Her service used to be faultless, but now she has become very forgetful. We are all fond of her; we all recognize that she cannot help the infirmity which age has brought her; the rest of the family do not scold her for her remissnesses, but at times I do--I can't seem to control myself. Don't I try? I do try. Now, then, when I was ready to dress, this morning, no clean clothes had been put out. I lost my temper; I lose it easiest and quickest in the early morning. I rang; and immediately began to warn myself not to show temper, and to be careful and speak gently. I safe-guarded myself most carefully. I even chose the very word I would use: "You've forgotten the clean clothes, Jane." When she appeared in the door I opened my mouth to say that phrase--and out of it, moved by an instant surge of passion which I was not expecting and hadn't time to put under control, came the hot rebuke, "You've forgotten them again!" You say a man always does the thing which will best please his Interior Master. Whence came the impulse to make careful preparation to save the girl the humiliation of a rebuke? Did that come from the Master, who is always primarily concerned about HIMSELF?

O.M. Unquestionably. There is no other source for any impulse. SECONDARILY you made preparation to save the girl, but PRIMARILY its object was to save yourself, by contenting the Master.

Y.M. How do you mean?

O.M. Has any member of the family ever implored you to watch your temper and not fly out at the girl?

Y.M. Yes. My mother.

O.M. You love her?

Y.M. Oh, more than that!

O.M. You would always do anything in your power to please her?

Y.M. It is a delight to me to do anything to please her!

O.M. Why? YOU WOULD DO IT FOR PAY, SOLELY--for PROFIT. What profit would you expect and certainly receive from the investment?

Y.M. Personally? None. To please HER is enough.

O.M. It appears, then, that your object, primarily, WASN'T to save the girl a humiliation, but to PLEASE YOUR MOTHER. It also appears that to please your mother gives YOU a strong pleasure. Is not that the profit which you get out of the investment? Isn't that the REAL profits and FIRST profit?

Y.M. Oh, well? Go on.

O.M. In ALL transactions, the Interior Master looks to it that YOU GET THE FIRST PROFIT. Otherwise there is no transaction.

Y.M. Well, then, if I was so anxious to get that profit and so intent upon it, why did I threw it away by losing my temper?

O.M. In order to get ANOTHER profit which suddenly superseded it in value.

Y.M. Where was it?

O.M. Ambushed behind your born temperament, and waiting for a chance. Your native warm temper suddenly jumped to the front, and FOR THE MOMENT its influence was more powerful than your mother's, and abolished it. In that instance you were eager to flash out a hot rebuke and enjoy it. You did enjoy it, didn't you?

Y.M. For--for a quarter of a second. Yes--I did.

O.M. Very well, it is as I have said: the thing which will give you the MOST pleasure, the most satisfaction, in any moment or FRACTION of a moment, is the thing you will always do. You must content the Master's LATEST whim, whatever it may be.

Y.M. But when the tears came into the old servant's eyes I could have cut my hand off for what I had done.

O.M. Right. You had humiliated YOURSELF, you see, you had given yourself PAIN. Nothing is of FIRST importance to a man except results which damage HIM or profit him--all the rest is SECONDARY. Your Master was displeased with you, although you had obeyed him. He required a prompt REPENTANCE; you obeyed again; you HAD to--there is never any escape from his commands. He is a hard master and fickle; he changes his mind in the fraction of a second, but you must be ready to obey, and you will obey, ALWAYS. If he requires repentance, you content him, you will always furnish it. He must be nursed, petted, coddled, and kept contented, let the terms be what they may.

Y.M. Training! Oh, what's the use of it? Didn't I, and didn't my mother try to train me up to where I would no longer fly out at that girl?

O.M. Have you never managed to keep back a scolding?

Y.M. Oh, certainly--many times.

O.M. More times this year than last?

Y.M. Yes, a good many more.

O.M. More times last year than the year before?

Y.M. Yes.

O.M. There is a large improvement, then, in the two years?

Y.M. Yes, undoubtedly.

O.M. Then your question is answered. You see there IS use in training. Keep on. Keeping faithfully on. You are doing well.

Y.M. Will my reform reach perfection?

O.M. It will. UP to YOUR limit.

Y.M. My limit? What do you mean by that?

O.M. You remember that you said that I said training was EVERYTHING. I corrected you, and said "training and ANOTHER thing." That other thing is TEMPERAMENT--that is, the disposition you were born with. YOU CAN'T ERADICATE YOUR DISPOSITION NOR ANY RAG OF IT--you can only put a pressure on it and keep it down and quiet. You have a warm temper?

Y.M. Yes.

O.M. You will never get rid of it; but by watching it you can keep it down nearly all the time. ITS PRESENCE IS YOUR LIMIT. Your reform will never quite reach perfection, for your temper will beat you now and then, but you come near enough. You have made valuable progress and can make more. There IS use in training. Immense use. Presently you will reach a new stage of development, then your progress will be easier; will proceed on a simpler basis, anyway.

Y.M. Explain.

O.M. You keep back your scoldings now, to please YOURSELF by pleasing your MOTHER; presently the mere triumphing over your temper will delight your vanity and confer a more delicious pleasure and satisfaction upon you than even the approbation of your MOTHER confers upon you now. You will then labor for yourself directly and at FIRST HAND, not by the roundabout way through your mother. It simplifies the matter, and it also strengthens the impulse.

Y.M. Ah, dear! But I sha'n't ever reach the point where I will spare the girl for HER sake PRIMARILY, not mine?

O.M. Why--yes. In heaven.

Y.M. (AFTER A REFLECTIVE PAUSE) Temperament. Well, I see one must allow for temperament. It is a large factor, sure enough. My mother is thoughtful, and not hot-tempered. When I was dressed I went to her room; she was not there; I called, she answered from the bathroom. I heard the water running. I inquired. She answered, without temper, that Jane had forgotten her bath, and she was preparing it herself. I offered to ring, but she said, "No, don't do that; it would only distress her to be confronted with her lapse, and would be a rebuke; she doesn't deserve that--she is not to blame for the tricks her memory serves her." I say--has my mother an Interior Master?--and where was he?

O.M. He was there. There, and looking out for his own peace and pleasure and contentment. The girl's distress would have pained YOUR MOTHER. Otherwise the girl would have been rung up, distress and all. I know women who would have gotten a No. 1 PLEASURE out of ringing Jane up--and so they would infallibly have pushed the button and obeyed the law of their make and training, which are the servants of their Interior Masters. It is quite likely that a part of your mother's forbearance came from training. The GOOD kind of training--whose best and highest function is to see to it that every time it confers a satisfaction upon its pupil a benefit shall fall at second hand upon others.

Y.M. If you were going to condense into an admonition your plan for the general betterment of the race's condition, how would you word it?

Admonition

O.M. Diligently train your ideals UPWARD and STILL UPWARD toward a summit where you will find your chiefest pleasure in conduct which, while contenting you, will be sure to confer benefits upon your neighbor and the community.

Y.M. Is that a new gospel?

O.M. No.

Y.M. It has been taught before?

O.M. For ten thousand years.

Y.M. By whom?

O.M. All the great religions--all the great gospels.

Y.M. Then there is nothing new about it?

O.M. Oh yes, there is. It is candidly stated, this time. That has not been done before.

Y.M. How do you mean?

O.M. Haven't I put YOU FIRST, and your neighbor and the community AFTERWARD?

Y.M. Well, yes, that is a difference, it is true.

O.M. The difference between straight speaking and crooked; the difference between frankness and shuffling.

Y.M. Explain.

O.M. The others offer your a hundred bribes to be good, thus conceding that the Master inside of you must be conciliated and contented first, and that you will do nothing at FIRST HAND but for his sake; then they turn square around and require you to do good for OTHER'S sake CHIEFLY; and to do your duty for duty's SAKE, chiefly; and to do acts of SELF-SACRIFICE. Thus at the outset we all stand upon the same ground--recognition of the supreme and absolute Monarch that resides in man, and we all grovel before him and appeal to him; then those others dodge and shuffle, and face around and unfrankly and inconsistently and illogically change the form of their appeal and direct its persuasions to man's SECOND-PLACE powers and to powers which have NO EXISTENCE in him, thus advancing them to FIRST place; whereas in my Admonition I stick logically and consistently to the original position: I place the Interior Master's requirements FIRST, and keep them there.

Y.M. If we grant, for the sake of argument, that your scheme and the other schemes aim at and produce the same result--RIGHT LIVING--has yours an advantage over the others?

O.M. One, yes--a large one. It has no concealments, no deceptions. When a man leads a right and valuable life under it he is not deceived as to the REAL chief motive which impels him to it--in those other cases he is.

Y.M. Is that an advantage? Is it an advantage to live a lofty life for a mean reason? In the other cases he lives the lofty life under the IMPRESSION that he is living for a lofty reason. Is not that an advantage?

O.M. Perhaps so. The same advantage he might get out of thinking himself a duke, and living a duke's life and parading in ducal fuss and feathers, when he wasn't a duke at all, and could find it out if he would only examine the herald's records.

Y.M. But anyway, he is obliged to do a duke's part; he puts his hand in his pocket and does his benevolences on as big a scale as he can stand, and that benefits the community.

O.M. He could do that without being a duke.

Y.M. But would he?

O.M. Don't you see where you are arriving?

Y.M. Where?

O.M. At the standpoint of the other schemes: That it is good morals to let an ignorant duke do showy benevolences for his pride's sake, a pretty low motive, and go on doing them unwarned, lest if he were made acquainted with the actual motive which prompted them he might shut up his purse and cease to be good?

Y.M. But isn't it best to leave him in ignorance, as long as he THINKS he is doing good for others' sake?

O.M. Perhaps so. It is the position of the other schemes. They think humbug is good enough morals when the dividend on it is good deeds and handsome conduct.

Y.M. It is my opinion that under your scheme of a man's doing a good deed for his OWN sake first-off, instead of first for the GOOD DEED'S sake, no man would ever do one.

O.M. Have you committed a benevolence lately?

Y.M. Yes. This morning.

O.M. Give the particulars.

Y.M. The cabin of the old negro woman who used to nurse me when I was a child and who saved my life once at the risk of her own, was burned last night, and she came mourning this morning, and pleading for money to build another one.

O.M. You furnished it?

Y.M. Certainly.

O.M. You were glad you had the money?

Y.M. Money? I hadn't. I sold my horse.

O.M. You were glad you had the horse?

Y.M. Of course I was; for if I hadn't had the horse I should have been incapable, and my MOTHER would have captured the chance to set old Sally up.

O.M. You were cordially glad you were not caught out and incapable?

Y.M. Oh, I just was!

O.M. Now, then--

Y.M. Stop where you are! I know your whole catalog of questions, and I could answer every one of them without your wasting the time to ask them; but I will summarize the whole thing in a single remark: I did the charity knowing it was because the act would give ME a splendid pleasure, and because old Sally's moving gratitude and delight would give ME another one; and because the reflection that she would be happy now and out of her trouble would fill ME full of happiness. I did the whole thing with my eyes open and recognizing and realizing that I was looking out for MY share of the profits FIRST. Now then, I have confessed. Go on.

O.M. I haven't anything to offer; you have covered the whole ground. Can you have been any MORE strongly moved to help Sally out of her trouble--could you have done the deed any more eagerly--if you had been under the delusion that you were doing it for HER sake and profit only?

Y.M. No! Nothing in the world could have made the impulse which moved me more powerful, more masterful, more thoroughly irresistible. I played the limit!

O.M. Very well. You begin to suspect--and I claim to KNOW -- that when a man is a shade MORE STRONGLY MOVED to do ONE of two things or of two dozen things than he is to do any one of the OTHERS, he will infallibly do that ONE thing, be it good or be it evil; and if it be good, not all the beguilements of all the casuistries can increase the strength of the impulse by a single shade or add a shade to the comfort and contentment he will get out of the act.

Y.M. Then you believe that such tendency toward doing good as is in men's hearts would not be diminished by the removal of the delusion that good deeds are done primarily for the sake of No. 2 instead of for the sake of No. 1?

O.M. That is what I fully believe.

Y.M. Doesn't it somehow seem to take from the dignity of the deed?

O.M. If there is dignity in falsity, it does. It removes that.

Y.M. What is left for the moralists to do?

O.M. Teach unreservedly what he already teaches with one side of his mouth and takes back with the other: Do right FOR YOUR OWN SAKE, and be happy in knowing that your NEIGHBOR will certainly share in the benefits resulting.

Y.M. Repeat your Admonition.

O.M. DILIGENTLY TRAIN YOUR IDEALS UPWARD AND STILL UPWARD TOWARD A SUMMIT WHERE YOU WILL FIND YOUR CHIEFEST PLEASURE IN CONDUCT WHICH, WHILE CONTENTING YOU, WILL BE SURE TO CONFER BENEFITS UPON YOUR NEIGHBOR AND THE COMMUNITY.

Y.M. One's EVERY act proceeds from EXTERIOR INFLUENCES, you think?

O.M. Yes.

Y.M. If I conclude to rob a person, I am not the ORIGINATOR of the idea, but it comes in from the OUTSIDE? I see him handling money--for instance--and THAT moves me to the crime?

O.M. That, by itself? Oh, certainly not. It is merely the LATEST outside influence of a procession of preparatory influences stretching back over a period of years. No SINGLE outside influence can make a man do a thing which is at war with his training. The most it can do is to start his mind on a new tract and open it to the reception of NEW influences--as in the case of Ignatius Loyola. In time these influences can train him to a point where it will be consonant with his new character to yield to the FINAL influence and do that thing. I will put the case in a form which will make my theory clear to you, I think. Here are two ingots of virgin gold. They shall represent a couple of characters which have been refined and perfected in the virtues by years of diligent right training. Suppose you wanted to break down these strong and well-compacted characters--what influence would you bring to bear upon the ingots?

Y.M. Work it out yourself. Proceed.

O.M. Suppose I turn upon one of them a steam-jet during a long succession of hours. Will there be a result?

Y.M. None that I know of.

O.M. Why?

Y.M. A steam-jet cannot break down such a substance.

O.M. Very well. The steam is an OUTSIDE INFLUENCE, but it is ineffective because the gold TAKES NO INTEREST IN IT. The ingot remains as it was. Suppose we add to the steam some quicksilver in a vaporized condition, and turn the jet upon the ingot, will there be an instantaneous result?

Y.M. No.

O.M. The QUICKSILVER is an outside influence which gold (by its peculiar nature--say TEMPERAMENT, DISPOSITION) CANNOT BE INDIFFERENT TO. It stirs up the interest of the gold, although we do not perceive it; but a SINGLE application of the influence works no damage. Let us continue the application in a steady stream, and call each minute a year. By the end of ten or twenty minutes--ten or twenty years--the little ingot is sodden with quicksilver, its virtues are gone, its character is degraded. At last it is ready to yield to a temptation which it would have taken no notice of, ten or twenty years ago. We will apply that temptation in the form of a pressure of my finger. You note the result?

Y.M. Yes; the ingot has crumbled to sand. I understand, now. It is not the SINGLE outside influence that does the work, but only the LAST one of a long and disintegrating accumulation of them. I see, now, how my SINGLE impulse to rob the man is not the one that makes me do it, but only the LAST one of a preparatory series. You might illustrate with a parable.

A Parable

O.M. I will. There was once a pair of New England boys-- twins. They were alike in good dispositions, feckless morals, and personal appearance. They were the models of the Sunday-school. At fifteen George had the opportunity to go as cabin-boy in a whale-ship, and sailed away for the Pacific. Henry remained at home in the village. At eighteen George was a sailor before the mast, and Henry was teacher of the advanced Bible class. At twenty-two George, through fighting-habits and drinking-habits acquired at sea and in the sailor boarding-houses of the European and Oriental ports, was a common rough in Hong-Kong, and out of a job; and Henry was superintendent of the Sunday-school. At twenty-six George was a wanderer, a tramp, and Henry was pastor of the village church. Then George came home, and was Henry's guest. One evening a man passed by and turned down the lane, and Henry said, with a pathetic smile, "Without intending me a discomfort, that man is always keeping me reminded of my pinching poverty, for he carries heaps of money about him, and goes by here every evening of his life." That OUTSIDE INFLUENCE--that remark-- was enough for George, but IT was not the one that made him ambush the man and rob him, it merely represented the eleven years' accumulation of such influences, and gave birth to the act for which their long gestation had made preparation. It had never entered the head of Henry to rob the man--his ingot had been subjected to clean steam only; but George's had been subjected to vaporized quicksilver.

V

More About the Machine

Note.--When Mrs. W. asks how can a millionaire give a single dollar to colleges and museums while one human being is destitute of bread, she has answered her question herself. Her feeling for the poor shows that she has a standard of benevolence; there she has conceded the millionaire's privilege of having a standard; since she evidently requires him to adopt her standard, she is by that act requiring herself to adopt his. The human being always looks down when he is examining another person's standard; he never find one that he has to examine by looking up.

The Man-Machine Again

Young Man. You really think man is a mere machine?

Old Man. I do.

Y.M. And that his mind works automatically and is independent of his control--carries on thought on its own hook?

O.M. Yes. It is diligently at work, unceasingly at work, during every waking moment. Have you never tossed about all night, imploring, beseeching, commanding your mind to stop work and let you go to sleep?--you who perhaps imagine that your mind is your servant and must obey your orders, think what you tell it to think, and stop when you tell it to stop. When it chooses to work, there is no way to keep it still for an instant. The brightest man would not be able to supply it with subjects if he had to hunt them up. If it needed the man's help it would wait for him to give it work when he wakes in the morning.

Y.M. Maybe it does.

O.M. No, it begins right away, before the man gets wide enough awake to give it a suggestion. He may go to sleep saying, "The moment I wake I will think upon such and such a subject," but he will fail. His mind will be too quick for him; by the time he has become nearly enough awake to be half conscious, he will find that it is already at work upon another subject. Make the experiment and see.

Y.M. At any rate, he can make it stick to a subject if he wants to.

O.M. Not if it find another that suits it better. As a rule it will listen to neither a dull speaker nor a bright one. It refuses all persuasion. The dull speaker wearies it and sends it far away in idle dreams; the bright speaker throws out stimulating ideas which it goes chasing after and is at once unconscious of him and his talk. You cannot keep your mind from wandering, if it wants to; it is master, not you.

After an Interval of Days

O.M. Now, dreams--but we will examine that later. Meantime, did you try commanding your mind to wait for orders from you, and not do any thinking on its own hook?

Y.M. Yes, I commanded it to stand ready to take orders when I should wake in the morning.

O.M. Did it obey?

Y.M. No. It went to thinking of something of its own initiation, without waiting for me. Also--as you suggested--at night I appointed a theme for it to begin on in the morning, and commanded it to begin on that one and no other.

O.M. Did it obey?

Y.M. No.

O.M. How many times did you try the experiment?

Y.M. Ten.

O.M. How many successes did you score?

Y.M. Not one.

O.M. It is as I have said: the mind is independent of the man. He has no control over it; it does as it pleases. It will take up a subject in spite of him; it will stick to it in spite of him; it will throw it aside in spite of him. It is entirely independent of him.

Y.M. Go on. Illustrate.

O.M. Do you know chess?

Y.M. I learned it a week ago.

O.M. Did your mind go on playing the game all night that first night?

Y.M. Don't mention it!

O.M. It was eagerly, unsatisfiably interested; it rioted in the combinations; you implored it to drop the game and let you get some sleep?

Y.M. Yes. It wouldn't listen; it played right along. It wore me out and I got up haggard and wretched in the morning.

O.M. At some time or other you have been captivated by a ridiculous rhyme-jingle?

Y.M. Indeed, yes!

"I saw Esau kissing Kate,
And she saw I saw Esau;
I saw Esau, he saw Kate,
And she saw--"

And so on. My mind went mad with joy over it. It repeated it all day and all night for a week in spite of all I could do to stop it, and it seemed to me that I must surely go crazy.

O.M. And the new popular song?

Y.M. Oh yes! "In the Swee-eet By and By"; etc. Yes, the new popular song with the taking melody sings through one's head day and night, asleep and awake, till one is a wreck. There is no getting the mind to let it alone.

O.M. Yes, asleep as well as awake. The mind is quite independent. It is master. You have nothing to do with it. It is so apart from you that it can conduct its affairs, sing its songs, play its chess, weave its complex and ingeniously constructed dreams, while you sleep. It has no use for your help, no use for your guidance, and never uses either, whether you be asleep or awake. You have imagined that you could originate a thought in your mind, and you have sincerely believed you could do it.

Y.M. Yes, I have had that idea.

O.M. Yet you can't originate a dream-thought for it to work out, and get it accepted?

Y.M. No.

O.M. And you can't dictate its procedure after it has originated a dream-thought for itself?

Y.M. No. No one can do it. Do you think the waking mind and the dream mind are the same machine?

O.M. There is argument for it. We have wild and fantastic day-thoughts? Things that are dream-like?

Y.M. Yes--like Mr. Wells's man who invented a drug that made him invisible; and like the Arabian tales of the Thousand Nights.

O.M. And there are dreams that are rational, simple, consistent, and unfantastic?

Y.M. Yes. I have dreams that are like that. Dreams that are just like real life; dreams in which there are several persons with distinctly differentiated characters--inventions of my mind and yet strangers to me: a vulgar person; a refined one; a wise person; a fool; a cruel person; a kind and compassionate one; a quarrelsome person; a peacemaker; old persons and young; beautiful girls and homely ones. They talk in character, each preserves his own characteristics. There are vivid fights, vivid and biting insults, vivid love-passages; there are tragedies and comedies, there are griefs that go to one's heart, there are sayings and doings that make you laugh: indeed, the whole thing is exactly like real life.

O.M. Your dreaming mind originates the scheme, consistently and artistically develops it, and carries the little drama creditably through--all without help or suggestion from you?

Y.M. Yes.

O.M. It is argument that it could do the like awake without help or suggestion from you--and I think it does. It is argument that it is the same old mind in both cases, and never needs your help. I think the mind is purely a machine, a thoroughly independent machine, an automatic machine. Have you tried the other experiment which I suggested to you?

Y.M. Which one?

O.M. The one which was to determine how much influence you have over your mind--if any.

Y.M. Yes, and got more or less entertainment out of it. I did as you ordered: I placed two texts before my eyes--one a dull one and barren of interest, the other one full of interest, inflamed with it, white-hot with it. I commanded my mind to busy itself solely with the dull one.

O.M. Did it obey?

Y.M. Well, no, it didn't. It busied itself with the other one.

O.M. Did you try hard to make it obey?

Y.M. Yes, I did my honest best.

O.M. What was the text which it refused to be interested in or think about?

Y.M. It was this question: If A owes B a dollar and a half, and B owes C two and three-quarter, and C owes A thirty- five cents, and D and A together owe E and B three-sixteenths of --of--I don't remember the rest, now, but anyway it was wholly uninteresting, and I could not force my mind to stick to it even half a minute at a time; it kept flying off to the other text.

O.M. What was the other text?

Y.M. It is no matter about that.

O.M. But what was it?

Y.M. A photograph.

O.M. Your own?

Y.M. No. It was hers.

O.M. You really made an honest good test. Did you make a second trial?

Y.M. Yes. I commanded my mind to interest itself in the morning paper's report of the pork-market, and at the same time I reminded it of an experience of mine of sixteen years ago. It refused to consider the pork and gave its whole blazing interest to that ancient incident.

O.M. What was the incident?

Y.M. An armed desperado slapped my face in the presence of twenty spectators. It makes me wild and murderous every time I think of it.

O.M. Good tests, both; very good tests. Did you try my other suggestion?

Y.M. The one which was to prove to me that if I would leave my mind to its own devices it would find things to think about without any of my help, and thus convince me that it was a machine, an automatic machine, set in motion by exterior influences, and as independent of me as it could be if it were in some one else's skull. Is that the one?

O.M. Yes.

Y.M. I tried it. I was shaving. I had slept well, and my mind was very lively, even gay and frisky. It was reveling in a fantastic and joyful episode of my remote boyhood which had suddenly flashed up in my memory--moved to this by the spectacle of a yellow cat picking its way carefully along the top of the garden wall. The color of this cat brought the bygone cat before me, and I saw her walking along the side-step of the pulpit; saw her walk on to a large sheet of sticky fly-paper and get all her feet involved; saw her struggle and fall down, helpless and dissatisfied, more and more urgent, more and more unreconciled, more and more mutely profane; saw the silent congregation quivering like jelly, and the tears running down their faces. I saw it all. The sight of the tears whisked my mind to a far distant and a sadder scene--in Terra del Fuego--and with Darwin's eyes I saw a naked great savage hurl his little boy against the rocks for a trifling fault; saw the poor mother gather up her dying child and hug it to her breast and weep, uttering no word. Did my mind stop to mourn with that nude black sister of mine? No--it was far away from that scene in an instant, and was busying itself with an ever-recurring and disagreeable dream of mine. In this dream I always find myself, stripped to my shirt, cringing and dodging about in the midst of a great drawing-room throng of finely dressed ladies and gentlemen, and wondering how I got there. And so on and so on, picture after picture, incident after incident, a drifting panorama of ever-changing, ever-dissolving views manufactured by my mind without any help from me--why, it would take me two hours to merely name the multitude of things my mind tallied off and photographed in fifteen minutes, let alone describe them to you.

O.M. A man's mind, left free, has no use for his help. But there is one way whereby he can get its help when he desires it.

Y.M. What is that way?

O.M. When your mind is racing along from subject to subject and strikes an inspiring one, open your mouth and begin talking upon that matter--or--take your pen and use that. It will interest your mind and concentrate it, and it will pursue the subject with satisfaction. It will take full charge, and furnish the words itself.

Y.M. But don't I tell it what to say?

O.M. There are certainly occasions when you haven't time. The words leap out before you know what is coming.

Y.M. For instance?

O.M. Well, take a "flash of wit"--repartee. Flash is the right word. It is out instantly. There is no time to arrange the words. There is no thinking, no reflecting. Where there is a wit-mechanism it is automatic in its action and needs no help. Where the whit-mechanism is lacking, no amount of study and reflection can manufacture the product.

Y.M. You really think a man originates nothing, creates nothing.

The Thinking-Process

O.M. I do. Men perceive, and their brain-machines automatically combine the things perceived. That is all.

Y.M. The steam-engine?

O.M. It takes fifty men a hundred years to invent it. One meaning of invent is discover. I use the word in that sense. Little by little they discover and apply the multitude of details that go to make the perfect engine. Watt noticed that confined steam was strong enough to lift the lid of the teapot. He didn't create the idea, he merely discovered the fact; the cat had noticed it a hundred times. From the teapot he evolved the cylinder--from the displaced lid he evolved the piston-rod. To attach something to the piston-rod to be moved by it, was a simple matter--crank and wheel. And so there was a working engine. [1]

One by one, improvements were discovered by men who used their eyes, not their creating powers--for they hadn't any--and now, after a hundred years the patient contributions of fifty or a hundred observers stand compacted in the wonderful machine which drives the ocean liner.

Y.M. A Shakespearean play?

O.M. The process is the same. The first actor was a savage. He reproduced in his theatrical war-dances, scalp- dances, and so on, incidents which he had seen in real life. A more advanced civilization produced more incidents, more episodes; the actor and the story-teller borrowed them. And so the drama grew, little by little, stage by stage. It is made up of the facts of life, not creations. It took centuries to develop the Greek drama. It borrowed from preceding ages; it lent to the ages that came after. Men observe and combine, that is all. So does a rat.

Y.M. How?

O.M. He observes a smell, he infers a cheese, he seeks and finds. The astronomer observes this and that; adds his this and that to the this-and-thats of a hundred predecessors, infers an invisible planet, seeks it and finds it. The rat gets into a trap; gets out with trouble; infers that cheese in traps lacks value, and meddles with that trap no more. The astronomer is very proud of his achievement, the rat is proud of his. Yet both are machines; they have done machine work, they have originated nothing, they have no right to be vain; the whole credit belongs to their Maker. They are entitled to no honors, no praises, no monuments when they die, no remembrance. One is a complex and elaborate machine, the other a simple and limited machine, but they are alike in principle, function, and process, and neither of them works otherwise than automatically, and neither of them may righteously claim a PERSONAL superiority or a personal dignity above the other.

Y.M. In earned personal dignity, then, and in personal merit for what he does, it follows of necessity that he is on the same level as a rat?

O.M. His brother the rat; yes, that is how it seems to me. Neither of them being entitled to any personal merit for what he does, it follows of necessity that neither of them has a right to arrogate to himself (personally created) superiorities over his brother.

Y.M. Are you determined to go on believing in these insanities? Would you go on believing in them in the face of able arguments backed by collated facts and instances?

O.M. I have been a humble, earnest, and sincere Truth-Seeker.

Y.M. Very well?

O.M. The humble, earnest, and sincere Truth-Seeker is always convertible by such means.

Y.M. I am thankful to God to hear you say this, for now I know that your conversion--

O.M. Wait. You misunderstand. I said I have BEEN a Truth-Seeker.

Y.M. Well?

O.M. I am not that now. Have your forgotten? I told you that there are none but temporary Truth-Seekers; that a permanent one is a human impossibility; that as soon as the Seeker finds what he is thoroughly convinced is the Truth, he seeks no further, but gives the rest of his days to hunting junk to patch it and caulk it and prop it with, and make it weather-proof and keep it from caving in on him. Hence the Presbyterian remains a Presbyterian, the Mohammedan a Mohammedan, the Spiritualist a Spiritualist, the Democrat a Democrat, the Republican a Republican, the Monarchist a Monarchist; and if a humble, earnest, and sincere Seeker after Truth should find it in the proposition that the moon is made of green cheese nothing could ever budge him from that position; for he is nothing but an automatic machine, and must obey the laws of his construction.

Y.M. After so--

O.M. Having found the Truth; perceiving that beyond question man has but one moving impulse--the contenting of his own spirit-- and is merely a machine and entitled to no personal merit for anything he does, it is not humanly possible for me to seek further. The rest of my days will be spent in patching and painting and puttying and caulking my priceless possession and in looking the other way when an imploring argument or a damaging fact approaches.

1. The Marquess of Worcester had done all of this more than a century earlier.

VI

Instinct and Thought

Young Man. It is odious. Those drunken theories of yours, advanced a while ago--concerning the rat and all that--strip Man bare of all his dignities, grandeurs, sublimities.

Old Man. He hasn't any to strip--they are shams, stolen clothes. He claims credits which belong solely to his Maker.

Y.M. But you have no right to put him on a level with a rat.

O.M. I don't--morally. That would not be fair to the rat. The rat is well above him, there.

Y.M. Are you joking?

O.M. No, I am not.

Y.M. Then what do you mean?

O.M. That comes under the head of the Moral Sense. It is a large question. Let us finish with what we are about now, before we take it up.

Y.M. Very well. You have seemed to concede that you place Man and the rat on A level. What is it? The intellectual?

O.M. In form--not a degree.

Y.M. Explain.

O.M. I think that the rat's mind and the man's mind are the same machine, but of unequal capacities--like yours and Edison's; like the African pygmy's and Homer's; like the Bushman's and Bismarck's.

Y.M. How are you going to make that out, when the lower animals have no mental quality but instinct, while man possesses reason?

O.M. What is instinct?

Y.M. It is merely unthinking and mechanical exercise of inherited habit.

O.M. What originated the habit?

Y.M. The first animal started it, its descendants have inherited it.

O.M. How did the first one come to start it?

Y.M. I don't know; but it didn't THINK it out.

O.M. How do you know it didn't?

Y.M. Well--I have a right to suppose it didn't, anyway.

O.M. I don't believe you have. What is thought?

Y.M. I know what you call it: the mechanical and automatic putting together of impressions received from outside, and drawing an inference from them.

O.M. Very good. Now my idea of the meaningless term "instinct" is, that it is merely PETRIFIED THOUGHT; solidified and made inanimate by habit; thought which was once alive and awake, but it become unconscious--walks in its sleep, so to speak.

Y.M. Illustrate it.

O.M. Take a herd of cows, feeding in a pasture. Their heads are all turned in one direction. They do that instinctively; they gain nothing by it, they have no reason for it, they don't know why they do it. It is an inherited habit which was originally thought-- that is to say, observation of an exterior fact, and a valuable inference drawn from that observation and confirmed by experience. The original wild ox noticed that with the wind in his favor he could smell his enemy in time to escape; then he inferred that it was worth while to keep his nose to the wind. That is the process which man calls reasoning. Man's thought-machine works just like the other animals', but it is a better one and more Edisonian. Man, in the ox's place, would go further, reason wider: he would face part of the herd the other way and protect both front and rear.

Y.M. Did you stay the term instinct is meaningless?

O.M. I think it is a bastard word. I think it confuses us; for as a rule it applies itself to habits and impulses which had a far-off origin in thought, and now and then breaks the rule and applies itself to habits which can hardly claim a thought-origin.

Y.M. Give an instance.

O.M. Well, in putting on trousers a man always inserts the same old leg first--never the other one. There is no advantage in that, and no sense in it. All men do it, yet no man thought it out and adopted it of set purpose, I imagine. But it is a habit which is transmitted, no doubt, and will continue to be transmitted.

Y.M. Can you prove that the habit exists?

O.M. You can prove it, if you doubt. If you will take a man to a clothing-store and watch him try on a dozen pairs of trousers, you will see.

Y.M. The cow illustration is not--

O.M. Sufficient to show that a dumb animal's mental machine is just the same as a man's and its reasoning processes the same? I will illustrate further. If you should hand Mr. Edison a box which you caused to fly open by some concealed device he would infer a spring, and would hunt for it and find it. Now an uncle of mine had an old horse who used to get into the closed lot where the corn-crib was and dishonestly take the corn. I got the punishment myself, as it was supposed that I had heedlessly failed to insert the wooden pin which kept the gate closed. These persistent punishments fatigued me; they also caused me to infer the existence of a culprit, somewhere; so I hid myself and watched the gate. Presently the horse came and pulled the pin out with his teeth and went in. Nobody taught him that; he had observed--then thought it out for himself. His process did not differ from Edison's; he put this and that together and drew an inference--and the peg, too; but I made him sweat for it.

Y.M. It has something of the seeming of thought about it. Still it is not very elaborate. Enlarge.

O.M. Suppose Mr. Edison has been enjoying some one's hospitalities. He comes again by and by, and the house is vacant. He infers that his host has moved. A while afterward, in another town, he sees the man enter a house; he infers that that is the new home, and follows to inquire. Here, now, is the experience of a gull, as related by a naturalist. The scene is a Scotch fishing village where the gulls were kindly treated. This particular gull visited a cottage; was fed; came next day and was fed again; came into the house, next time, and ate with the family; kept on doing this almost daily, thereafter. But, once the gull was away on a journey for a few days, and when it returned the house was vacant. Its friends had removed to a village three miles distant. Several months later it saw the head of the family on the street there, followed him home, entered the house without excuse or apology, and became a daily guest again. Gulls do not rank high mentally, but this one had memory and the reasoning faculty, you see, and applied them Edisonially.

Y.M. Yet it was not an Edison and couldn't be developed into one.

O.M. Perhaps not. Could you?

Y.M. That is neither here nor there. Go on.

O.M. If Edison were in trouble and a stranger helped him out of it and next day he got into the same difficulty again, he would infer the wise thing to do in case he knew the stranger's address. Here is a case of a bird and a stranger as related by a naturalist. An Englishman saw a bird flying around about his dog's head, down in the grounds, and uttering cries of distress. He went there to see about it. The dog had a young bird in his mouth--unhurt. The gentleman rescued it and put it on a bush and brought the dog away. Early the next morning the mother bird came for the gentleman, who was sitting on his veranda, and by its maneuvers persuaded him to follow it to a distant part of the grounds--flying a little way in front of him and waiting for him to catch up, and so on; and keeping to the winding path, too, instead of flying the near way across lots. The distance covered was four hundred yards. The same dog was the culprit; he had the young bird again, and once more he had to give it up. Now the mother bird had reasoned it all out:

since the stranger had helped her once, she inferred that he would do it again; she knew where to find him, and she went upon her errand with confidence. Her mental processes were what Edison's would have been. She put this and that together--and that is all that thought IS--and out of them built her logical arrangement of inferences. Edison couldn't have done it any better himself.

Y.M. Do you believe that many of the dumb animals can think?

O.M. Yes--the elephant, the monkey, the horse, the dog, the parrot, the macaw, the mocking-bird, and many others. The elephant whose mate fell into a pit, and who dumped dirt and rubbish into the pit till bottom was raised high enough to enable the captive to step out, was equipped with the reasoning quality. I conceive that all animals that can learn things through teaching and drilling have to know how to observe, and put this and that together and draw an inference--the process of thinking. Could you teach an idiot of manuals of arms, and to advance, retreat, and go through complex field maneuvers at the word of command?

Y.M. Not if he were a thorough idiot.

O.M. Well, canary-birds can learn all that; dogs and elephants learn all sorts of wonderful things. They must surely be able to notice, and to put things together, and say to themselves, "I get the idea, now: when I do so and so, as per order, I am praised and fed; when I do differently I am punished." Fleas can be taught nearly anything that a Congressman can.

Y.M. Granting, then, that dumb animals are able to think upon a low plane, is there any that can think upon a high one? Is there one that is well up toward man?

O.M. Yes. As a thinker and planner the ant is the equal of any savage race of men; as a self-educated specialist in several arts she is the superior of any savage race of men; and in one or two high mental qualities she is above the reach of any man, savage or civilized!

Y.M. Oh, come! you are abolishing the intellectual frontier which separates man and beast.

O.M. I beg your pardon. One cannot abolish what does not exist.

Y.M. You are not in earnest, I hope. You cannot mean to seriously say there is no such frontier.

O.M. I do say it seriously. The instances of the horse, the gull, the mother bird, and the elephant show that those creatures put their this's and thats together just as Edison would have done it and drew the same inferences that he would have drawn. Their mental machinery was just like his, also its manner of working. Their equipment was as inferior to the Strasburg clock, but that is the only difference--there is no frontier.

Y.M. It looks exasperatingly true; and is distinctly offensive. It elevates the dumb beasts to--to--

O.M. Let us drop that lying phrase, and call them the Unrevealed Creatures; so far as we can know, there is no such thing as a dumb beast.

Y.M. On what grounds do you make that assertion?

O.M. On quite simple ones. "Dumb" beast suggests an animal that has no thought-machinery, no understanding, no speech, no way of communicating what is in its mind. We know that a hen HAS speech. We cannot understand everything she says, but we easily learn two or three of her phrases. We know when she is saying, "I have laid an egg"; we know when she is saying to the chicks, "Run here, dears, I've found a worm"; we know what she is saying when she voices a warning: "Quick! hurry! gather yourselves under mamma, there's a hawk coming!" We understand the cat when she stretches herself out, purring with affection and contentment and lifts up a soft voice and says, "Come, kitties, supper's ready"; we understand her when she goes mourning about and says, "Where can they be? They are lost. Won't you help me hunt for them?" and we understand the disreputable Tom when he challenges at midnight from his shed, "You come over here, you product of immoral commerce, and I'll make your fur fly!" We understand a few of a dog's phrases and we learn to understand a few of the remarks and gestures of any bird or other animal that we domesticate and observe. The clearness and exactness of the few of the hen's speeches which we understand is argument that she can communicate to her kind a hundred things which we cannot comprehend--in a word, that she can converse. And this argument is also applicable in the case of others of the great army of the Unrevealed. It is just like man's vanity and impertinence to call an animal dumb because it is dumb to his dull perceptions. Now as to the ant--

Y.M. Yes, go back to the ant, the creature that--as you seem to think--sweeps away the last vestige of an intellectual frontier between man and the Unrevealed.

O.M. That is what she surely does. In all his history the aboriginal Australian never thought out a house for himself and built it. The ant is an amazing architect. She is a wee little creature, but she builds a strong and enduring house eight feet high--a house which is as large in proportion to her size as is the largest capitol or cathedral in the world compared to man's size. No savage race has produced architects who could approach the air in genius or culture. No civilized race has produced architects who could plan a house better for the uses proposed than can hers. Her house contains a throne-room; nurseries for her young; granaries; apartments for her soldiers, her workers, etc.; and they and the multifarious halls and corridors which communicate with them are arranged and distributed with an educated and experienced eye for convenience and adaptability.

Y.M. That could be mere instinct.

O.M. It would elevate the savage if he had it. But let us look further before we decide. The ant has soldiers--battalions, regiments, armies; and they have their appointed captains and generals, who lead them to battle.

Y.M. That could be instinct, too.

O.M. We will look still further. The ant has a system of government; it is well planned, elaborate, and is well carried on.

Y.M. Instinct again.

O.M. She has crowds of slaves, and is a hard and unjust employer of forced labor.

Y.M. Instinct.

O.M. She has cows, and milks them.

Y.M. Instinct, of course.

O.M. In Texas she lays out a farm twelve feet square, plants it, weeds it, cultivates it, gathers the crop and stores it away.

Y.M. Instinct, all the same.

O.M. The ant discriminates between friend and stranger. Sir John Lubbock took ants from two different nests, made them drunk with whiskey and laid them, unconscious, by one of the nests, near some water. Ants from the nest came and examined and discussed these disgraced creatures, then carried their friends home and threw the strangers overboard. Sir John repeated the experiment a number of times. For a time the sober ants did as they had done at first--carried their friends home and threw the strangers overboard. But finally they lost patience, seeing that their reformatory efforts went for nothing, and threw both friends and strangers overboard. Come--is this instinct, or is it thoughtful and intelligent discussion of a thing new-- absolutely new--to their experience; with a verdict arrived at, sentence passed, and judgment executed? Is it instinct?--thought petrified by ages of habit--or isn't it brand-new thought, inspired by the new occasion, the new circumstances?

Y.M. I have to concede it. It was not a result of habit; it has all the look of reflection, thought, putting this and that together, as you phrase it. I believe it was thought.

O.M. I will give you another instance of thought. Franklin had a cup of sugar on a table in his room. The ants got at it. He tried several preventives; and ants rose superior to them. Finally he contrived one which shut off access--probably set the table's legs in pans of water, or drew a circle of tar around the cup, I don't remember. At any rate, he watched to see what they would do. They tried various schemes--failures, every one. The ants were badly puzzled. Finally they held a consultation, discussed the problem, arrived at a decision--and this time they beat that great philosopher. They formed in procession, cross the floor, climbed the wall, marched across the ceiling to a point just over the cup, then one by one they let go and fell down into it! Was that instinct--thought petrified by ages of inherited habit?

Y.M. No, I don't believe it was. I believe it was a newly reasoned scheme to meet a new emergency.

O.M. Very well. You have conceded the reasoning power in two instances. I come now to a mental detail wherein the ant is a long way the superior of any human being. Sir John Lubbock proved by many experiments that an ant knows a stranger ant of her own species in a moment, even when the stranger is disguised --with paint. Also he proved that an ant knows every individual in her hive of five hundred thousand souls. Also, after a year's absence one of the five hundred thousand she will straightway recognize the returned absentee and grace the recognition with a affectionate welcome. How are these recognitions made? Not by color, for painted ants were recognized. Not by smell, for ants that had been dipped in chloroform were recognized. Not by speech and not by antennae signs nor contacts, for the drunken and motionless ants were recognized and the friend discriminated from the stranger. The ants were all of the same species, therefore the friends had to be recognized by form and feature-- friends who formed part of a hive of five hundred thousand! Has any man a memory for form and feature approaching that?

Y.M. Certainly not.

O.M. Franklin's ants and Lubbuck's ants show fine capacities of putting this and that together in new and untried emergencies and deducting smart conclusions from the combinations--a man's mental process exactly. With memory to help, man preserves his observations and reasonings, reflects upon them, adds to them, recombines, and so proceeds, stage by stage, to far results--from the teakettle to the ocean greyhound's complex engine; from personal labor to slave labor; from wigwam to palace; from the capricious chase to agriculture and stored food; from nomadic life to stable government and concentrated authority; from incoherent hordes to massed armies. The ant has observation, the reasoning faculty, and the preserving adjunct of a prodigious memory; she has duplicated man's development and the essential features of his civilization, and you call it all instinct!

Y.M. Perhaps I lacked the reasoning faculty myself.

O.M. Well, don't tell anybody, and don't do it again.

Y.M. We have come a good way. As a result--as I understand it-- I am required to concede that there is absolutely no intellectual frontier separating Man and the Unrevealed Creatures?

O.M. That is what you are required to concede. There is no such frontier--there is no way to get around that. Man has a finer and more capable machine in him than those others, but it is the same machine and works in the same way. And neither he nor those others can command the machine--it is strictly automatic, independent of control, works when it pleases, and when it doesn't please, it can't be forced.

Y.M. Then man and the other animals are all alike, as to mental machinery, and there isn't any difference of any stupendous magnitude between them, except in quality, not in kind.

O.M. That is about the state of it--intellectuality. There are pronounced limitations on both sides. We can't learn to understand much of their language, but the dog, the elephant, etc., learn to understand a very great deal of ours. To that extent they are our superiors. On the other hand, they can't learn reading, writing, etc., nor any of our fine and high things, and there we have a large advantage over them.

Y.M. Very well, let them have what they've got, and welcome; there is still a wall, and a lofty one. They haven't got the Moral Sense; we have it, and it lifts us immeasurably above them.

O.M. What makes you think that?

Y.M. Now look here--let's call a halt. I have stood the other infamies and insanities and that is enough; I am not going to have man and the other animals put on the same level morally.

O.M. I wasn't going to hoist man up to that.

Y.M. This is too much! I think it is not right to jest about such things.

O.M. I am not jesting, I am merely reflecting a plain and simple truth--and without uncharitableness. The fact that man knows right from wrong proves his INTELLECTUAL superiority to the other creatures; but the fact that he can DO wrong proves his MORAL inferiority to any creature that CANNOT. It is my belief that this position is not assailable.

Free Will

Y.M. What is your opinion regarding Free Will?

O.M. That there is no such thing. Did the man possess it who gave the old woman his last shilling and trudged home in the storm?

Y.M. He had the choice between succoring the old woman and leaving her to suffer. Isn't it so?

O.M. Yes, there was a choice to be made, between bodily comfort on the one hand and the comfort of the spirit on the other. The body made a strong appeal, of course--the body would be quite sure to do that; the spirit made a counter appeal. A choice had to be made between the two appeals, and was made. Who or what determined that choice?

Y.M. Any one but you would say that the man determined it, and that in doing it he exercised Free Will.

O.M. We are constantly assured that every man is endowed with Free Will, and that he can and must exercise it where he is offered a choice between good conduct and less-good conduct. Yet we clearly saw that in that man's case he really had no Free Will: his temperament, his training, and the daily influences which had molded him and made him what he was, COMPELLED him to rescue the old woman and thus save HIMSELF--save himself from spiritual pain, from unendurable wretchedness. He did not make the choice, it was made FOR him by forces which he could not control. Free Will has always existed in WORDS, but it stops there, I think--stops short of FACT. I would not use those words--Free Will--but others.

Y.M. What others?

O.M. Free Choice.

Y.M. What is the difference?

O.M. The one implies untrammeled power to ACT as you please, the other implies nothing beyond a mere MENTAL PROCESS: the critical ability to determine which of two things is nearest right and just.

Y.M. Make the difference clear, please.

O.M. The mind can freely SELECT, CHOOSE, POINT OUT the right and just one--its function stops there. It can go no further in the matter. It has no authority to say that the right one shall be acted upon and the wrong one discarded. That authority is in other hands.

Y.M. The man's?

O.M. In the machine which stands for him. In his born disposition and the character which has been built around it by training and environment.

Y.M. It will act upon the right one of the two?

O.M. It will do as it pleases in the matter. George Washington's machine would act upon the right one; Pizarro would act upon the wrong one.

Y.M. Then as I understand it a bad man's mental machinery calmly and judicially points out which of two things is right and just--

O.M. Yes, and his MORAL machinery will freely act upon the other or the other, according to its make, and be quite indifferent to the MIND'S feeling concerning the matter--that is, WOULD be, if the mind had any feelings; which it hasn't. It is merely a thermometer: it registers the heat and the cold, and cares not a farthing about either.

Y.M. Then we must not claim that if a man KNOWS which of two things is right he is absolutely BOUND to do that thing?

O.M. His temperament and training will decide what he shall do, and he will do it; he cannot help himself, he has no authority over the mater. Wasn't it right for David to go out and slay Goliath?

Y.M. Yes.

O.M. Then it would have been equally RIGHT for any one else to do it?

Y.M. Certainly.

O.M. Then it would have been RIGHT for a born coward to attempt it?

Y.M. It would--yes.

O.M. You know that no born coward ever would have attempted it, don't you?

Y.M. Yes.

O.M. You know that a born coward's make and temperament would be an absolute and insurmountable bar to his ever essaying such a thing, don't you?

Y.M. Yes, I know it.

O.M. He clearly perceives that it would be RIGHT to try it?

Y.M. Yes.

O.M. His mind has Free Choice in determining that it would be RIGHT to try it?

Y.M. Yes.

O.M. Then if by reason of his inborn cowardice he simply can NOT essay it, what becomes of his Free Will? Where is his Free Will? Why claim that he has Free Will when the plain facts show that he hasn't? Why content that because he and David SEE the right alike, both must ACT alike? Why impose the same laws upon goat and lion?

Y.M. There is really no such thing as Free Will?

O.M. It is what I think. There is WILL. But it has nothing to do with INTELLECTUAL PERCEPTIONS OF RIGHT AND WRONG, and is not under their command. David's temperament and training had Will, and it was a compulsory force; David had to obey its decrees, he had no choice. The coward's temperament and training possess Will, and IT is compulsory; it commands him to avoid danger, and he obeys, he has no choice. But neither the Davids nor the cowards possess Free Will--will that may do the right or do the wrong, as their MENTAL verdict shall decide.

Not Two Values, But Only One

Y.M. There is one thing which bothers me: I can't tell where you draw the line between MATERIAL covetousness and SPIRITUAL covetousness.

O.M. I don't draw any.

Y.M. How do you mean?

O.M. There is no such thing as MATERIAL covetousness. All covetousness is spiritual

Y.M. ALL longings, desires, ambitions SPIRITUAL, never material?

O.M. Yes. The Master in you requires that in ALL cases you shall content his SPIRIT--that alone. He never requires anything else, he never interests himself in any other matter.

Y.M. Ah, come! When he covets somebody's money--isn't that rather distinctly material and gross?

O.M. No. The money is merely a symbol--it represents in visible and concrete form a SPIRITUAL DESIRE. Any so-called material thing that you want is merely a symbol: you want it not for ITSELF, but because it will content your spirit for the moment.

Y.M. Please particularize.

O.M. Very well. Maybe the thing longed for is a new hat. You get it and your vanity is pleased, your spirit contented. Suppose your friends deride the hat, make fun of it: at once it loses its value; you are ashamed of it, you put it out of your sight, you never want to see it again.

Y.M. I think I see. Go on.

O.M. It is the same hat, isn't it? It is in no way altered. But it wasn't the HAT you wanted, but only what it stood for--a something to please and content your SPIRIT. When it failed of that, the whole of its value was gone. There are no MATERIAL values; there are only spiritual ones. You will hunt in vain for a material value that is ACTUAL, REAL--there is no such thing. The only value it possesses, for even a moment, is the spiritual value back of it: remove that end and it is at once worthless--like the hat.

Y.M. Can you extend that to money?

O.M. Yes. It is merely a symbol, it has no MATERIAL value; you think you desire it for its own sake, but it is not so. You desire it for the spiritual content it will bring; if it fail of that, you discover that its value is gone. There is that pathetic tale of the man who labored like a slave, unresting, unsatisfied, until he had accumulated a fortune, and was happy over it, jubilant about it; then in a single week a pestilence swept away all whom he held dear and left him desolate. His money's value was gone. He realized that his joy in it came not from the money itself, but from the spiritual contentment he got out of his family's enjoyment of the pleasures and delights it lavished upon them. Money has no MATERIAL value; if you remove its spiritual value nothing is left but dross. It is so with all things, little or big, majestic or trivial--there are no exceptions. Crowns, scepters, pennies, paste jewels, village notoriety, world-wide fame--they are all the same, they have no MATERIAL value: while they content the SPIRIT they are precious, when this fails they are worthless.

A Difficult Question

Y.M. You keep me confused and perplexed all the time by your elusive terminology. Sometimes you divide a man up into two or three separate personalities, each with authorities, jurisdictions, and responsibilities of its own, and when he is in that condition I can't grasp it. Now when _I_ speak of a man, he is THE WHOLE THING IN ONE, and easy to hold and contemplate.

O.M. That is pleasant and convenient, if true. When you speak of "my body" who is the "my"?

Y.M. It is the "me."

O.M. The body is a property then, and the Me owns it. Who is the Me?

Y.M. The Me is THE WHOLE THING; it is a common property; an undivided ownership, vested in the whole entity.

O.M. If the Me admires a rainbow, is it the whole Me that admires it, including the hair, hands, heels, and all?

Y.M. Certainly not. It is my MIND that admires it.

O.M. So YOU divide the Me yourself. Everybody does; everybody must. What, then, definitely, is the Me?

Y.M. I think it must consist of just those two parts-- the body and the mind.

O.M. You think so? If you say "I believe the world is round," who is the "I" that is speaking?

Y.M. The mind.

O.M. If you say "I grieve for the loss of my father," who is the "I"?

Y.M. The mind.

O.M. Is the mind exercising an intellectual function when it examines and accepts the evidence that the world is round?

Y.M. Yes.

O.M. Is it exercising an intellectual function when it grieves for the loss of your father?

Y.M. That is not cerebration, brain-work, it is a matter of FEELING.

O.M. Then its source is not in your mind, but in your MORAL territory?

Y.M. I have to grant it.

O.M. Is your mind a part of your PHYSICAL equipment?

Y.M. No. It is independent of it; it is spiritual.

O.M. Being spiritual, it cannot be affected by physical influences?

Y.M. No.

O.M. Does the mind remain sober with the body is drunk?

Y.M. Well--no.

O.M. There IS a physical effect present, then?

Y.M. It looks like it.

O.M. A cracked skull has resulted in a crazy mind. Why should it happen if the mind is spiritual, and INDEPENDENT of physical influences?

Y.M. Well--I don't know.

O.M. When you have a pain in your foot, how do you know it?

Y.M. I feel it.

O.M. But you do not feel it until a nerve reports the hurt to the brain. Yet the brain is the seat of the mind, is it not?

Y.M. I think so.

O.M. But isn't spiritual enough to learn what is happening in the outskirts without the help of the PHYSICAL messenger? You perceive that the question of who or what the Me is, is not a simple one at all. You say "I admire the rainbow," and "I believe the world is round," and in these cases we find that the Me is not speaking, but only the MENTAL part. You say, "I grieve," and again the Me is not all speaking, but only the MORAL part. You say the mind is wholly spiritual; then you say "I have a pain" and find that this time the Me is mental AND spiritual combined. We all use the "I" in this indeterminate fashion, there is no help for it. We imagine a Master and King over what you call The Whole Thing, and we speak of him as "I," but when we try to define him we find we cannot do it. The intellect and the feelings can act quite INDEPENDENTLY of each other; we recognize that, and we look around for a Ruler who is master over both, and can serve as a DEFINITE AND INDISPUTABLE "I," and enable us to know what we mean and who or what we are talking about when we use that pronoun, but we have to give it up and confess that we cannot find him. To me, Man is a machine, made up of many mechanisms, the moral and mental ones acting automatically in accordance with the impulses of an interior Master who is built out of born-temperament and an accumulation of multitudinous outside influences and trainings; a machine whose ONE function is to secure the spiritual contentment of the Master, be his desires good or be they evil; a machine whose Will is absolute and must be obeyed, and always IS obeyed.

Y.M. Maybe the Me is the Soul?

O.M. Maybe it is. What is the Soul?

Y.M. I don't know.

O.M. Neither does any one else.

The Master Passion

Y.M. What is the Master?--or, in common speech, the Con-science? Explain it.

O.M. It is that mysterious autocrat, lodged in a man, which compels the man to content its desires. It may be called the Master Passion--the hunger for Self-Approval.

Y.M. Where is its seat?

O.M. In man's moral constitution.

Y.M. Are its commands for the man's good?

O.M. It is indifferent to the man's good; it never concerns itself about anything but the satisfying of its own desires. It can be TRAINED to prefer things which will be for the man's good, but it will prefer them only because they will content IT better than other things would.

Y.M. Then even when it is trained to high ideals it is still looking out for its own contentment, and not for the man's good.

O.M. True. Trained or untrained, it cares nothing for the man's good, and never concerns itself about it.

Y.M. It seems to be an IMMORAL force seated in the man's moral constitution.

O.M. It is a COLORLESS force seated in the man's moral constitution. Let us call it an instinct--a blind, unreasoning instinct, which cannot and does not distinguish between good morals and bad ones, and cares nothing for results to the man provided its own contentment be secured; and it will ALWAYS secure that.

Y.M. It seeks money, and it probably considers that that is an advantage for the man?

O.M. It is not always seeking money, it is not always seeking power, nor office, nor any other MATERIAL advantage. In ALL cases it seeks a SPIRITUAL contentment, let the MEANS be what they may. Its desires are determined by the man's tempera-ment-- and it is lord over that. Temperament, Conscience, Susceptibility, Spiritual Appetite, are, in fact, the same thing. Have you ever heard of a person who cared nothing for money?

Y.M. Yes. A scholar who would not leave his garret and his books to take a place in a business house at a large salary.

O.M. He had to satisfy his master--that is to say, his temperament, his Spiritual Appetite--and it preferred books to money. Are there other cases?

Y.M. Yes, the hermit.

O.M. It is a good instance. The hermit endures solitude, hunger, cold, and manifold perils, to content his autocrat, who prefers these things, and prayer and contemplation, to money or to any show or luxury that money can buy. Are there others?

Y.M. Yes. The artist, the poet, the scientist.

O.M. Their autocrat prefers the deep pleasures of these occupations, either well paid or ill paid, to any others in the market, at any price. You REALIZE that the Master Passion--the contentment of the spirit--concerns itself with many things besides so-called material advantage, material prosperity, cash, and all that?

Y.M. I think I must concede it.

O.M. I believe you must. There are perhaps as many Temperaments that would refuse the burdens and vexations and distinctions of public office as there are that hunger after them. The one set of Temperaments seek the contentment of the spirit, and that alone; and this is exactly the case with the other set. Neither set seeks anything BUT the contentment of the spirit. If the one is sordid, both are sordid; and equally so, since the end in view is precisely the same in both cases. And in both cases Temperament decides the preference--and Temperament is BORN, not made.

Conclusion

O.M. You have been taking a holiday?

Y.M. Yes; a mountain tramp covering a week. Are you ready to talk?

O.M. Quite ready. What shall we begin with?

Y.M. Well, lying abed resting up, two days and nights, I have thought over all these talks, and passed them carefully in review. With this result: that . . . that . . . are you intending to publish your notions about Man some day?

O.M. Now and then, in these past twenty years, the Master inside of me has half-intended to order me to set them to paper and publish them. Do I have to tell you why the order has remained unissued, or can you explain so simply a thing without my help?

Y.M. By your doctrine, it is simplicity itself: outside influences moved your interior Master to give the order; stronger outside influences deterred him. Without the outside influences, neither of these impulses could ever have been born, since a person's brain is incapable or originating an idea within itself.

O.M. Correct. Go on.

Y.M. The matter of publishing or withholding is still in your Master's hands. If some day an outside influence shall determine him to publish, he will give the order, and it will be obeyed.

O.M. That is correct. Well?

Y.M. Upon reflection I have arrived at the conviction that the publication of your doctrines would be harmful. Do you pardon me?

O.M. Pardon YOU? You have done nothing. You are an instrument--a speaking-trumpet. Speaking-trumpets are not responsible for what is said through them. Outside influences--in the form of lifelong teachings, trainings, notions, prejudices, and other second-hand importations--have persuaded the Master within you that the publication of these doctrines would be harmful. Very well, this is quite natural, and was to be expected; in fact, was inevitable. Go on; for the sake of ease and convenience, stick to habit: speak in the first person, and tell me what your Master thinks about it.

Y.M. Well, to begin: it is a desolating doctrine; it is not inspiring, enthusing, uplifting. It takes the glory out of man, it takes the pride out of him, it takes the heroism out of him, it denies him all personal credit, all applause; it not only degrades him to a machine, but allows him no control over the machine; makes a mere coffee-mill of him, and neither permits him to supply the coffee nor turn the crank, his sole and piteously humble function being to grind coarse or fine, according to his make, outside impulses doing the rest.

O.M. It is correctly stated. Tell me--what do men admire most in each other?

Y.M. Intellect, courage, majesty of build, beauty of counten-ance, charity, benevolence, magnanimity, kindliness, heroism, and--and--

O.M. I would not go any further. These are ELEMENTALS. Virtue, fortitude, holiness, truthfulness, loyalty, high ideals--these, and all the related qualities that are named in the dictionary, are MADE OF THE ELEMENTALS, by blendings, combinations, and shadings of the elementals, just as one makes green by blending blue and yellow, and makes several shades and tints of red by modifying the elemental red. There are several elemental colors; they are all in the rainbow; out of them we manufacture and name fifty shades of them. You have named the elementals of the human rainbow, and also one BLEND--heroism, which is made out of courage and magnanimity. Very well, then; which of these elements does the possessor of it manufacture for himself? Is it intellect?

Y.M. No.

O.M. Why?

Y.M. He is born with it.

O.M. Is it courage?

Y.M. No. He is born with it.

O.M. Is it majesty of build, beauty of countenance?

Y.M. No. They are birthrights.

O.M. Take those others--the elemental moral qualities-- charity, benevolence, magnanimity, kindliness; fruitful seeds, out of which spring, through cultivation by outside influences, all the manifold blends and combinations of virtues named in the dictionaries: does man manufacture any of those seeds, or are they all born in him?

Y.M. Born in him.

O.M. Who manufactures them, then?

Y.M. God.

O.M. Where does the credit of it belong?

Y.M. To God.

O.M. And the glory of which you spoke, and the applause?

Y.M. To God.

O.M. Then it is YOU who degrade man. You make him claim glory, praise, flattery, for every valuable thing he possesses-- BORROWED finery, the whole of it; no rag of it earned by himself, not a detail of it produced by his own labor. YOU make man a humbug; have I done worse by him?

Y.M. You have made a machine of him.

O.M. Who devised that cunning and beautiful mechanism, a man's hand?

Y.M. God.

O.M. Who devised the law by which it automatically hammers out of a piano an elaborate piece of music, without error, while the man is thinking about something else, or talking to a friend?

Y.M. God.

O.M. Who devised the blood? Who devised the wonderful machinery which automatically drives its renewing and refreshing streams through the body, day and night, without assistance or advice from the man? Who devised the man's mind, whose machinery works automatically, interests itself in what it pleases, regardless of its will or desire, labors all night when it likes, deaf to his appeals for mercy? God devised all these things. _I_ have not made man a machine, God made him a machine. I am merely calling attention to the fact, nothing more. Is it wrong to call attention to the fact? Is it a crime?

Y.M. I think it is wrong to EXPOSE a fact when harm can come of it.

O.M. Go on.

Y.M. Look at the matter as it stands now. Man has been taught that he is the supreme marvel of the Creation; he believes it; in all the ages he has never doubted it, whether he was a naked savage, or clothed in purple and fine linen, and civilized. This has made his heart buoyant, his life cheery. His pride in himself, his sincere admiration of himself, his joy in what he supposed were his own and unassisted achievements, and his exultation over the praise and applause which they evoked--these have exalted him, enthused him, ambitioned him to higher and higher flights; in a word, made his life worth the living. But by your scheme, all this is abolished; he is degraded to a machine, he is a nobody, his noble prides wither to mere vanities; let him strive as he may, he can never be any better than his humblest and stupidest neighbor; he would never be cheerful again, his life would not be worth the living.

O.M. You really think that?

Y.M. I certainly do.

O.M. Have you ever seen me uncheerful, unhappy.

Y.M. No.

O.M. Well, _I_ believe these things. Why have they not made me unhappy?

Y.M. Oh, well--temperament, of course! You never let THAT escape from your scheme.

O.M. That is correct. If a man is born with an unhappy temperament, nothing can make him happy; if he is born with a happy temperament, nothing can make him unhappy.

Y.M. What--not even a degrading and heart-chilling system of beliefs?

O.M. Beliefs? Mere beliefs? Mere convictions? They are powerless. They strive in vain against inborn temperament.

Y.M. I can't believe that, and I don't.

O.M. Now you are speaking hastily. It shows that you have not studiously examined the facts. Of all your intimates, which one is the happiest? Isn't it Burgess?

Y.M. Easily.

O.M. And which one is the unhappiest? Henry Adams?

Y.M. Without a question!

O.M. I know them well. They are extremes, abnormals; their temperaments are as opposite as the poles. Their life-histories are about alike--but look at the results! Their ages are about the same--about around fifty. Burgess had always been buoyant, hopeful, happy; Adams has always been cheerless, hopeless, despondent. As young fellows both tried country journalism--and failed. Burgess didn't seem to mind it; Adams couldn't smile, he could only mourn and groan over what had happened and torture himself with vain regrets for not having done so and so instead of so and so--THEN he would have succeeded. They tried the law-- and failed. Burgess remained happy--because he couldn't help it. Adams was wretched--because he couldn't help it. From that day to this, those two men have gone on trying things and failing: Burgess has come out happy and cheerful every time; Adams the reverse. And we do absolutely know that these men's inborn temperaments have remained unchanged through all the vicissitudes of their material affairs. Let us see how it is with their immaterials. Both have been zealous Democrats; both have been zealous Republicans; both have been zealous Mugwumps. Burgess has always found happiness and Adams unhappiness in these several political beliefs and in their migrations out of them. Both of these men have been Presbyterians, Universalists, Methodists, Catholics--then Presbyterians again, then Methodists again. Burgess has always found rest in these excursions, and Adams unrest. They are trying Christian Science, now, with the customary result, the inevitable result. No political or religious belief can make Burgess unhappy or the other man happy. I assure you it is purely a matter of temperament. Beliefs are ACQUIREMENTS, temperaments are BORN; beliefs are subject to change, nothing whatever can change temperament.

Y.M. You have instanced extreme temperaments.

O.M. Yes, the half-dozen others are modifications of the extremes. But the law is the same. Where the temperament is two-thirds happy, or two-thirds unhappy, no political or religious beliefs can change the proportions. The vast majority of temperaments are pretty equally balanced; the intensities are absent, and this enables a nation to learn to accommodate itself to its political and religious circumstances and like them, be satisfied with them, at last prefer them. Nations do not THINK, they only FEEL. They get their feelings at second hand through their temperaments, not their brains. A nation can be brought-- by force of circumstances, not argument--to reconcile itself to ANY KIND OF GOVERNMENT OR RELIGION THAT CAN BE DEVISED; in time it will fit itself to the required conditions; later, it will prefer them and will fiercely fight for them. As instances, you have all history: the Greeks, the Romans, the Persians, the Egyptians, the Russians, the Germans, the French, the English, the Spaniards, the Americans, the South Americans, the Japanese, the Chinese, the Hindus, the Turks--a thousand wild and tame religions, every kind of government that can be thought of, from tiger to house-cat, each nation KNOWING it has the only true religion and the only sane system of govern-ment, each despising all the others, each an ass and not suspecting it, each proud of its fancied supremacy, each perfectly sure it is the pet of God, each without undoubting confidence summoning Him to take command in time of war, each surprised when He goes over to the enemy, but by habit able to excuse it and resume compliments--in a word, the whole human race content, always content, persistently content, indestructibly content, happy, thankful, proud, NO MATTER WHAT ITS RELIGION IS, NOR WHETHER ITS MASTER BE TIGER OR HOUSE-CAT. Am I stating facts? You know I am. Is the human race cheerful? You know it is. Considering what it can stand, and be happy, you do me too much honor when you think that _I_ can place before it a system of plain cold facts that can take the cheerfulness out of it. Nothing can do that. Everything has been tried. Without success. I beg you not to be troubled.

THE DEATH OF JEAN

THE death of Jean Clemens occurred early in the morning of December 24, 1909. Mr. Clemens was in great stress of mind when I first saw him, but a few hours later I found him writing steadily.

"I am setting it down," he said, "everything. It is a relief to me to write it. It furnishes me an excuse for thinking." At intervals during that day and the next I looked in, and usually found him writing. Then on the evening of the 26th, when he knew that Jean had been laid to rest in Elmira, he came to my room with the manuscript in his hand.

"I have finished it," he said; "read it. I can form no opinion of it myself. If you think it worthy, some day--at the proper time--it can end my autobiography. It is the final chapter."

Four months later--almost to the day--(April 21st) he was with Jean.

Albert Bigelow Paine.

Stormfield, Christmas Eve, 11 A.M., 1909.

JEAN IS DEAD!

Has any one ever tried to put upon paper all the little happenings connected with a dear one--happenings of the twenty- four hours preceding the sudden and unexpected death of that dear one? Would a book contain them? Would two books contain them? I think not. They pour into the mind in a flood. They are little things that have been always happening every day, and were always so unimportant and easily forgettable before--but now! Now, how different! how precious they are, now dear, how unforgettable, how pathetic, how sacred, how clothed with dignity!

Last night Jean, all flushed with splendid health, and I the same, from the wholesome effects of my Bermuda holiday, strolled hand in hand from the dinner-table and sat down in the library and chatted, and planned, and discussed, cheerily and happily (and how unsuspectingly!)--until nine--which is late for us--then went upstairs, Jean's friendly German dog following. At my door Jean said, "I can't kiss you good night, father: I have a cold, and you could catch it." I bent and kissed her hand. She was moved--I saw it in her eyes--and she impulsively kissed my hand in return. Then with the usual gay "Sleep well, dear!" from both, we parted.

At half past seven this morning I woke, and heard voices outside my door. I said to myself, "Jean is starting on her usual horseback flight to the station for the mail." Then Katy [1] entered, stood quaking and gasping at my bedside a moment, then found her tongue:

"MISS JEAN IS DEAD!"

Possibly I know now what the soldier feels when a bullet crashes through his heart.

In her bathroom there she lay, the fair young creature, stretched upon the floor and covered with a sheet. And looking so placid, so natural, and as if asleep. We knew what had happened. She was an epileptic: she had been seized with a convulsion and heart failure in her bath. The doctor had to come several miles. His efforts, like our previous ones, failed to bring her back to life.

It is noon, now. How lovable she looks, how sweet and how tranquil! It is a noble face, and full of dignity; and that was a good heart that lies there so still.

In England, thirteen years ago, my wife and I were stabbed to the heart with a cablegram which said, "Susy was mercifully released today." I had to send a like shot to Clara, in Berlin, this morning. With the peremptory addition, "You must not come home." Clara and her husband sailed from here on the 11th of this month. How will Clara bear it? Jean, from her babyhood, was a worshiper of Clara.

Four days ago I came back from a month's holiday in Bermuda in perfected health; but by some accident the reporters failed to perceive this. Day before yesterday, letters and telegrams began to arrive from friends and strangers which indicated that I was supposed to be dangerously ill. Yesterday Jean begged me to explain my case through the Associated Press. I said it was not important enough; but she was distressed and said I must think of Clara. Clara would see the report in the German papers, and as she had been nursing her husband day and night for four months [2] and was worn out and feeble, the shock might be disastrous. There was reason in that; so I sent a humorous paragraph by telephone to the Associated Press denying the "charge" that I was "dying," and saying "I would not do such a thing at my time of life."

Jean was a little troubled, and did not like to see me treat the matter so lightly; but I said it was best to treat it so, for there was nothing serious about it. This morning I sent the sorrowful facts of this day's irremediable disaster to the Associated Press.

Will both appear in this evening's papers?-- the one so blithe, the other so tragic?

I lost Susy thirteen years ago; I lost her mother--her incomparable mother!--five and a half years ago; Clara has gone away to live in Europe; and now I have lost Jean. How poor I am, who was once so rich! Seven months ago Mr. Roger died--one of the best friends I ever had, and the nearest perfect, as man and gentleman, I have yet met among my race; within the last six weeks Gilder has passed away, and Laffan--old, old friends of mine. Jean lies yonder, I sit here; we are strangers under our own roof; we kissed hands good-by at this door last night--and it was forever, we never suspecting it. She lies there, and I sit here--writing, busying myself, to keep my heart from breaking. How dazzlingly the sunshine is flooding the hills around! It is like a mockery.

Seventy-four years ago twenty-four days ago. Seventy-four years old yesterday. Who can estimate my age today?

I have looked upon her again. I wonder I can bear it. She looks just as her mother looked when she lay dead in that Florentine villa so long ago. The sweet placidity of death! it is more beautiful than sleep.

I saw her mother buried. I said I would never endure that horror again; that I would never again look into the grave of any one dear to me. I have kept to that. They will take Jean from this house tomorrow, and bear her to Elmira, New York, where lie those of us that have been released, but I shall not follow.

Jean was on the dock when the ship came in, only four days ago. She was at the door, beaming a welcome, when I reached this house the next evening. We played cards, and she tried to teach me a new game called "Mark Twain." We sat chatting cheerily in the library last night, and she wouldn't let me look into the loggia, where she was making Christmas preparations. She said she would finish them in the morning, and then her little French friend would arrive from New York--the surprise would follow; the surprise she had been working over for days. While she was out for a moment I disloyally stole a look. The loggia floor was clothed with rugs and furnished with chairs and sofas; and the uncompleted surprise was there: in the form of a Christmas tree that was drenched with silver film in a most wonderful way; and on a table was prodigal profusion of bright things which she was going to hang upon it today. What desecrating hand will ever banish that eloquent unfinished surprise from that place? Not mine, surely. All these little matters have happened in the last four days. "Little." Yes-- THEN. But not now. Nothing she said or thought or did is little now. And all the lavish humor!--what is become of it? It is pathos, now. Pathos, and the thought of it brings tears.

All these little things happened such a few hours ago--and now she lies yonder. Lies yonder, and cares for nothing any more. Strange--marvelous--incredible! I have had this experience before; but it would still be incredible if I had had it a thousand times.

"MISS JEAN IS DEAD!"

That is what Katy said. When I heard the door open behind the bed's head without a preliminary knock, I supposed it was Jean coming to kiss me good morning, she being the only person who was used to entering without formalities.

And so--

I have been to Jean's parlor. Such a turmoil of Christmas presents for servants and friends! They are everywhere; tables, chairs, sofas, the floor--everything is occupied, and over-occupied. It is many and many a year since I have seen the like. In that ancient day Mrs. Clemens and I used to slip softly into the nursery at midnight on Christmas Eve and look the array of presents over. The children were little then. And now here is Jean's parlor looking just as that nursery used to look. The presents are not labeled--the hands are forever idle that would have labeled them today. Jean's mother always worked herself down with her Christmas preparations. Jean did the same yesterday and the preceding days, and the fatigue has cost her her life. The fatigue caused the convulsion that attacked her this morning. She had had no attack for months.

Jean was so full of life and energy that she was constantly is danger of overtaxing her strength. Every morning she was in the saddle by half past seven, and off to the station for her mail. She examined the letters and I distributed them: some to her, some to Mr. Paine, the others to the stenographer and myself. She dispatched her share and then mounted her horse again and went around superintending her farm and her poultry the rest of the day. Sometimes she played billiards with me after dinner, but she was usually too tired to play, and went early to bed.

Yesterday afternoon I told her about some plans I had been devising while absent in Bermuda, to lighten her burdens. We would get a housekeeper; also we would put her share of the secretary-work into Mr. Paine's hands.

No--she wasn't willing. She had been making plans herself. The matter ended in a compromise, I submitted. I always did. She wouldn't audit the bills and let Paine fill out the checks-- she would continue to attend to that herself. Also, she would continue to be housekeeper, and let Katy assist. Also, she would continue to answer the letters of personal friends for me. Such was the compromise. Both of us called it by that name, though I was not able to see where my formidable change had been made.

However, Jean was pleased, and that was sufficient for me. She was proud of being my secretary, and I was never able to persuade her to give up any part of her share in that unlovely work.

In the talk last night I said I found everything going so smoothly that if she were willing I would go back to Bermuda in February and get blessedly out of the clash and turmoil again for another month. She was urgent that I should do it, and said that if I would put off the trip until March she would take Katy and go with me. We struck hands upon that, and said it was settled. I had a mind to write to Bermuda by tomorrow's ship and secure a furnished house and servants. I meant to write the letter this morning. But it will never be written, now.

For she lies yonder, and before her is another journey than that.

Night is closing down; the rim of the sun barely shows above the sky-line of the hills.

I have been looking at that face again that was growing dearer and dearer to me every day. I was getting acquainted with Jean in these last nine months. She had been long an exile from home when she came to us three-quarters of a year ago. She had been shut up in sanitariums, many miles from us. How eloquent glad and grateful she was to cross her father's threshold again!

Would I bring her back to life if I could do it? I would not. If a word would do it, I would beg for strength to withhold the word. And I would have the strength; I am sure of it. In her loss I am almost bankrupt, and my life is a bitterness, but I am content: for she has been enriched with the most precious of all gifts--that gift which makes all other gifts mean and poor-- death. I have never wanted any released friend of mine restored to life since I reached manhood. I felt in this way when Susy passed away; and later my wife, and later Mr. Rogers. When Clara met me at the station in New York and told me Mr. Rogers had died suddenly that morning, my thought was, Oh, favorite of fortune-- fortunate all his long and lovely life-- fortunate to his latest moment! The reporters said there were tears of sorrow in my eyes. True--but they were for ME, not for him. He had suffered no loss. All the fortunes he had ever made before were poverty compared with this one.

Why did I build this house, two years ago? To shelter this vast emptiness? How foolish I was! But I shall stay in it. The spirits of the dead hallow a house, for me. It was not so with other members of the family. Susy died in the house we built in Hartford. Mrs. Clemens would never enter it again. But it made the house dearer to me. I have entered it once since, when it was tenantless and silent and forlorn, but to me it was a holy place and beautiful. It seemed to me that the spirits of the dead were all about me, and would speak to me and welcome me if they could: Livy, and Susy, and George, and Henry Robinson, and Charles Dudley Warner. How good and kind they were, and how lovable their lives! In fancy I could see them all again, I could call the children back and hear them romp again with George--that peerless black ex-slave and children's idol who came one day--a flitting stranger--to wash windows, and stayed eighteen years. Until he died. Clara and Jean would never enter again the New York hotel which their mother had frequented in earlier days. They could not bear it. But I shall stay in this house. It is dearer to me tonight than ever it was before. Jean's spirit will make it beautiful for me always. Her lonely and tragic death--but I will not think of that now.

Jean's mother always devoted two or three weeks to Christmas shopping, and was always physically exhausted when Christmas Eve came. Jean was her very own child--she wore herself out present- hunting in New York these latter days. Paine has just found on her desk a long list of names--fifty, he thinks--people to whom she sent presents last night. Apparently she forgot no one. And Katy found there a roll of bank-notes, for the servants.

Her dog has been wandering about the grounds today, comradeless and forlorn. I have seen him from the windows. She got him from Germany. He has tall ears and looks exactly like a wolf. He was educated in Germany, and knows no language but the German. Jean gave him no orders save in that tongue. And so when the burglar-alarm made a fierce clamor at midnight a fortnight ago, the butler, who is French and knows no German, tried in vain to interest the dog in the supposed burglar. Jean wrote me, to Bermuda, about the incident. It was the last letter I was ever to receive from her bright head and her competent hand. The dog will not be neglected.

There was never a kinder heart than Jean's. From her childhood up she always spent the most of her allowance on charities of one kind or another. After she became secretary and had her income doubled she spent her money upon these things with a free hand. Mine too, I am glad and grateful to say.

She was a loyal friend to all animals, and she loved them all, birds, beasts, and everything--even snakes--an inheritance from me. She knew all the birds; she was high up in that lore. She became a member of various humane societies when she was still a little girl--both here and abroad--and she remained an active member to the last. She founded two or three societies for the protection of animals, here and in Europe.

She was an embarrassing secretary, for she fished my corres-pondence out of the waste-basket and answered the letters. She thought all letters deserved the courtesy of an answer. Her mother brought her up in that kindly error.

She could write a good letter, and was swift with her pen. She had but an indifferent ear music, but her tongue took to languages with an easy facility. She never allowed her Italian, French, and German to get rusty through neglect.

The telegrams of sympathy are flowing in, from far and wide, now, just as they did in Italy five years and a half ago, when this child's mother laid down her blameless life. They cannot heal the hurt, but they take away some of the pain. When Jean and I kissed hands and parted at my door last, how little did we imagine that in twenty-two hours the telegraph would be bringing words like these:

"From the bottom of our hearts we send out sympathy, dearest of friends."

For many and many a day to come, wherever I go in this house, remembrancers of Jean will mutely speak to me of her. Who can count the number of them?

She was in exile two years with the hope of healing her malady--epilepsy. There are no words to express how grateful I am that she did not meet her fate in the hands of strangers, but in the loving shelter of her own home.

"MISS JEAN IS DEAD!"

It is true. Jean is dead.

A month ago I was writing bubbling and hilarious articles for magazines yet to appear, and now I am writing--this.

CHRISTMAS DAY. NOON.--Last night I went to Jean's room at intervals, and turned back the sheet and looked at the peaceful face, and kissed the cold brow, and remembered that heartbreaking night in Florence so long ago, in that cavernous and silent vast villa, when I crept downstairs so many times, and turned back a sheet and looked at a face just like this one-- Jean's mother's face--and kissed a brow that was just like this one. And last night I saw again what I had seen then--that strange and lovely miracle--the sweet, soft contours of early maidenhood restored by the gracious hand of death! When Jean's mother lay dead, all trace of care, and trouble, and suffering, and the corroding years had vanished out of the face, and I was looking again upon it as I had known and worshipped it in its young bloom and beauty a whole generation before.

About three in the morning, while wandering about the house in the deep silences, as one dies in times like these, when there is a dumb sense that something has been lost that will never be found again, yet must be sought, if only for the employment the useless seeking gives, I came upon Jean's dog in the hall downstairs, and noted that he did not spring to greet me, according to his hospitable habit, but came slow and sorrowful- ly; also I remembered that he had not visited Jean's apartment since the tragedy. Poor fellow, did he know? I think so. Always when Jean was abroad in the open he was with her; always when she was in the house he was with her, in the night as well as in the day. Her parlor was his bedroom. Whenever I happened upon him on the ground floor he always followed me about, and when I went upstairs he went too--in a tumultuous gallop. But now it was different: after patting him a little I went to the library--he remained behind; when I went upstairs he did not follow me, save with his wistful eyes. He has wonderful eyes--big, and kind, and eloquent. He can talk with them. He is a beautiful creature, and is of the breed of the New York police-dogs. I do not like dogs, because they bark when there is no occasion for it; but I have liked this one from the beginning, because he belonged to Jean, and because he never barks except when there is occasion-- which is not oftener than twice a week.

In my wanderings I visited Jean's parlor. On a shelf I found a pile of my books, and I knew what it meant. She was waiting for me to come home from Bermuda and autograph them, then she would send them away. If I only knew whom she intended them for! But I shall never know. I will keep them. Her hand has touched them--it is an accolade--they are noble, now.

And in a closet she had hidden a surprise for me--a thing I have often wished I owned: a noble big globe. I couldn't see it for the tears. She will never know the pride I take in it, and the pleasure. Today the mails are full of loving remembrances for her: full of those old, old kind words she loved so well, "Merry Christmas to Jean!" If she could only have lived one day longer!

At last she ran out of money, and would not use mine. So she sent to one of those New York homes for poor girls all the clothes she could spare--and more, most likely.

CHRISTMAS NIGHT.--This afternoon they took her away from her room. As soon as I might, I went down to the library, and there she lay, in her coffin, dressed in exactly the same clothes she wore when she stood at the other end of the same room on the 6th of October last, as Clara's chief bridesmaid. Her face was radiant with happy excitement then; it was the same face now, with the dignity of death and the peace of God upon it.

They told me the first mourner to come was the dog. He came uninvited, and stood up on his hind legs and rested his fore paws upon the trestle, and took a last long look at the face that was so dear to him, then went his way as silently as he had come. HE KNOWS.

At mid-afternoon it began to snow. The pity of it--that Jean could not see it! She so loved the snow.

The snow continued to fall. At six o'clock the hearse drew up to the door to bear away its pathetic burden. As they lifted the casket, Paine began playing on the orchestrelle Schubert's "Impromptu," which was Jean's favorite. Then he played the Intermezzo; that was for Susy; then he played the Largo; that was for their mother. He did this at my request. Elsewhere in my Autobiography I have told how the Intermezzo and the Largo came to be associated in my heart with Susy and Livy in their last hours in this life.

From my windows I saw the hearse and the carriages wind along the road and gradually grow vague and spectral in the falling snow, and presently disappear. Jean was gone out of my life, and would not come back any more. Jervis, the cousin she had played with when they were babies together--he and her beloved old Katy--were conducting her to her distant childhood home, where she will lie by her mother's side once more, in the company of Susy and Langdon.

DECEMBER 26TH. The dog came to see me at eight o'clock this morning. He was very affectionate, poor orphan! My room will be his quarters hereafter.

The storm raged all night. It has raged all the morning. The snow drives across the landscape in vast clouds, superb, sublime--and Jean not here to see.

2:30 P.M.--It is the time appointed. The funeral has begun. Four hundred miles away, but I can see it all, just as if I were there. The scene is the library in the Langdon homestead. Jean's coffin stands where her mother and I stood, forty years ago, and were married; and where Susy's coffin stood thirteen years ago; where her mother's stood five years and a half ago; and where mine will stand after a little time.

FIVE O'CLOCK.--It is all over.

When Clara went away two weeks ago to live in Europe, it was hard, but I could bear it, for I had Jean left. I said WE would be a family. We said we would be close comrades and happy--just we two. That fair dream was in my mind when Jean met me at the steamer last Monday; it was in my mind when she received me at the door last Tuesday evening. We were together; WE WERE A FAMILY! the dream had come true--oh, precisely true, contentedly, true, satisfyingly true! and remained true two whole days.

And now? Now Jean is in her grave!

In the grave--if I can believe it. God rest her sweet spirit!

-----

1. Katy Leary, who had been in the service of the Clemens family for twenty-nine years.

2. Mr. Gabrilowitsch had been operated on for appendicitis.

THE TURNING-POINT OF MY LIFE

I

IF I understand the idea, the BAZAR invites several of us to write upon the above text. It means the change in my life's course which introduced what must be regarded by me as the most IMPORTANT condition of my career. But it also implies--without intention, perhaps--that that turning-point ITSELF was the creator of the new condition. This gives it too much distinction, too much prominence, too much credit. It is only the LAST link in a very long chain of turning-points commissioned to produce the cardinal result; it is not any more important than the humblest of its ten thousand predecessors. Each of the ten thousand did its appointed share, on its appointed date, in forwarding the scheme, and they were all necessary; to have left out any one of them would have defeated the scheme and brought about SOME OTHER result. It know we have a fashion of saying "such and such an event was the turning-point in my life," but we shouldn't say it. We should merely grant that its place as LAST link in the chain makes it the most CONSPICUOUS link; in real importance it has no advantage over any one of its predecessors.

Perhaps the most celebrated turning-point recorded in history was the crossing of the Rubicon. Suetonius says:

Coming up with his troops on the banks of the Rubicon, he halted for a while, and, revolving in his mind the importance of the step he was on the point of taking, he turned to those about him and said, "We may still retreat; but if we pass this little bridge, nothing is left for us but to fight it out in arms."

This was a stupendously important moment. And all the incidents, big and little, of Caesar's previous life had been leading up to it, stage by stage, link by link. This was the LAST link--merely the last one, and no bigger than the others; but as we gaze back at it through the inflating mists of our imagination, it looks as big as the orbit of Neptune.

You, the reader, have a PERSONAL interest in that link, and so have I; so has the rest of the human race. It was one of the links in your life-chain, and it was one of the links in mine. We may wait, now, with baited breath, while Caesar reflects. Your fate and mine are involved in his decision.

While he was thus hesitating, the following incident occurred. A person remarked for his noble mien and graceful aspect appeared close at hand, sitting and playing upon a pipe. When not only the shepherds, but a number of soldiers also, flocked to listen to him, and some trumpeters among them, he snatched a trumpet from one of them, ran to the river with it, and, sounding the advance with a piercing blast, crossed to the other side. Upon this, Caesar exclaimed: "Let us go whither the omens of the gods and the iniquity of our enemies call up. THE DIE IS CAST."

So he crossed--and changed the future of the whole human race, for all time. But that stranger was a link in Caesar's life-chain, too; and a necessary one. We don't know his name, we never hear of him again; he was very casual; he acts like an accident; but he was no accident, he was there by compulsion of HIS life-chain, to blow the electrifying blast that was to make up Caesar's mind for him, and thence go piping down the aisles of history forever.

If the stranger hadn't been there! But he WAS. And Caesar crossed. With such results! Such vast events--each a link in the HUMAN RACE'S life-chain; each event producing the next one, and that one the next one, and so on: the destruction of the republic; the founding of the empire; the breaking up of the empire; the rise of Christianity upon its ruins; the spread of the religion to other lands--and so on; link by link took its appointed place at its appointed time, the discovery of America being one of them; our Revolution another; the inflow of English and other immigrants another; their drift westward (my ancestors among them) another; the settlement of certain of them in Missouri, which resulted in ME. For I was one of the unavoidable results of the crossing of the Rubicon. If the stranger, with his trumpet blast, had stayed away (which he COULDN'T, for he was the appointed link) Caesar would not have crossed. What would have happened, in that case, we can never guess. We only know that the things that did happen would not have happened. They might have been replaced by equally prodigious things, of course, but their nature and results are beyond our guessing. But the matter that interests me personally is that I would not be HERE now, but somewhere else; and probably black--there is no telling. Very well, I am glad he crossed. And very really and thankfully glad, too, though I never cared anything about it before.

II

To me, the most important feature of my life is its literary feature. I have been professionally literary something more than forty years. There have been many turning-points in my life, but the one that was the link in the chain appointed to conduct me to the literary guild is the most CONSPICUOUS link in that chain. BECAUSE it was the last one. It was not any more important than its predecessors. All the other links have an inconspicuous look, except the crossing of the Rubicon; but as factors in making me literary they are all of the one size, the crossing of the Rubicon included.

I know how I came to be literary, and I will tell the steps that lead up to it and brought it about.

The crossing of the Rubicon was not the first one, it was hardly even a recent one; I should have to go back ages before Caesar's day to find the first one. To save space I will go back only a couple of generations and start with an incident of my boyhood. When I was twelve and a half years old, my father died. It was in the spring. The summer came, and brought with it an epidemic of measles. For a time a child died almost every day. The village was paralyzed with fright, distress, despair. Children that were not smitten with the disease were imprisoned in their homes to save them from the infection. In the homes there were no cheerful faces, there was no music, there was no singing but of solemn hymns, no voice but of prayer, no romping was allowed, no noise, no laughter, the family moved spectrally about on tiptoe, in a ghostly hush. I was a prisoner. My soul was steeped in this awful dreariness--and in fear. At some time or other every day and every night a sudden shiver shook me to the marrow, and I said to myself, "There, I've got it! and I shall die." Life on these miserable terms was not worth living, and at last I made up my mind to get the disease and have it over, one way or the other. I escaped from the house and went to the house of a neighbor where a playmate of mine was very ill with the malady. When the chance offered I crept into his room and got into bed with him. I was discovered by his mother and sent back into captivity. But I had the disease; they could not take that from me. I came near to dying. The whole village was interested, and anxious, and sent for news of me every day; and not only once a day, but several times. Everybody believed I would die; but on the fourteenth day a change came for the worse and they were disappointed.

This was a turning-point of my life. (Link number one.) For when I got well my mother closed my school career and apprenticed me to a printer. She was tired of trying to keep me out of mischief, and the adventure of the measles decided her to put me into more masterful hands than hers.

I became a printer, and began to add one link after another to the chain which was to lead me into the literary profession. A long road, but I could not know that; and as I did not know what its goal was, or even that it had one, I was indifferent. Also contented.

A young printer wanders around a good deal, seeking and finding work; and seeking again, when necessity commands. N. B. Necessity is a CIRCUMSTANCE; Circumstance is man's master--and when Circumstance commands, he must obey; he may argue the matter--that is his privilege, just as it is the honorable privilege of a falling body to argue with the attraction of gravitation--but it won't do any good, he must OBEY. I wandered for ten years, under the guidance and dictatorship of Circumstance, and finally arrived in a city of Iowa, where I worked several months. Among the books that interested me in those days was one about the Amazon. The traveler told an alluring tale of his long voyage up the great river from Para to the sources of the Madeira, through the heart of an enchanted land, a land wastefully rich in tropical wonders, a romantic land where all the birds and flowers and animals were of the museum varieties, and where the alligator and the crocodile and the monkey seemed as much at home as if they were in the Zoo. Also, he told an astonishing tale about COCA, a vegetable

product of miraculous powers, asserting that it was so nourish-
ing and so strength-giving that the native of the mountains of
the Madeira region would tramp up hill and down all day on a
pinch of powdered coca and require no other sustenance.

I was fired with a longing to ascend the Amazon. Also with a
longing to open up a trade in coca with all the world. During
months I dreamed that dream, and tried to contrive ways to get
to Para and spring that splendid enterprise upon an unsuspect-
ing planet. But all in vain. A person may PLAN as much as he
wants to, but nothing of consequence is likely to come of it until
the magician CIRCUMSTANCE steps in and takes the matter off
his hands. At last Circumstance came to my help. It was in this
way. Circumstance, to help or hurt another man, made him
lose a fifty-dollar bill in the street; and to help or hurt me, made
me find it. I advertised the find, and left for the Amazon the
same day. This was another turning-point, another link.

Could Circumstance have ordered another dweller in that town
to go to the Amazon and open up a world-trade in coca on a
fifty- dollar basis and been obeyed? No, I was the only one.
There were other fools there--shoals and shoals of them--but
they were not of my kind. I was the only one of my kind.

Circumstance is powerful, but it cannot work alone; it has to
have a partner. Its partner is man's TEMPERAMENT--his natural
disposition. His temperament is not his invention, it is BORN in
him, and he has no authority over it, neither is he responsible
for its acts. He cannot change it, nothing can change it, nothing
can modify it--except temporarily. But it won't stay modified. It
is permanent, like the color of the man's eyes and the shape of
his ears. Blue eyes are gray in certain unusual lights; but they
resume their natural color when that stress is removed.

A Circumstance that will coerce one man will have no effect upon a man of a different temperament. If Circumstance had thrown the bank-note in Caesar's way, his temperament would not have made him start for the Amazon. His temperament would have compelled him to do something with the money, but not that. It might have made him advertise the note--and WAIT. We can't tell. Also, it might have made him go to New York and buy into the Government, with results that would leave Tweed nothing to learn when it came his turn.

Very well, Circumstance furnished the capital, and my temperament told me what to do with it. Sometimes a temperament is an ass. When that is the case of the owner of it is an ass, too, and is going to remain one. Training, experience, association, can temporarily so polish him, improve him, exalt him that people will think he is a mule, but they will be mistaken. Artificially he IS a mule, for the time being, but at bottom he is an ass yet, and will remain one.

By temperament I was the kind of person that DOES things. Does them, and reflects afterward. So I started for the Amazon without reflecting and without asking any questions. That was more than fifty years ago. In all that time my temperament has not changed, by even a shade. I have been punished many and many a time, and bitterly, for doing things and reflecting afterward, but these tortures have been of no value to me; I still do the thing commanded by Circumstance and Temperament, and reflect afterward. Always violently. When I am reflecting, on these occasions, even deaf persons can hear me think.

I went by the way of Cincinnati, and down the Ohio and Mississippi. My idea was to take ship, at New Orleans, for Para. In New Orleans I inquired, and found there was no ship leaving for Para. Also, that there never had BEEN one leaving for Para. I reflected. A policeman came and asked me what I was doing, and I told him. He made me move on, and said if he caught me reflecting in the public street again he would run me in.

After a few days I was out of money. Then Circumstance arrived, with another turning-point of my life--a new link. On my way down, I had made the acquaintance of a pilot. I begged him to teach me the river, and he consented. I became a pilot.

By and by Circumstance came again--introducing the Civil War, this time, in order to push me ahead another stage or two toward the literary profession. The boats stopped running, my livelihood was gone.

Circumstance came to the rescue with a new turning-point and a fresh link. My brother was appointed secretary to the new Territory of Nevada, and he invited me to go with him and help him in his office. I accepted.

In Nevada, Circumstance furnished me the silver fever and I went into the mines to make a fortune, as I supposed; but that was not the idea. The idea was to advance me another step toward literature. For amusement I scribbled things for the Virginia City ENTERPRISE. One isn't a printer ten years without setting up acres of good and bad literature, and learning-- unconsciously at first, consciously later--to discriminate between the two, within his mental limitations; and meantime he is unconsciously acquiring what is called a "style." One of my efforts attracted attention, and the ENTERPRISE sent for me and put me on its staff.

And so I became a journalist--another link. By and by Circums- tance and the Sacramento UNION sent me to the Sandwich Islands for five or six months, to write up sugar. I did it; and threw in a good deal of extraneous matter that hadn't anything to do with sugar. But it was this extraneous matter that helped me to another link.

It made me notorious, and San Francisco invited me to lecture. Which I did. And profitably. I had long had a desire to travel and see the world, and now Circumstance had most kindly and unexpectedly hurled me upon the platform and furnished me the means. So I joined the "Quaker City Excursion."

When I returned to America, Circumstance was waiting on the pier-- with the LAST link--the conspicuous, the consummating, the victorious link: I was asked to WRITE A BOOK, and I did it, and called it THE INNOCENTS ABROAD. Thus I became at last a member of the literary guild. That was forty-two years ago, and I have been a member ever since. Leaving the Rubicon incident away back where it belongs, I can say with truth that the reason I am in the literary profession is because I had the measles when I was twelve years old.

III

Now what interests me, as regards these details, is not the details themselves, but the fact that none of them was foreseen by me, none of them was planned by me, I was the author of none of them. Circumstance, working in harness with my temperament, created them all and compelled them all. I often offered help, and with the best intentions, but it was rejected-- as a rule, uncourteously. I could never plan a thing and get it to come out the way I planned it. It came out some other way-- some way I had not counted upon.

And so I do not admire the human being--as an intellectual marvel--as much as I did when I was young, and got him out of books, and did not know him personally. When I used to read that such and such a general did a certain brilliant thing, I believed it. Whereas it was not so. Circumstance did it by help of his temperament. The circumstances would have failed of effect with a general of another temperament: he might see the chance, but lose the advantage by being by nature too slow or too quick or too doubtful. Once General Grant was asked a question about a matter which had been much debated by the public and the newspapers; he answered the question without any hesitancy. "General, who planned the the march through Georgia?" "The enemy!" He added that the enemy usually makes your plans for you. He meant that the enemy by neglect or through force of circumstances leaves an opening for you, and you see your chance and take advantage of it.

Circumstances do the planning for us all, no doubt, by help of our temperaments. I see no great difference between a man and a watch, except that the man is conscious and the watch isn't, and the man TRIES to plan things and the watch doesn't. The watch doesn't wind itself and doesn't regulate itself--these things are done exteriorly. Outside influences, outside circumstances, wind the MAN and regulate him. Left to himself, he wouldn't get regulated at all, and the sort of time he would keep would not be valuable. Some rare men are wonderful watches, with gold case, compensation balance, and all those things, and some men are only simple and sweet and humble Waterburys. I am a Waterbury. A Waterbury of that kind, some say.

A nation is only an individual multiplied. It makes plans and Circumstances comes and upsets them--or enlarges them. Some patriots throw the tea overboard; some other patriots destroy a Bastille. The PLANS stop there; then Circumstance comes in, quite unexpectedly, and turns these modest riots into a revolution.

And there was poor Columbus. He elaborated a deep plan to find a new route to an old country. Circumstance revised his plan for him, and he found a new WORLD. And HE gets the credit of it to this day. He hadn't anything to do with it.

Necessarily the scene of the real turning-point of my life (and of yours) was the Garden of Eden. It was there that the first link was forged of the chain that was ultimately to lead to the emptying of me into the literary guild. Adam's TEMPERAMENT was the first command the Deity ever issued to a human being on this planet. And it was the only command Adam would NEVER be able to disobey. It said, "Be weak, be water, be characterless, be cheaply persuadable." The latter command, to let the fruit alone, was certain to be disobeyed. Not by Adam himself, but by his TEMPERAMENT--which he did not create and had no authority over. For the TEMPERAMENT is the man; the thing tricked out with clothes and named Man is merely its Shadow, nothing more. The law of the tiger's temperament is, Thou shalt kill; the law of the sheep's temperament is Thou shalt not kill. To issue later commands requiring the tiger to let the fat stranger alone, and requiring the sheep to imbue its hands in the blood of the lion is not worth while, for those commands CAN'T be obeyed. They would invite to violations of the law of TEMPERAMENT, which is supreme, and take precedence of all other authorities. I cannot help feeling disappointed in Adam and Eve. That is, in their temperaments. Not in THEM, poor helpless young creatures-- afflicted with temperaments made out of butter; which butter was com-manded to get into contact with fire and BE MELTED. What I cannot help wishing is, that Adam had been postponed, and Martin Luther and Joan of Arc put in their place--that splendid pair equipped with temperaments not made of butter, but of asbestos. By neither sugary persuasions nor by hell fire could Satan have beguiled THEM to eat the apple. There would have been results! Indeed, yes. The apple would be intact today;

there would be no human race; there would be no YOU; there would be no ME. And the old, old creation-dawn scheme of ultimately launching me into the literary guild would have been defeated.

HOW TO MAKE HISTORY DATES STICK

THESE chapters are for children, and I shall try to make the words large enough to command respect. In the hope that you are listening, and that you have confidence in me, I will proceed. Dates are difficult things to acquire; and after they are acquired it is difficult to keep them in the head. But they are very valuable. They are like the cattle-pens of a ranch--they shut in the several brands of historical cattle, each within its own fence, and keep them from getting mixed together. Dates are hard to remember because they consist of figures; figures are monotonously unstriking in appearance, and they don't take hold, they form no pictures, and so they give the eye no chance to help. Pictures are the thing. Pictures can make dates stick. They can make nearly anything stick-- particularly IF YOU MAKE THE PICTURES YOURSELF. Indeed, that is the great point--make the pictures YOURSELF. I know about this from experience. Thirty years ago I was delivering a memorized lecture every night, and every night I had to help myself with a page of notes to keep from getting myself mixed. The notes consisted of beginnings of sentences, and were eleven in number, and they ran something like this:

"IN THAT REGION THE WEATHER--"

"AT THAT TIME IT WAS A CUSTOM--"

"BUT IN CALIFORNIA ONE NEVER HEARD--"

Eleven of them. They initialed the brief divisions of the lecture and protected me against skipping. But they all looked about alike on the page; they formed no picture; I had them by heart, but I could never with certainty remember the order of their succession; therefore I always had to keep those notes by me and look at them every little while. Once I mislaid them; you will not be able to imagine the terrors of that evening. I now saw that I must invent some other protection. So I got ten of the initial letters by heart in their proper order--I, A, B, and so on--and I went on the platform the next night with these marked in ink on my ten finger-nails. But it didn't answer. I kept track of the figures for a while; then I lost it, and after that I was never quite sure which finger I had used last. I couldn't lick off a letter after using it, for while that would have made success certain it also would have provoked too much curiosity. There was curiosity enough without that. To the audience I seemed more interested in my fingernails than I was in my subject; one or two persons asked me afterward what was the matter with my hands.

It was now that the idea of pictures occurred to me; then my troubles passed away. In two minutes I made six pictures with a pen, and they did the work of the eleven catch-sentences, and did it perfectly. I threw the pictures away as soon as they were made, for I was sure I could shut my eyes and see them any time. That was a quarter of a century ago; the lecture vanished out of my head more than twenty years ago, but I would rewrite it from the pictures--for they remain. Here are three of them: (Fig. 1).

The first one is a haystack--below it a rattlesnake--and it told me where to begin to talk ranch-life in Carson Valley. The second one told me where to begin the talk about a strange and violent wind that used to burst upon Carson City from the Sierra Nevadas every afternoon at two o'clock and try to blow the town away. The third picture, as you easily perceive, is lightning; its duty was to remind me when it was time to begin to talk about San Francisco weather, where there IS no lightning--nor thunder, either--and it never failed me.

I will give you a valuable hint. When a man is making a speech and you are to follow him don't jot down notes to speak from, jot down PICTURES. It is awkward and embarrassing to have to keep referring to notes; and besides it breaks up your speech and makes it ragged and non-coherent; but you can tear up your pictures as soon as you have made them--they will stay fresh and strong in your memory in the order and sequence in which you scratched them down. And many will admire to see what a good memory you are furnished with, when perhaps your memory is not any better than mine.

Sixteen years ago when my children were little creatures the governess was trying to hammer some primer histories into their heads. Part of this fun--if you like to call it that--consisted in the memorizing of the accession dates of the thirty-seven personages who had ruled England from the Conqueror down. These little people found it a bitter, hard contract. It was all dates, and all looked alike, and they wouldn't stick. Day after day of the summer vacation dribbled by, and still the kings held the fort; the children couldn't conquer any six of them.

With my lecture experience in mind I was aware that I could invent some way out of the trouble with pictures, but I hoped a way could be found which would let them romp in the open air while they learned the kings. I found it, and they mastered all the monarchs in a day or two.

The idea was to make them SEE the reigns with their eyes; that would be a large help. We were at the farm then. From the house-porch the grounds sloped gradually down to the lower fence and rose on the right to the high ground where my small work-den stood. A carriage-road wound through the grounds and up the hill. I staked it out with the English monarchs, beginning with the Conqueror, and you could stand on the porch and clearly see every reign and its length, from the Conquest down to Victoria, then in the forty-sixth year of her reign--EIGHT HUNDRED AND SEVENTEEN YEARS OF English history under your eye at once!

English history was an unusually live topic in America just then. The world had suddenly realized that while it was not noticing the Queen had passed Henry VIII., passed Henry VI. and Elizabeth, and gaining in length every day. Her reign had entered the list of the long ones; everybody was interested now-- it was watching a race. Would she pass the long Edward? There was a possibility of it. Would she pass the long Henry? Doubtful, most people said. The long George? Impossible! Everybody said it. But we have lived to see her leave him two years behind.

I measured off 817 feet of the roadway, a foot representing a year, and at the beginning and end of each reign I drove a three-foot white-pine stake in the turf by the roadside and wrote the name and dates on it. Abreast the middle of the porch-front stood a great granite flower-vase overflowing with a cataract of bright-yellow flowers--I can't think of their name. The vase of William the Conqueror. We put his name on it and his accession date, 1066. We started from that and measured off twenty-one feet of the road, and drove William Rufus's state; then thirteen feet and drove the first Henry's stake; then thirty-five feet and drove Stephen's; then nineteen feet, which brought us just past the summer-house on the left; then we staked out thirty-five, ten, and seventeen for the second Henry and Richard and John; turned the curve and entered upon just what was needed for Henry III.--a level, straight stretch of fifty-six feet of road without a crinkle in it. And it lay exactly in front of the house, in the middle of the grounds. There couldn't have been a better place for that long reign; you could stand on the porch and see those two wide-apart stakes almost with your eyes shut. (Fig. 2.)

That isn't the shape of the road--I have bunched it up like that to save room. The road had some great curves in it, but their gradual sweep was such that they were no mar to history. No, in our road one could tell at a glance who was who by the size of the vacancy between stakes--with LOCALITY to help, of course.

Although I am away off here in a Swedish village [1] and those stakes did not stand till the snow came, I can see them today as plainly as ever; and whenever I think of an English monarch his stakes rise before me of their own accord and I notice the large or small space which he takes up on our road. Are your kings spaced off in your mind? When you think of Richard III. and of James II. do the durations of their reigns seem about alike to you? It isn't so to me; I always notice that there's a foot's difference. When you think of Henry III. do you see a great long stretch of straight road? I do; and just at the end where it joins on to Edward I. I always see a small pear-bush with its green fruit hanging down. When I think of the Commonwealth I see a shady little group of these small saplings which we called the oak parlor; when I think of George III. I see him stretching up the hill, part of him occupied by a flight of stone steps; and I can locate Stephen to an inch when he comes into my mind, for he just filled the stretch which went by the summer-house. Victoria's reign reached almost to my study door on the first little summit; there's sixteen feet to be added now; I believe that that would carry it to a big pine-tree that was shattered by some lightning one summer when it was trying to hit me.

We got a good deal of fun out of the history road; and exercise, too. We trotted the course from the conqueror to the study, the children calling out the names, dates, and length of reigns as we passed the stakes, going a good gait along the long reigns, but slowing down when we came upon people like Mary and Edward VI., and the short Stuart and Plantagenet, to give time to get in the statistics. I offered prizes, too--apples. I threw one as far as I could send it, and the child that first shouted the reign it fell in got the apple.

The children were encouraged to stop locating things as being "over by the arbor," or "in the oak parlor," or "up at the stone steps," and say instead that the things were in Stephen, or in the Commonwealth, or in George III. They got the habit without trouble. To have the long road mapped out with such exactness was a great boon for me, for I had the habit of leaving books and other articles lying around everywhere, and had not previously been able to definitely name the place, and so had often been obliged to go to fetch them myself, to save time and failure; but now I could name the reign I left them in, and send the children.

Next I thought I would measure off the French reigns, and peg them alongside the English ones, so that we could always have contemporaneous French history under our eyes as we went our English rounds. We pegged them down to the Hundred Years' War, then threw the idea aside, I do not now remember why. After that we made the English pegs fence in European and American history as well as English, and that answered very well. English and alien poets, statesmen, artists, heroes, battles, plagues, cataclysms, revolutions--we shoveled them all into the English fences according to their dates. Do you understand? We gave Washington's birth to George II.'s pegs and his death to George III.'s; George II. got the Lisbon earthquake and George III. the Declaration of Independence. Goethe, Shakespeare, Napoleon, Savonarola, Joan of Arc, the French Revolution, the Edict of Nantes, Clive, Wellington, Waterloo, Plassey, Patay, Cowpens, Saratoga, the Battle of the Boyne, the invention of the logarithms, the microscope, the steam-engine, the telegraph-- anything and everything all over the world--we dumped it all in among the English pegs according to it date and regardless of its nationality.

If the road-pegging scheme had not succeeded I should have lodged the kings in the children's heads by means of pictures-- that is, I should have tried. It might have failed, for the pictures could only be effective WHEN MADE BY THE PUPIL; not the master, for it is the work put upon the drawing that makes the drawing stay in the memory, and my children were too little to make drawings at that time. And, besides, they had no talent for art, which is strange, for in other ways they are like me.

But I will develop the picture plan now, hoping that you will be able to use it. It will come good for indoors when the weather is bad and one cannot go outside and peg a road. Let us imagine that the kings are a procession, and that they have come out of the Ark and down Ararat for exercise and are now starting back again up the zigzag road. This will bring several of them into view at once, and each zigzag will represent the length of a king's reign.

And so on. You will have plenty of space, for by my project you will use the parlor wall. You do not mark on the wall; that would cause trouble. You only attach bits of paper to it with pins or thumb-tacks. These will leave no mark.

Take your pen now, and twenty-one pieces of white paper, each two inches square, and we will do the twenty-one years of the Conqueror's reign. On each square draw a picture of a whale and write the dates and term of service. We choose the whale for several reasons: its name and William's begin with the same letter; it is the biggest fish that swims, and William is the most conspicuous figure in English history in the way of a landmark; finally, a whale is about the easiest thing to draw. By the time you have drawn twenty-one wales and written "William I.-- 1066-1087--twenty-one years" twenty-one times, those details will be your property; you cannot dislodge them from your memory with anything but dynamite. I will make a sample for you to copy: (Fig. 3).

I have got his chin up too high, but that is no matter; he is looking for Harold. It may be that a whale hasn't that fin up there on his back, but I do not remember; and so, since there is a doubt, it is best to err on the safe side. He looks better, anyway, than he would without it.

Be very careful and ATTENTIVE while you are drawing your first whale from my sample and writing the word and figures under it, so that you will not need to copy the sample any more. Compare your copy with the sample; examine closely; if you find you have got everything right and can shut your eyes and see the picture and call the words and figures, then turn the sample and copy upside down and make the next copy from memory; and also the next and next, and so on, always drawing and writing from memory until you have finished the whole twenty-one. This will take you twenty minutes, or thirty, and by that time you will find that you can make a whale in less time than an unpracticed person can make a sardine; also, up to the time you die you will always be able to furnish William's dates to any ignorant person that inquires after them.

You will now take thirteen pieces of BLUE paper, each two inches square, and do William II. (Fig. 4.)

Make him spout his water forward instead of backward; also make him small, and stick a harpoon in him and give him that sick look in the eye. Otherwise you might seem to be continuing the other William, and that would be confusing and a damage. It is quite right to make him small; he was only about a No. 11 whale, or along there somewhere; there wasn't room in him for his father's great spirit. The barb of that harpoon ought not to show like that, because it is down inside the whale and ought to be out of sight, but it cannot be helped; if the barb were removed people would think some one had stuck a whip-stock into the whale. It is best to leave the barb the way it is, then every one will know it is a harpoon and attending to business. Remember--draw from the copy only once; make your other twelve and the inscription from memory.

Now the truth is that whenever you have copied a picture and its inscription once from my sample and two or three times from memory the details will stay with you and be hard to forget. After that, if you like, you may make merely the whale's HEAD and WATER-SPOUT for the Conqueror till you end his reign, each time SAYING the inscription in place of writing it; and in the case of William II. make the HARPOON alone, and say over the inscription each time you do it. You see, it will take nearly twice as long to do the first set as it will to do the second, and that will give you a marked sense of the difference in length of the two reigns.

Next do Henry I. on thirty-five squares of RED paper. (Fig. 5.)

That is a hen, and suggests Henry by furnishing the first syllable. When you have repeated the hen and the inscription until you are perfectly sure of them, draw merely the hen's head the rest of the thirty-five times, saying over the inscription each time. Thus: (Fig. 6).

You begin to understand how how this procession is going to look when it is on the wall. First there will be the Conqueror's twenty-one whales and water-spouts, the twenty-one white squares joined to one another and making a white stripe three and one- half feet long; the thirteen blue squares of William II. will be joined to that--a blue stripe two feet, two inches long, followed by Henry's red stripe five feet, ten inches long, and so on. The colored divisions will smartly show to the eye the difference in the length of the reigns and impress the propor- tions on the memory and the understanding. (Fig. 7.)

Stephen of Blois comes next. He requires nineteen two-inch squares of YELLOW paper. (Fig. 8.)

That is a steer. The sound suggests the beginning of Stephen's name. I choose it for that reason. I can make a better steer than that when I am not excited. But this one will do. It is a good-enough steer for history. The tail is defective, but it only wants straightening out.

Next comes Henry II. Give him thirty-five squares of RED paper. These hens must face west, like the former ones. (Fig. 9.)

This hen differs from the other one. He is on his way to inquire what has been happening in Canterbury.

How we arrive at Richard I., called Richard of the Lion- heart because he was a brave fighter and was never so contented as when he was leading crusades in Palestine and neglecting his affairs at home. Give him ten squares of WHITE paper. (Fig. 10).

That is a lion. His office is to remind you of the lion- hearted Richard. There is something the matter with his legs, but I do not quite know what it is, they do not seem right. I think the hind ones are the most unsatisfactory; the front ones are well enough, though it would be better if they were rights and lefts.

Next comes King John, and he was a poor circumstance. He was called Lackland. He gave his realm to the Pope. Let him have seventeen squares of YELLOW paper. (Fig. 11.)

That creature is a jamboree. It looks like a trademark, but that is only an accident and not intentional. It is prehistoric and extinct. It used to roam the earth in the Old Silurian times, and lay eggs and catch fish and climb trees and live on fossils; for it was of a mixed breed, which was the fashion then. It was very fierce, and the Old Silurians were afraid of it, but this is a tame one. Physically it has no representative now, but its mind has been transmitted. First I drew it sitting down, but have turned it the other way now because I think it looks more attractive and spirited when one end of it is galloping. I love to think that in this attitude it gives us a pleasant idea of John coming all in a happy excitement to see what the barons have been arranging for him at Runnymede, while the other one gives us an idea of him sitting down to wring his hands and grieve over it.

We now come to Henry III.; RED squares again, of course-- fifty-six of them. We must make all the Henrys the same color; it will make their long reigns show up handsomely on the wall. Among all the eight Henrys there were but two short ones. A lucky name, as far as longevity goes. The reigns of six of the Henrys cover 227 years. It might have been well to name all the royal princes Henry, but this was overlooked until it was too late. (Fig. 12.)

This is the best one yet. He is on his way (1265) to have a look at the first House of Commons in English history. It was a monumental event, the situation in the House, and was the second great liberty landmark which the century had set up. I have made Henry looking glad, but this was not intentional. Edward I. comes next; LIGHT-BROWN paper, thirty-five squares. (Fig. 13.)

That is an editor. He is trying to think of a word. He props his feet on a chair, which is the editor's way; then he can think better. I do not care much for this one; his ears are not alike; still, editor suggests the sound of Edward, and he will do. I could make him better if I had a model, but I made this one from memory. But is no particular matter; they all look alike, anyway. They are conceited and troublesome, and don't pay enough. Edward was the first really English king that had yet occupied the throne. The editor in the picture probably looks just as Edward looked when it was first borne in upon him that this was so. His whole attitude expressed gratification and pride mixed with stupefaction and astonishment.

Edward II. now; twenty BLUE squares. (Fig. 14.)

Another editor. That thing behind his ear is his pencil. Whenever he finds a bright thing in your manuscript he strikes it out with that. That does him good, and makes him smile and show his teeth, the way he is doing in the picture. This one has just been striking out a smart thing, and now he is sitting there with his thumbs in his vest-holes, gloating. They are full of envy and malice, editors are. This picture will serve to remind you that Edward II. was the first English king who was DEPOSED. Upon demand, he signed his deposition himself. He had found kingship a most aggravating and disagreeable occupation, and you can see by the look of him that he is glad he resigned. He has put his blue pencil up for good now. He had struck out many a good thing with it in his time.

Edward III. next; fifty RED squares. (Fig. 15.)

This editor is a critic. He has pulled out his carving- knife and his tomahawk and is starting after a book which he is going to have for breakfast. This one's arms are put on wrong. I did not notice it at first, but I see it now. Somehow he has got his right arm on his left shoulder, and his left arm on his right shoulder, and this shows us the back of his hands in both instances. It makes him left-handed all around, which is a thing which has never happened before, except perhaps in a museum. That is the way with art, when it is not acquired but born to you: you start in to make some simple little thing, not suspecting that your genius is beginning to work and swell and strain in secret, and all of a sudden there is a convulsion and you fetch out something astonishing. This is called inspiration. It is an accident; you never know when it is coming. I might have tried as much as a year to think of such a strange thing as an all-around left-handed man and I could not have done it, for the more you try to think of an unthinkable thing the more it eludes you; but it can't elude inspiration; you have only to bait with inspiration and you will get it every time. Look at Botticelli's "Spring." Those snaky women were unthinkable, but inspiration secured them for us, thanks to goodness. It is too late to reorganize this editor-critic now; we will leave him as he is. He will serve to remind us.

Richard II. next; twenty-two WHITE squares. (Fig. 16.)

We use the lion again because this is another Richard. Like Edward II., he was DEPOSED. He is taking a last sad look at his crown before they take it away. There was not room enough and I have made it too small; but it never fitted him, anyway.

Now we turn the corner of the century with a new line of monarchs--the Lancastrian kings.

Henry IV.; fourteen squares of YELLOW paper. (Fig. 17.)

This hen has laid the egg of a new dynasty and realizes the magnitude of the event. She is giving notice in the usual way. You notice I am improving in the construction of hens. At first I made them too much like other animals, but this one is orthodox. I mention this to encourage you. You will find that the more you practice the more accurate you will become. I could always draw animals, but before I was educated I could not tell what kind they were when I got them done, but now I can. Keep up your courage; it will be the same with you, although you may not think it. This Henry died the year after Joan of Arc was born.

Henry V.; nine BLUE squares. (Fig. 18)

There you see him lost in meditation over the monument which records the amazing figures of the battle of Agincourt. French history says 20,000 Englishmen routed 80,000 Frenchmen there; and English historians say that the French loss, in killed and wounded, was 60,000.

Henry VI.; thirty-nine RED squares. (Fig. 19)

This is poor Henry VI., who reigned long and scored many misfortunes and humiliations. Also two great disasters: he lost France to Joan of Arc and he lost the throne and ended the dynasty which Henry IV. had started in business with such good prospects. In the picture we see him sad and weary and downcast, with the scepter falling from his nerveless grasp. It is a pathetic quenching of a sun which had risen in such splendor.

Edward IV.; twenty-two LIGHT-BROWN squares. (Fig. 20.)

That is a society editor, sitting there elegantly dressed, with his legs crossed in that indolent way, observing the clothes the ladies wear, so that he can describe them for his paper and make them out finer than they are and get bribes for it and become wealthy. That flower which he is wearing in his buttonhole is a rose--a white rose, a York rose--and will serve to remind us of the War of the Roses, and that the white one was the winning color when Edward got the throne and dispossessed the Lancastrian dynasty.

Edward V.; one-third of a BLACK square. (Fig. 21.)

His uncle Richard had him murdered in the tower. When you get the reigns displayed upon the wall this one will be conspicuous and easily remembered. It is the shortest one in English history except Lady Jane Grey's, which was only nine days. She is never officially recognized as a monarch of England, but if you or I should ever occupy a throne we should like to have proper notice taken of it; and it would be only fair and right, too, particularly if we gained nothing by it and lost our lives besides.

Richard III.; two WHITE squares. (Fig. 22.)

That is not a very good lion, but Richard was not a very good king. You would think that this lion has two heads, but that is not so; one is only a shadow. There would be shadows for the rest of him, but there was not light enough to go round, it being a dull day, with only fleeting sun-glimpses now and then. Richard had a humped back and a hard heart, and fell at the battle of Bosworth. I do not know the name of that flower in the pot, but we will use it as Richard's trade-mark, for it is said that it grows in only one place in the world--Bosworth Field-- and tradition says it never grew there until Richard's royal blood warmed its hidden seed to life and made it grow.

Henry VII.; twenty-four BLUE squares. (Fig. 23.)

Henry VII. had no liking for wars and turbulence; he preferred peace and quiet and the general prosperity which such conditions create. He liked to sit on that kind of eggs on his own private account as well as the nation's, and hatch them out and count up their result. When he died he left his heir 2,000,000 pounds, which was a most unusual fortune for a king to possess in those days. Columbus's great achievement gave him the discovery-fever, and he sent Sebastian Cabot to the New World to search out some foreign territory for England. That is Cabot's ship up there in the corner. This was the first time that England went far abroad to enlarge her estate--but not the last.

Henry VIII.; thirty-eight RED squares. (Fig. 24.)

That is Henry VIII. suppressing a monastery in his arrogant fashion.

Edward VI.; six squares of YELLOW paper. (Fig. 25.)

He is the last Edward to date. It is indicated by that thing over his head, which is a LAST--shoemaker's last.

Mary; five squares of BLACK paper. (Fig. 26.)

The picture represents a burning martyr. He is in back of the smoke. The first three letters of Mary's name and the first three of the word martyr are the same. Martyrdom was going out in her day and martyrs were becoming scarcer, but she made several. For this reason she is sometimes called Bloody Mary.

This brings us to the reign of Elizabeth, after passing through a period of nearly five hundred years of England's history--492 to be exact. I think you may now be trusted to go the rest of the way without further lessons in art or inspirations in the matter of ideas. You have the scheme now, and something in the ruler's name or career will suggest the pictorial symbol. The effort of inventing such things will not only help your memory, but will develop originality in art. See what it has done for me. If you do not find the parlor wall big enough for all of England's history, continue it into the dining- room and into other rooms. This will make the walls interesting and instructive and really worth something instead of being just flat things to hold the house together.

-----

1. Summer of 1899.

THE MEMORABLE ASSASSINATION

N OTE.--The assassination of the Empress of Austria at Geneva, September 10, 1898, occurred during Mark Twain's Austrian residence. The news came to him at Kaltenleutgeben, a summer resort a little way out of Vienna. To his friend, the Rev. Jos. H. Twichell, he wrote:

"That good and unoffending lady, the Empress, is killed by a madman, and I am living in the midst of world-history again. The Queen's Jubilee last year, the invasion of the Reichsrath by the police, and now this murder, which will still be talked of and described and painted a thousand a thousand years from now. To have a personal friend of the wearer of two crowns burst in at the gate in the deep dusk of the evening and say, in a voice broken with tears, 'My God! the Empress is murdered,' and fly toward her home before we can utter a question--why, it brings the giant event home to you, makes you a part of it and personally interested; it is as if your neighbor, Antony, should come flying and say, 'Caesar is butchered--the head of the world is fallen!'

"Of course there is no talk but of this. The mourning is universal and genuine, the consternation is stupefying. The Austrian Empire is being draped with black. Vienna will be a spectacle to see by next Saturday, when the funeral cort`ege marches."

He was strongly moved by the tragedy, impelled to write concerning it. He prepared the article which follows, but did not offer it for publication, perhaps feeling that his own close association with the court circles at the moment prohibited this personal utterance. There appears no such reason for withholding its publication now.

A. B. P.

The more one thinks of the assassination, the more imposing and tremendous the event becomes. The destruction of a city is a large event, but it is one which repeats itself several times in a thousand years; the destruction of a third part of a nation by plague and famine is a large event, but it has happened several times in history; the murder of a king is a large event, but it has been frequent.

The murder of an empress is the largest of all events. One must go back about two thousand years to find an instance to put with this one. The oldest family of unchallenged descent in Christendom lives in Rome and traces its line back seventeen hundred years, but no member of it has been present in the earth when an empress was murdered, until now. Many a time during these seventeen centuries members of that family have been startled with the news of extraordinary events--the destruction of cities, the fall of thrones, the murder of kings, the wreck of dynasties, the extinction of religions, the birth of new systems of government; and their descendants have been by to hear of it and talk about it when all these things were repeated once, twice, or a dozen times--but to even that family has come news at last which is not staled by use, has no duplicates in the long reach of its memory.

It is an event which confers a curious distinction upon every individual now living in the world: he has stood alive and breathing in the presence of an event such as has not fallen within the experience of any traceable or untraceable ancestor of his for twenty centuries, and it is not likely to fall within the experience of any descendant of his for twenty more.

Time has made some great changes since the Roman days. The murder of an empress then--even the assassination of Caesar himself--could not electrify the world as this murder has electrified it. For one reason, there was then not much of a world to electrify; it was a small world, as to known bulk, and it had rather a thin population, besides; and for another reason, the news traveled so slowly that its tremendous initial thrill wasted away, week by week and month by month, on the journey, and by the time it reached the remoter regions there was but little of it left. It was no longer a fresh event, it was a thing of the far past; it was not properly news, it was history. But the world is enormous now, and prodigiously populated-- that is one change; and another is the lightning swiftness of the flight of tidings, good and bad. "The Empress is murdered!" When those amazing words struck upon my ear in this Austrian village last Saturday, three hours after the disaster, I knew that it was already old news in London, Paris, Berlin, New York, San Francisco, Japan, China, Melbourne, Cape Town, Bombay, Madras, Calcutta, and that the entire globe with a single voice, was cursing the perpetrator of it. Since the telegraph first began to stretch itself wider and wider about the earth, larger and increasingly larger areas of the world have, as time went on, received simultaneously the shock of a great calamity; but this is the first time in history that the entire surface of the globe has been swept in a single instant with the thrill of so gigantic an event.

And who is the miracle-worker who has furnished to the world this spectacle? All the ironies are compacted in the answer. He is at the bottom of the human ladder, as the accepted estimates of degree and value go: a soiled and patched young loafer, without gifts, without talents, without education, without morals, without character, without any born charm or any acquired one that wins or beguiles or attracts; without a single grace of mind or heart or hand that any tramp or prostitute could envy him; an unfaithful private in the ranks, an incompetent stone- cutter, an inefficient lackey; in a word, a mangy, offensive, empty, unwashed, vulgar, gross, mephitic, timid, sneaking, human polecat. And it was within the privileges and powers of this sarcasm upon the human race to reach up--up--up--and strike from its far summit in the social skies the world's accepted ideal of Glory and Might and Splendor and Sacredness! It realizes to us what sorry shows and shadows we are. Without our clothes and our pedestals we are poor things and much of a size; our dignities are not real, our pomps are shams. At our best and stateliest we are not suns, as we pretended, and teach, and believe, but only candles; and any bummer can blow us out.

And now we get realized to us once more another thing which we often forget--or try to: that no man has a wholly undiseased mind; that in one way or another all men are mad. Many are mad for money. When this madness is in a mild form it is harmless and the man passes for sane; but when it develops powerfully and takes possession of the man, it can make him cheat, rob, and kill; and when he has got his fortune and lost it again it can land him in the asylum or the suicide's coffin. Love is a madness; if thwarted it develops fast; it can grow to a frenzy of despair and make an otherwise sane and highly gifted prince, like Rudolph, throw away the crown of an empire and snuff out his own life. All the whole list of desires, predilections, aversions, ambitions, passions, cares, griefs, regrets, remorses, are incipient madness, and ready to grow, spread, and consume, when the occasion comes. There are no healthy minds, and nothing saves any man but accident--the accident of not having his malady put to the supreme test.

One of the commonest forms of madness is the desire to be noticed, the pleasure derived from being noticed. Perhaps it is not merely common, but universal. In its mildest form it doubtless is universal. Every child is pleased at being noticed; many intolerable children put in their whole time in distressing and idiotic effort to attract the attention of visitors; boys are always "showing off"; apparently all men and women are glad and grateful when they find that they have done a thing which has lifted them for a moment out of obscurity and caused wondering talk. This common madness can develop, by nurture, into a hunger for notoriety in one, for fame in another. It is this madness for being noticed and talked about which has invented kingship and the thousand other dignities, and tricked them out with pretty and showy fineries; it has made kings pick one another's pockets, scramble for one another's crowns and estates, slaughter one another's subjects; it has raised up prize-fighters, and poets, and villages mayors, and little and big politicians, and big and little charity-founders, and bicycle champions, and banditti chiefs, and frontier desperadoes, and Napoleons. Anything to get notoriety; anything to set the village, or the township, or the city, or the State, or the nation, or the planet shouting, "Look--there he goes--that is the man!" And in five minutes' time, at no cost of brain, or labor, or genius this mangy Italian tramp has beaten them all, transcended them all, outstripped them all, for in time their names will perish; but by the friendly help of the insane newspapers and courts and kings and historians, his is safe and live and thunder in the world all down the ages as long as human speech shall endure! Oh, if it were not so tragic how ludicrous it would be!

She was so blameless, the Empress; and so beautiful, in mind and heart, in person and spirit; and whether with a crown upon her head or without it and nameless, a grace to the human race, and almost a justification of its creation; WOULD be, indeed, but that the animal that struck her down re-establishes the doubt.

In her character was every quality that in woman invites and engages respect, esteem, affection, and homage. Her tastes, her instincts, and her aspirations were all high and fine and all her life her heart and brain were busy with activities of a noble sort. She had had bitter griefs, but they did not sour her spirit, and she had had the highest honors in the world's gift, but she went her simple way unspoiled. She knew all ranks, and won them all, and made them her friends. An English fisherman's wife said, "When a body was in trouble she didn't send her help, she brought it herself." Crowns have adorned others, but she adorned her crowns.

It was a swift celebrity the assassin achieved. And it is marked by some curious contrasts. At noon last, Saturday there was no one in the world who would have considered acquaintanceship with him a thing worth claiming or mentioning; no one would have been vain of such an acquaintanceship; the humblest honest boot-black would not have valued the fact that he had met him or seen him at some time or other; he was sunk in abysmal obscurity, he was away beneath the notice of the bottom grades of officialdom. Three hours later he was the one subject of conversation in the world, the gilded generals and admirals and governors were discussing him, all the kings and queens and emperors had put aside their other interests to talk about him. And wherever there was a man, at the summit of the world or the bottom of it, who by chance had at some time or other come across that creature, he remembered it with a secret satisfaction, and MENTIONED it--for it was a distinction, now! It brings human dignity pretty low, and for a moment the thing is not quite realizable--but it is perfectly true. If there is a king who can remember, now, that he once saw that creature in a time past, he has let that fact out, in a more or less studiedly casual and indifferent way, some dozens of times during the past week. For a king is merely human; the inside of him is exactly like the inside of any other person; and it is human to find satisfaction in being in a kind of personal way connected with amazing events. We are all privately vain of such a thing; we are all alike; a king is a king by accident; the reason the rest of us are not kings is merely due to another accident; we are all made out of the same clay, and it is a sufficient poor quality.

Below the kings, these remarks are in the air these days; I know it well as if I were hearing them:

THE COMMANDER: "He was in my army."

THE GENERAL: "He was in my corps."

THE COLONEL: "He was in my regiment. A brute. I remember him well."

THE CAPTAIN: "He was in my company. A troublesome scoundrel. I remember him well."

THE SERGEANT: "Did I know him? As well as I know you. Why, every morning I used to--" etc., etc.; a glad, long story, told to devouring ears.

THE LANDLADY: "Many's the time he boarded with me. I can show you his very room, and the very bed he slept in. And the charcoal mark there on the wall--he made that. My little Johnny saw him do it with his own eyes. Didn't you, Johnny?"

It is easy to see, by the papers, that the magistrate and the constables and the jailer treasure up the assassin's daily remarks and doings as precious things, and as wallowing this week in seas of blissful distinction. The interviewer, too; he tried to let on that he is not vain of his privilege of contact with this man whom few others are allowed to gaze upon, but he is human, like the rest, and can no more keep his vanity corked in than could you or I.

Some think that this murder is a frenzied revolt against the criminal militarism which is impoverishing Europe and driving the starving poor mad. That has many crimes to answer for, but not this one, I think. One may not attribute to this man a generous indignation against the wrongs done the poor; one may not dignify him with a generous impulse of any kind. When he saw his photograph and said, "I shall be celebrated," he laid bare the impulse that prompted him. It was a mere hunger for notoriety. There is another confessed case of the kind which is as old as history--the burning of the temple of Ephesus.

Among the inadequate attempts to account for the assassination we must concede high rank to the many which have described it as a "peculiarly brutal crime" and then added that it was "ordained from above." I think this verdict will not be popular "above." If the deed was ordained from above, there is no rational way of making this prisoner even partially responsible for it, and the Genevan court cannot condemn him without manifestly committing a crime. Logic is logic, and by disregarding its laws even the most pious and showy theologian may be beguiled into preferring charges which should not be ventured upon except in the shelter of plenty of lightning-rods.

I witnessed the funeral procession, in company with friends, from the windows of the Krantz, Vienna's sumptuous new hotel. We came into town in the middle of the forenoon, and I went on foot from the station. Black flags hung down from all the houses; the aspects were Sunday-like; the crowds on the sidewalks were quiet and moved slowly; very few people were smoking; many ladies wore deep mourning, gentlemen were in black as a rule; carriages were speeding in all directions, with footmen and coachmen in black clothes and wearing black cocked hats; the shops were closed; in many windows were pictures of the Empress: as a beautiful young bride of seventeen; as a serene and majestic lady with added years; and finally in deep black and without ornaments--the costume she always wore after the tragic death of her son nine years ago, for her heart broke then, and life lost almost all its value for her. The people stood grouped before these pictures, and now and then one saw women and girls turn away wiping the tears from their eyes.

In front of the Krantz is an open square; over the way was the church where the funeral services would be held. It is small and old and severely plain, plastered outside and whitewashed or painted, and with no ornament but a statue of a monk in a niche over the door, and above that a small black flag. But in its crypt lie several of the great dead of the House of Habsburg, among them Maria Theresa and Napoleon's son, the Duke of Reichstadt. Hereabouts was a Roman camp, once, and in it the Emperor Marcus Aurelius died a thousand years before the first Habsburg ruled in Vienna, which was six hundred years ago and more.

The little church is packed in among great modern stores and houses, and the windows of them were full of people. Behind the vast plate-glass windows of the upper floors of the house on the corner one glimpsed terraced masses of fine-clothed men and women, dim and shimmery, like people under water. Under us the square was noiseless, but it was full of citizens; officials in fine uniforms were flitting about on errands, and in a doorstep sat a figure in the uttermost raggedness of poverty, the feet bare, the head bent humbly down; a youth of eighteen or twenty, he was, and through the field-glass one could see that he was tearing apart and munching riffraff that he had gathered somewhere. Blazing uniforms flashed by him, making a sparkling contrast with his drooping ruin of moldy rags, but he took not notice; he was not there to grieve for a nation's disaster; he had his own cares, and deeper. From two directions two long files of infantry came plowing through the pack and press in silence; there was a low, crisp order and the crowd vanished, the square save the sidewalks was empty, the private mourner was gone. Another order, the soldiers fell apart and enclosed the square in a double-ranked human fence. It was all so swift, noiseless, exact--like a beautifully ordered machine.

It was noon, now. Two hours of stillness and waiting followed. Then carriages began to flow past and deliver the two and three hundred court personages and high nobilities privileged to enter the church. Then the square filled up; not with civilians, but with army and navy officers in showy and beautiful uniforms. They filled it compactly, leaving only a narrow carriage path in front of the church, but there was no civilian among them. And it was better so; dull clothes would have marred the radiant spectacle. In the jam in front of the church, on its steps, and on the sidewalk was a bunch of uniforms which made a blazing splotch of color--intense red, gold, and white--which dimmed the brilliancies around them; and opposite them on the other side of the path was a bunch of cascaded bright-green plumes above pale-blue shoulders which made another splotch of splendor emphatic and conspicuous in its glowing surroundings. It was a sea of flashing color all about, but these two groups were the high notes. The green plumes were worn by forty or fifty Austrian generals, the group opposite them were chiefly Knights of Malta and knights of a German order. The mass of heads in the square were covered by gilt helmets and by military caps roofed with a mirror-like gaze, and the movements of the wearers caused these things to catch the sun-rays, and the effect was fine to see--the square was like a garden of richly colored flowers with a multitude of blinding and flashing little suns distributed over it.

Think of it--it was by command of that Italian loafer yonder on his imperial throne in the Geneva prison that this splendid multitude was assembled there; and the kings and emperors that were entering the church from a side street were there by his will. It is so strange, so unrealizable.

At three o'clock the carriages were still streaming by in single file. At three-five a cardinal arrives with his attendants; later some bishops; then a number of archdeacons--all in striking colors that add to the show. At three-ten a procession of priests passed along, with crucifix. Another one, presently; after an interval, two more; at three-fifty another one--very long, with many crosses, gold-embroidered robes, and much white lace; also great pictured banners, at intervals, receding into the distance.

A hum of tolling bells makes itself heard, but not sharply. At three-fifty-eight a waiting interval. Presently a long procession of gentlemen in evening dress comes in sight and approaches until it is near to the square, then falls back against the wall of soldiers at the sidewalk, and the white shirt-fronts show like snowflakes and are very conspicuous where so much warm color is all about.

A waiting pause. At four-twelve the head of the funeral procession comes into view at last. First, a body of cavalry, four abreast, to widen the path. Next, a great body of lancers, in blue, with gilt helmets. Next, three six-horse mourning-coaches; outriders and coachmen in black, with cocked hats and white wigs. Next, troops in splendid uniforms, red, gold, and white, exceedingly showy.

Now the multitude uncover. The soldiers present arms; there is a low rumble of drums; the sumptuous great hearse approaches, drawn at a walk by eight black horses plumed with black bunches of nodding ostrich feathers; the coffin is borne into the church, the doors are closed.

The multitude cover their heads, and the rest of the procession moves by; first the Hungarian Guard in their indescribably brilliant and picturesque and beautiful uniform, inherited from the ages of barbaric splendor, and after them other mounted forces, a long and showy array.

Then the shining crown in the square crumbled apart, a wrecked rainbow, and melted away in radiant streams, and in the turn of a wrist the three dirtiest and raggedest and cheerfulest little slum-girls in Austria were capering about in the spacious vacancy. It was a day of contrasts.

Twice the Empress entered Vienna in state. The first time was in 1854, when she was a bride of seventeen, and then she rode in measureless pomp and with blare of music through a fluttering world of gay flags and decorations, down streets walled on both hands with a press of shouting and welcoming subjects; and the second time was last Wednesday, when she entered the city in her coffin and moved down the same streets in the dead of the night under swaying black flags, between packed human walls again; but everywhere was a deep stillness, now--a stillness emphasized, rather than broken, by the muffled hoofbeats of the long cavalcade over pavements cushioned with sand, and the low sobbing of gray-headed women who had witnessed the first entry forty-four years before, when she and they were young--and unaware!

A character in Baron von Berger's recent fairy drama "Habsburg" tells about the first coming of the girlish Empress- Queen,
and in his history draws a fine picture: I cannot make a close
translation of it, but will try to convey the spirit of the verses:

I saw the stately pageant pass: In her high place I saw the
Empress-Queen: I could not take my eyes away From that fair
vision, spirit-like and pure, That rose serene, sublime, and
figured to my sense A noble Alp far lighted in the blue, That in
the flood of morning rends its veil of cloud And stands a dream
of glory to the gaze Of them that in the Valley toil and plod.

A SCRAP OF CURIOUS HISTORY

MARION City, on the Mississippi River, in the State of Missouri--a village; time, 1845.   La Bourboule-les-Bains, France --a village; time, the end of June, 1894. I was in the one village in that early time; I am in the other now. These times and places are sufficiently wide apart, yet today I have the strange sense of being thrust back into that Missourian village and of reliving certain stirring days that I lived there so long ago.

Last Saturday night the life of the President of the French Republic was taken by an Italian assassin. Last night a mob surrounded our hotel, shouting, howling, singing the "Marseillaise," and pelting our windows with sticks and stones; for we have Italian waiters, and the mob demanded that they be turned out of the house instantly--to be drubbed, and then driven out of the village. Everybody in the hotel remained up until far into the night, and experienced the several kinds of terror which one reads about in books which tell of nigh attacks by Italians and by French mobs: the growing roar of the oncoming crowd; the arrival, with rain of stones and a crash of glass; the withdrawal to rearrange plans--followed by a silence ominous, threatening, and harder to bear than even the active siege and the noise. The landlord and the two village policemen stood their ground, and at last the mob was persuaded to go away and leave our Italians in peace. Today four of the ringleaders have been sentenced to heavy punishment of a public sort--and are become local heroes, by consequence.

That is the very mistake which was at first made in the Missourian village half a century ago.   The mistake was repeated and repeated--just as France is doing in these later months.

In our village we had our Ravochals, our Henrys, our Vaillants; and in a humble way our Cesario--I hope I have spelled this name wrong.   Fifty years ago we passed through, in all essentials, what France has been passing through during the past two or three years, in the matter of periodical frights, horrors, and shudderings.

In several details the parallels are quaintly exact.   In that day, for a man to speak out openly and proclaim himself an enemy of negro slavery was simply to proclaim himself a madman. For he was blaspheming against the holiest thing known to a Missourian, and could NOT be in his right mind.   For a man to proclaim himself an anarchist in France, three years ago, was to proclaim himself a madman--he could not be in his right mind.

Now the original first blasphemer against any institution profoundly venerated by a community is quite sure to be in earnest; his followers and imitators may be humbugs and self-seekers, but he himself is sincere--his heart is in his protest.

Robert Hardy was our first ABOLITIONIST--awful name!   He was a journeyman cooper, and worked in the big cooper-shop belonging to the great pork-packing establishment which was Marion City's chief pride and sole source of prosperity.   He was a New- Englander, a stranger.   And, being a stranger, he was of course regarded as an inferior person--for that has been human nature from Adam down--and of course, also, he was made to feel unwelcome, for this is the ancient law with man and the other animals.   Hardy was thirty years old, and a bachelor; pale, given to reverie and reading. He was reserved, and seemed to prefer the isolation which had fallen to his lot. He was treated to many side remarks by his fellows, but as he did not resent them it was decided that he was a coward.

All of a sudden he proclaimed himself an abolitionist-- straight out and publicly! He said that negro slavery was a crime, an infamy. For a moment the town was paralyzed with astonishment; then it broke into a fury of rage and swarmed toward the cooper-shop to lynch Hardy. But the Methodist minister made a powerful speech to them and stayed their hands. He proved to them that Hardy was insane and not responsible for his words; that no man COULD be sane and utter such words.

So Hardy was saved. Being insane, he was allowed to go on talking. He was found to be good entertainment. Several nights running he made abolition speeches in the open air, and all the town flocked to hear and laugh. He implored them to believe him sane and sincere, and have pity on the poor slaves, and take measurements for the restoration of their stolen rights, or in no long time blood would flow--blood, blood, rivers of blood!

It was great fun. But all of a sudden the aspect of things changed. A slave came flying from Palmyra, the county-seat, a few miles back, and was about to escape in a canoe to Illinois and freedom in the dull twilight of the approaching dawn, when the town constable seized him. Hardy happened along and tried to rescue the negro; there was a struggle, and the constable did not come out of it alive. Hardly crossed the river with the negro, and then came back to give himself up. All this took time, for the Mississippi is not a French brook, like the Seine, the Loire, and those other rivulets, but is a real river nearly a mile wide. The town was on hand in force by now, but the Methodist preacher and the sheriff had already made arrangements in the interest of order; so Hardy was surrounded by a strong guard and safely conveyed to the village calaboose in spite of all the effort of the mob to get hold of him. The reader will have begun to perceive that this Methodist minister was a prompt man; a prompt man, with active hands and a good headpiece. Williams was his name--Damon Williams; Damon Williams in public, Damnation Williams in private, because he was so powerful on that theme and so frequent.

The excitement was prodigious. The constable was the first man who had ever been killed in the town. The event was by long odds the most imposing in the town's history. It lifted the humble village into sudden importance; its name was in everybody's mouth for twenty miles around. And so was the name of Robert Hardy--Robert Hardy, the stranger, the despised. In a day he was become the person of most conse-quence in the region, the only person talked about. As to those other coopers, they found their position curiously changed-- they were important people, or unimportant, now, in propor-tion as to how large or how small had been their intercourse with the new celebrity. The two or three who had really been on a sort of familiar footing with him found themselves objects of admiring interest with the public and of envy with their shopmates.

The village weekly journal had lately gone into new hands. The new man was an enterprising fellow, and he made the most of the tragedy. He issued an extra. Then he put up posters promising to devote his whole paper to matters connected with the great event--there would be a full and intensely interesting biography of the murderer, and even a portrait of him. He was as good as his word. He carved the portrait himself, on the back of a wooden type--and a terror it was to look at. It made a great commotion, for this was the first time the village paper had ever contained a picture. The village was very proud. The output of the paper was ten times as great as it had ever been before, yet every copy was sold.

When the trial came on, people came from all the farms around, and from Hannibal, and Quincy, and even from Keokuk; and the court-house could hold only a fraction of the crowd that applied for admission. The trial was published in the village paper, with fresh and still more trying pictures of the accused.

Hardy was convicted, and hanged--a mistake. People came from miles around to see the hanging; they brought cakes and cider, also the women and children, and made a picnic of the matter. It was the largest crowd the village had ever seen. The rope that hanged Hardy was eagerly bought up, in inch samples, for everybody wanted a memento of the memorable event.

Martyrdom gilded with notoriety has its fascinations. Within one week afterward four young lightweights in the village proclaimed themselves abolitionists! In life Hardy had not been able to make a convert; everybody laughed at him; but nobody could laugh at his legacy. The four swaggered around with their slouch-hats pulled down over their faces, and hinted darkly at awful possibilities. The people were troubled and afraid, and showed it. And they were stunned, too; they could not understand it. "Abolitionist" had always been a term of shame and horror; yet here were four young men who were not only not ashamed to bear that name, but were grimly proud of it. Respectable young men they were, too--of good families, and brought up in the church. Ed Smith, the printer's apprentice, nineteen, had been the head Sunday-school boy, and had once recited three thousand Bible verses without making a break. Dick Savage, twenty, the baker's apprentice; Will Joyce, twenty-two, journeyman blacksmith; and Henry Taylor, twenty-four, tobacco-stemmer--were the other three. They were all of a sentimental cast; they were all romance-readers; they all wrote poetry, such as it was; they were all vain and foolish; but they had never before been suspected of having anything bad in them.

They withdrew from society, and grew more and more mysterious and dreadful. They presently achieved the distinction of being denounced by names from the pulpit--which made an immense stir! This was grandeur, this was fame. They were envied by all the other young fellows now. This was natural. Their company grew--grew alarmingly. They took a name. It was a secret name, and was divulged to no outsider; publicly they were simply the abolitionists. They had pass-words, grips, and signs; they had secret meetings; their initiations were conducted with gloomy pomps and ceremonies, at midnight.

They always spoke of Hardy as "the Martyr," and every little while they moved through the principal street in procession--at midnight, black-robed, masked, to the measured tap of the solemn drum--on pilgrimage to the Martyr's grave, where they went through with some majestic fooleries and swore ven-geance upon his murderers. They gave previous notice of the pilgrimage by small posters, and warned everybody to keep indoors and darken all houses along the route, and leave the road empty. These warnings were obeyed, for there was a skull and crossbones at the top of the poster.

When this kind of thing had been going on about eight weeks, a quite natural thing happened. A few men of character and grit woke up out of the nightmare of fear which had been stupefy-ing their faculties, and began to discharge scorn and scoffings at themselves and the community for enduring this child's-play; and at the same time they proposed to end it straightway. Everybody felt an uplift; life was breathed into their dead spirits; their courage rose and they began to feel like men again. This was on a Saturday. All day the new feeling grew and strengthened; it grew with a rush; it brought inspiration and cheer with it. Midnight saw a united community, full of zeal and pluck, and with a clearly defined and welcome piece of work in front of it. The best organizer and strongest and bitterest talker on that great Saturday was the Presbyterian clergyman who had denounced the original four from his pulpit--Rev. Hiram Fletcher--and he promised to use his pulpit in the public interest again now. On the morrow he had revelations to make, he said--secrets of the dreadful society.

But the revelations were never made. At half past two in the morning the dead silence of the village was broken by a crashing explosion, and the town patrol saw the preacher's house spring in a wreck of whirling fragments into the sky. The preacher was killed, together with a negro woman, his only slave and servant.

The town was paralyzed again, and with reason. To struggle against a visible enemy is a thing worth while, and there is a plenty of men who stand always ready to undertake it; but to struggle against an invisible one--an invisible one who sneaks in and does his awful work in the dark and leaves no trace--that is another matter. That is a thing to make the bravest tremble and hold back.

The cowed populace were afraid to go to the funeral. The man who was to have had a packed church to hear him expose and denounce the common enemy had but a handful to see him buried. The coroner's jury had brought in a verdict of "death by the visitation of God," for no witness came forward; if any existed they prudently kept out of the way. Nobody seemed sorry. Nobody wanted to see the terrible secret society provoked into the commission of further outrages. Everybody wanted the tragedy hushed up, ignored, forgotten, if possible.

And so there was a bitter surprise and an unwelcome one when Will Joyce, the blacksmith's journeyman, came out and proclaimed himself the assassin! Plainly he was not minded to be robbed of his glory. He made his proclamation, and stuck to it. Stuck to it, and insisted upon a trial. Here was an ominous thing; here was a new and peculiarly formidable terror, for a motive was revealed here which society could not hope to deal with successfully--VANITY, thirst for notoriety. If men were going to kill for notoriety's sake, and to win the glory of newspaper renown, a big trial, and a showy execution, what possible invention of man could discourage or deter them? The town was in a sort of panic; it did not know what to do.

However, the grand jury had to take hold of the matter--it had no choice. It brought in a true bill, and presently the case went to the county court. The trial was a fine sensation. The prisoner was the principal witness for the prosecution. He gave a full account of the assassination; he furnished even the minutest particulars: how he deposited his keg of powder and laid his train--from the house to such-and-such a spot; how George Ronalds and Henry Hart came along just then, smoking, and he borrowed Hart's cigar and fired the train with it, shouting, "Down with all slave-tyrants!" and how Hart and Ronalds made no effort to capture him, but ran away, and had never come forward to testify yet.

But they had to testify now, and they did--and pitiful it was to see how reluctant they were, and how scared. The crowded house listened to Joyce's fearful tale with a profound and breathless interest, and in a deep hush which was not broken till he broke it himself, in concluding, with a roaring repetition of his "Death to all slave-tyrants!"--which came so unexpectedly and so startlingly that it made everyone present catch his breath and gasp.

The trial was put in the paper, with biography and large portrait, with other slanderous and insane pictures, and the edition sold beyond imagination.

The execution of Joyce was a fine and picturesque thing. It drew a vast crowd. Good places in trees and seats on rail fences sold for half a dollar apiece; lemonade and gingerbread-stands had great prosperity. Joyce recited a furious and fantastic and denunciatory speech on the scaffold which had imposing passages of school-boy eloquence in it, and gave him a reputation on the spot as an orator, and his name, later, in the society's records, of the "Martyr Orator." He went to his death breathing slaughter and charging his society to "avenge his murder." If he knew anything of human nature he knew that to plenty of young fellows present in that great crowd he was a grand hero--and enviably situated.

He was hanged. It was a mistake. Within a month from his death the society which he had honored had twenty new members, some of them earnest, determined men. They did not court distinction in the same way, but they celebrated his martyrdom. The crime which had been obscure and despised had become lofty and glorified.

Such things were happening all over the country. Wild- brained martyrdom was succeeded by uprising and organization. Then, in natural order, followed riot, insurrection, and the wrack and restitutions of war. It was bound to come, and it would naturally come in that way. It has been the manner of reform since the beginning of the world.

SWITZERLAND, THE CRADLE OF LIBERTY

Interlaken, Switzerland, 1891.

It is a good many years since I was in Switzerland last. In that remote time there was only one ladder railway in the country. That state of things is all changed. There isn't a mountain in Switzerland now that hasn't a ladder railroad or two up its back like suspenders; indeed, some mountains are latticed with them, and two years hence all will be. In that day the peasant of the high altitudes will have to carry a lantern when he goes visiting in the night to keep from stumbling over railroads that have been built since his last round. And also in that day, if there shall remain a high-altitude peasant whose potato-patch hasn't a railroad through it, it would make him as conspicuous as William Tell.

However, there are only two best ways to travel through Switzerland. The first best is afloat. The second best is by open two-horse carriage. One can come from Lucerne to Interlaken over the Brunig by ladder railroad in an hour or so now, but you can glide smoothly in a carriage in ten, and have two hours for luncheon at noon--for luncheon, not for rest. There is no fatigue connected with the trip. One arrives fresh in spirit and in person in the evening--no fret in his heart, no grime on his face, no grit in his hair, not a cinder in his eye. This is the right condition of mind and body, the right and due preparation for the solemn event which closed the day--stepping with meta-phorically uncovered head into the presence of the most impressive mountain mass that the globe can show--the Jungfrau. The stranger's first feeling, when suddenly confronted by that towering and awful apparition wrapped in its shroud of snow, is breath-taking astonishment. It is as if heaven's gates had swung open and exposed the throne.

It is peaceful here and pleasant at Interlaken. Nothing going on--at least nothing but brilliant life-giving sunshine. There are floods and floods of that. One may properly speak of it as "going on," for it is full of the suggestion of activity; the light pours down with energy, with visible enthusiasm. This is a good atmosphere to be in, morally as well as physically. After trying the political atmosphere of the neighboring monarchies, it is healing and refreshing to breathe air that has known no taint of slavery for six hundred years, and to come among a people whose political history is great and fine, and worthy to be taught in all schools and studied by all races and peoples. For the struggle here throughout the centuries has not been in the interest of any private family, or any church, but in the interest of the whole body of the nation, and for shelter and protection of all forms of belief. This fact is colossal. If one would realize how colossal it is, and of what dignity and majesty, let him contrast it with the purposes and objects of the Crusades, the siege of York, the War of the Roses, and other historic comedies of that sort and size.

Last week I was beating around the Lake of Four Cantons, and I saw Rutli and Altorf. Rutli is a remote little patch of meadow, but I do not know how any piece of ground could be holier or better worth crossing oceans and continents to see, since it was there that the great trinity of Switzerland joined hands six centuries ago and swore the oath which set their enslaved and insulted country forever free; and Altorf is also honorable ground and worshipful, since it was there that William, surnamed Tell (which interpreted means "The foolish talker"--that is to say, the too-daring talker), refused to bow to Gessler's hat. Of late years the prying student of history has been delighting himself beyond measure over a wonderful find which he has made-- to wit, that Tell did not shoot the apple from his son's head. To hear the students jubilate, one would suppose that the question of whether Tell shot the apple or didn't was an important matter; whereas it ranks in importance exactly with the question of whether Washington chopped down the cherry-tree or didn't. The deeds of Washington, the patriot, are the essential thing; the cherry-tree incident is of no conse-quence. To prove that Tell did shoot the apple from his son's head would merely prove that he had better nerve than most men and was skillful with a bow as a million others who preceded and followed him, but not one whit more so. But Tell was more and better than a mere marksman, more and better than a mere cool head; he was a type; he stands for Swiss patriotism; in his person was represented a whole people; his spirit was their spirit--the spirit which would bow to none but God, the spirit which said this in words and confirmed it with deeds. There have always been Tells in Switzerland--people who would not bow. There was a sufficiency of them at Rutli; there were plenty of them at Murten; plenty at Grandson; there are plenty today. And the first of them all--the very first, earliest banner-bearer of human freedom in this world--was not a man, but a woman--Stauffacher's wife. There she looms dim and great, through the haze of the centuries, delivering into her husband's ear that gospel of revolt which was to bear fruit in the conspiracy of Rutli and the birth of the first free government the world had ever seen.

From this Victoria Hotel one looks straight across a flat of trifling width to a lofty mountain barrier, which has a gateway in it shaped like an inverted pyramid. Beyond this gateway arises the vast bulk of the Jungfrau, a spotless mass of gleaming snow, into the sky. The gateway, in the dark-colored barrier, makes a strong frame for the great picture. The somber frame and the glowing snow-pile are startlingly contrasted. It is this frame which concentrates and emphasizes the glory of the Jungfrau and makes it the most engaging and beguiling and fascinating spectacle that exists on the earth. There are many mountains of snow that are as lofty as the Jungfrau and as nobly proportioned, but they lack the fame. They stand at large; they are intruded upon and elbowed by neighboring domes and summits, and their grandeur is diminished and fails of effect.

It is a good name, Jungfrau--Virgin. Nothing could be whiter; nothing could be purer; nothing could be saintlier of aspect. At six yesterday evening the great intervening barrier seen through a faint bluish haze seemed made of air and substanceless, so soft and rich it was, so shimmering where the wandering lights touched it and so dim where the shadows lay. Apparently it was a dream stuff, a work of the imagination, nothing real about it. The tint was green, slightly varying shades of it, but mainly very dark. The sun was down--as far as that barrier was concerned, but not for the Jungfrau, towering into the heavens beyond the gateway. She was a roaring conflagration of blinding white.

It is said the Fridolin (the old Fridolin), a new saint, but formerly a missionary, gave the mountain its gracious name. He was an Irishman, son of an Irish king--there were thirty thousand kings reigning in County Cork alone in his time, fifteen hundred years ago. It got so that they could not make a living, there was so much competition and wages got cut so. Some of them were out of work months at a time, with wife and little children to feed, and not a crust in the place. At last a particularly severe winter fell upon the country, and hundreds of them were reduced to mendicancy and were to be seen day after day in the bitterest weather, standing barefoot in the snow, holding out their crowns for alms. Indeed, they would have been obliged to emigrate or starve but for a fortunate idea of Prince Fridolin's, who started a labor-union, the first one in history, and got the great bulk of them to join it. He thus won the general gratitude, and they wanted to make him emperor--emperor over them all--emperor of County Cork, but he said, No, walking delegate was good enough for him. For behold! he was modest beyond his years, and keen as a whip. To this day in Germany and Switzerland, where St. Fridolin is revered and honored, the peasantry speak of him affectionately as the first walking delegate.

The first walk he took was into France and Germany, missionarying--for missionarying was a better thing in those days than it is in ours. All you had to do was to cure the savage's sick daughter by a "miracle"--a miracle like the miracle of Lourdes in our day, for instance--and immediately that head savage was your convert, and filled to the eyes with a new convert's enthusiasm. You could sit down and make yourself easy, now. He would take an ax and convert the rest of the nation himself. Charlemagne was that kind of a walking delegate.

Yes, there were great missionaries in those days, for the methods were sure and the rewards great. We have no such missionaries now, and no such methods.

But to continue the history of the first walking delegate, if you are interested. I am interested myself because I have seen his relics in Sackingen, and also the very spot where he worked his great miracle--the one which won him his sainthood in the papal court a few centuries later. To have seen these things makes me feel very near to him, almost like a member of the family, in fact. While wandering about the Continent he arrived at the spot on the Rhine which is now occupied by Sackingen, and proposed to settle there, but the people warned him off. He appealed to the king of the Franks, who made him a present of the whole region, people and all. He built a great cloister there for women and proceeded to teach in it and accumulate more land. There were two wealthy brothers in the neighborhood, Urso and Landulph. Urso died and Fridolin claimed his estates. Landulph asked for documents and papers. Fridolin had none to show. He said the bequest had been made to him by word of mouth. Landulph suggested that he produce a witness and said it in a way which he thought was very witty, very sarcastic. This shows that he did not know the walking delegate. Fridolin was not disturbed. He said:

"Appoint your court. I will bring a witness."

The court thus created consisted of fifteen counts and barons. A day was appointed for the trial of the case. On that day the judges took their seats in state, and proclamation was made that the court was ready for business. Five minutes, ten minutes, fifteen minutes passed, and yet no Fridolin appeared. Landulph rose, and was in the act of claiming judgment by default when a strange clacking sound was heard coming up the stairs. In another moment Fridolin entered at the door and came walking in a deep hush down the middle aisle, with a tall skeleton stalking in his rear.

Amazement and terror sat upon every countenance, for everybody suspected that the skeleton was Urso's. It stopped before the chief judge and raised its bony arm aloft and began to speak, while all the assembled shuddered, for they could see the words leak out between its ribs. It said:

"Brother, why dost thou disturb my blessed rest and withhold by robbery the gift which I gave thee for the honor of God?"

It seems a strange thing and most irregular, but the verdict was actually given against Landulph on the testimony of this wandering rack-heap of unidentified bones. In our day a skeleton would not be allowed to testify at all, for a skeleton has no moral responsibility, and its word could not be believed on oath, and this was probably one of them. However, the incident is valuable as preserving to us a curious sample of the quaint laws of evidence of that remote time--a time so remote, so far back toward the beginning of original idiocy, that the difference between a bench of judges and a basket of vegetables was as yet so slight that we may say with all confidence that it didn't really exist.

During several afternoons I have been engaged in an interesting, maybe useful, piece of work--that is to say, I have been trying to make the mighty Jungfrau earn her living--earn it in a most humble sphere, but on a prodigious scale, on a prodigious scale of necessity, for she couldn't do anything in a small way with her size and style. I have been trying to make her do service on a stupendous dial and check off the hours as they glide along her pallid face up there against the sky, and tell the time of day to the populations lying within fifty miles of her and to the people in the moon, if they have a good telescope there.

Until late in the afternoon the Jungfrau's aspect is that of a spotless desert of snow set upon edge against the sky. But by mid-afternoon some elevations which rise out of the western border of the desert, whose presence you perhaps had not detected or suspected up to that time, began to cast black shadows eastward across the gleaming surface. At first there is only one shadow; later there are two. Toward 4 P.M. the other day I was gazing and worshiping as usual when I chanced to notice that shadow No. 1 was beginning to take itself something of the shape of the human profile. By four the back of the head was good, the military cap was pretty good, the nose was bold and strong, the upper lip sharp, but not pretty, and there was a great goatee that shot straight aggressively forward from the chin.

At four-thirty the nose had changed its shape considerably, and the altered slant of the sun had revealed and made conspicuous a huge buttress or barrier of naked rock which was so located as to answer very well for a shoulder or coat-collar to this swarthy and indiscreet sweetheart who had stolen out there right before everybody to pillow his head on the Virgin's white breast and whisper soft sentimentalities to her in the sensuous music of the crashing ice-domes and the boom and thunder of the passing avalanche--music very familiar to his ear, for he had heard it every afternoon at this hour since the day he first came courting this child of the earth, who lives in the sky, and that day is far, yes--for he was at this pleasant sport before the Middle Ages drifted by him in the valley; before the Romans marched past, and before the antique and recordless barbarians fished and hunted here and wondered who he might be, and were probably afraid of him; and before primeval man himself, just emerged from his four-footed estate, stepped out upon this plain, first sample of his race, a thousand centuries ago, and cast a glad eye up there, judging he had found a brother human being and consequently something to kill; and before the big saurians wallowed here, still some eons earlier. Oh yes, a day so far back that the eternal son was present to see that first visit; a day so far back that neither tradition nor history was born yet and a whole weary eternity must come and go before the restless little creature, of whose face this stupendous Shadow Face was the prophecy, would arrive in the earth and begin his shabby career and think of a big thing. Oh, indeed yes; when you talk about your poor Roman and Egyptian day-before-yesterday antiquities, you should choose a time when the hoary Shadow Face of the Jungfrau is not by. It antedates all antiquities known or imaginable; for it was here the world itself created the theater of future antiquities. And it is the only witness with a human face that was there to see the marvel, and remains to us a memorial of it.

By 4:40 P.M. the nose of the shadow is perfect and is beautiful. It is black and is powerfully marked against the upright canvas of glowing snow, and covers hundreds of acres of that resplendent surface.

Meantime shadow No. 2 has been creeping out well to the rear of the face west of it--and at five o'clock has assumed a shape that has rather a poor and rude semblance of a shoe.

Meantime, also, the great Shadow Face has been gradually changing for twenty minutes, and now, 5 P.M., it is becoming a quite fair portrait of Roscoe Conkling. The likeness is there, and is unmistakable. The goatee is shortened, now, and has an end; formerly it hadn't any, but ran off eastward and arrived nowhere.

By 6 P.M. the face has dissolved and gone, and the goatee has become what looks like the shadow of a tower with a pointed roof, and the shoe had turned into what the printers call a "fist" with a finger pointing.

If I were now imprisoned on a mountain summit a hundred miles northward of this point, and was denied a timepiece, I could get along well enough from four till six on clear days, for I could keep trace of the time by the changing shapes of these mighty shadows of the Virgin's front, the most stupendous dial I am acquainted with, the oldest clock in the world by a couple of million years.

I suppose I should not have noticed the forms of the shadows if I hadn't the habit of hunting for faces in the clouds and in mountain crags--a sort of amusement which is very entertaining even when you don't find any, and brilliantly satisfying when you do. I have searched through several bushels of photographs of the Jungfrau here, but found only one with the Face in it, and in this case it was not strictly recognizable as a face, which was evidence that the picture was taken before four o'clock in the afternoon, and also evidence that all the photographers have persistently overlooked one of the most fascinating features of the Jungfrau show. I say fascinating, because if you once detect a human face produced on a great plan by unconscious nature, you never get tired of watching it. At first you can't make another person see it at all, but after he has made it out once he can't see anything else afterward.

The King of Greece is a man who goes around quietly enough when off duty. One day this summer he was traveling in an ordinary first-class compartment, just in his other suit, the one which he works the realm in when he is at home, and so he was not looking like anybody in particular, but a good deal like everybody in general. By and by a hearty and healthy German-American got in and opened up a frank and interesting and sympathetic conversation with him, and asked him a couple of thousand questions about himself, which the king answered good- naturedly, but in a more or less indefinite way as to private particulars.

"Where do you live when you are at home?"

"In Greece."

"Greece! Well, now, that is just astonishing! Born there?"

"No."

"Do you speak Greek?"

"Yes."

"Now, ain't that strange! I never expected to live to see that. What is your trade? I mean how do you get your living? What is your line of business?"

"Well, I hardly know how to answer. I am only a kind of foreman, on a salary; and the business--well, is a very general kind of business."

"Yes, I understand--general jobbing--little of everything--anything that there's money in."

"That's about it, yes."

"Are you traveling for the house now?"

"Well, partly; but not entirely. Of course I do a stroke of business if it falls in the way--"

"Good! I like that in you! That's me every time. Go on."

"I was only going to say I am off on my vacation now."

"Well that's all right. No harm in that. A man works all the better for a little let-up now and then. Not that I've been used to having it myself; for I haven't. I reckon this is my first. I was born in Germany, and when I was a couple of weeks old shipped to America, and I've been there ever since, and that's sixty-four years by the watch. I'm an American in principle and a German at heart, and it's the boss combination. Well, how do you get along, as a rule--pretty fair?"

"I've a rather large family--"

"There, that's it--big family and trying to raise them on a salary. Now, what did you go to do that for?"

"Well, I thought--"

"Of course you did. You were young and confident and thought you could branch out and make things go with a whirl, and here you are, you see! But never mind about that. I'm not trying to discourage you. Dear me! I've been just where you are myself! You've got good grit; there's good stuff in you, I can see that. You got a wrong start, that's the whole trouble. But you hold your grip, and we'll see what can be done. Your case ain't half as bad as it might be. You are going to come out all right--I'm bail for that. Boys and girls?"

"My family? Yes, some of them are boys--"

"And the rest girls. It's just as I expected. But that's all right, and it's better so, anyway. What are the boys doing-- learning a trade?"

"Well, no--I thought--"

"It's a big mistake. It's the biggest mistake you ever made. You see that in your own case. A man ought always to have a trade to fall back on. Now, I was harness-maker at first. Did that prevent me from becoming one of the biggest brewers in America? Oh no. I always had the harness trick to fall back on in rough weather. Now, if you had learned how to make harness-- However, it's too late now; too late. But it's no good plan to cry over spilt milk. But as to the boys, you see--what's to become of them if anything happens to you?"

"It has been my idea to let the eldest one succeed me--"

"Oh, come! Suppose the firm don't want him?"

"I hadn't thought of that, but--"

"Now, look here; you want to get right down to business and stop dreaming. You are capable of immense things--man. You can make a perfect success in life. All you want is somebody to steady you and boost you along on the right road. Do you own anything in the business?"

"No--not exactly; but if I continue to give satisfaction, I suppose I can keep my--"

"Keep your place--yes. Well, don't you depend on anything of the kind. They'll bounce you the minute you get a little old and worked out; they'll do it sure. Can't you manage somehow to get into the firm? That's the great thing, you know."

"I think it is doubtful; very doubtful."

"Um--that's bad--yes, and unfair, too. Do you suppose that if I should go there and have a talk with your people-- Look here-- do you think you could run a brewery?"

"I have never tried, but I think I could do it after a little familiarity with the business."

The German was silent for some time. He did a good deal of thinking, and the king waited curiously to see what the result was going to be. Finally the German said:

"My mind's made up. You leave that crowd--you'll never amount to anything there. In these old countries they never give a fellow a show. Yes, you come over to America--come to my place in Rochester; bring the family along. You shall have a show in the business and the foremanship, besides. George-- you said your name was George?--I'll make a man of you. I give you my word. You've never had a chance here, but that's all going to change. By gracious! I'll give you a lift that'll make your hair curl!"

AT THE SHRINE OF ST. WAGNER

Bayreuth, Aug. 2d, 1891

It was at Nuremberg that we struck the inundation of music-mad strangers that was rolling down upon Bayreuth. It had been long since we had seen such multitudes of excited and struggling people. It took a good half-hour to pack them and pair them into the train--and it was the longest train we have yet seen in Europe. Nuremberg had been witnessing this sort of experience a couple of times a day for about two weeks. It gives one an impressive sense of the magnitude of this biennial pilgrimage. For a pilgrimage is what it is. The devotees come from the very ends of the earth to worship their prophet in his own Kaaba in his own Mecca.

If you are living in New York or San Francisco or Chicago or anywhere else in America, and you conclude, by the middle of May, that you would like to attend the Bayreuth opera two months and a half later, you must use the cable and get about it immediately or you will get no seats, and you must cable for lodgings, too. Then if you are lucky you will get seats in the last row and lodgings in the fringe of the town. If you stop to write you will get nothing. There were plenty of people in Nuremberg when we passed through who had come on pilgrimage without first securing seats and lodgings. They had found neither in Bayreuth; they had walked Bayreuth streets a while in sorrow, then had gone to Nuremberg and found neither beds nor standing room, and had walked those quaint streets all night, waiting for the hotels to open and empty their guests into trains, and so make room for these, their defeated brethren and sisters in the faith. They had endured from thirty to forty hours' railroading on the continent of Europe--with all which that implies of worry, fatigue, and financial impoverishment--and all they had got and all they were to get for it was handiness and accuracy in kicking themselves, acquired by practice in the back streets of the two towns when other people were in bed; for back they must go over that unspeakable journey with their pious mission unfulfilled. These humiliated outcasts had the frowsy and unbrushed and apologetic look of wet cats, and their eyes were glazed with drowsiness, their bodies were adroop from crown to sole, and all kind-hearted people refrained from asking them if they had been to Bayreuth and failed to connect, as knowing they would lie.

We reached here (Bayreuth) about mid-afternoon of a rainy Saturday. We were of the wise, and had secured lodgings and opera seats months in advance.

I am not a musical critic, and did not come here to write essays about the operas and deliver judgment upon their merits. The little children of Bayreuth could do that with a finer sympathy and a broader intelligence than I. I only care to bring four or five pilgrims to the operas, pilgrims able to appreciate them and enjoy them. What I write about the performance to put in my odd time would be offered to the public as merely a cat's view of a king, and not of didactic value.

Next day, which was Sunday, we left for the opera-house-- that is to say, the Wagner temple--a little after the middle of the afternoon. The great building stands all by itself, grand and lonely, on a high ground outside the town. We were warned that if we arrived after four o'clock we should be obliged to pay two dollars and a half extra by way of fine. We saved that; and it may be remarked here that this is the only opportunity that Europe offers of saving money. There was a big crowd in the grounds about the building, and the ladies' dresses took the sun with fine effect. I do not mean to intimate that the ladies were in full dress, for that was not so. The dresses were pretty, but neither sex was in evening dress.

The interior of the building is simple--severely so; but there is no occasion for color and decoration, since the people sit in the dark. The auditorium has the shape of a keystone, with the stage at the narrow end. There is an aisle on each side, but no aisle in the body of the house. Each row of seats extends in an unbroken curve from one side of the house to the other. There are seven entrance doors on each side of the theater and four at the butt, eighteen doors to admit and emit 1,650 persons. The number of the particular door by which you are to enter the house or leave it is printed on your ticket, and you can use no door but that one. Thus, crowding and confusion are impossible. Not so many as a hundred people use any one door. This is better than having the usual (and useless) elaborate fireproof arrangements. It is the model theater of the world. It can be emptied while the second hand of a watch makes its circuit. It would be entirely safe, even if it were built of lucifer matches.

If your seat is near the center of a row and you enter late you must work your way along a rank of about twenty-five ladies and gentlemen to get to it. Yet this causes no trouble, for everybody stands up until all the seats are full, and the filling is accomplished in a very few minutes. Then all sit down, and you have a solid mass of fifteen hundred heads, making a steep cellar-door slant from the rear of the house down to the stage.

All the lights were turned low, so low that the congregation sat in a deep and solemn gloom. The funereal rustling of dresses and the low buzz of conversation began to die swiftly down, and presently not the ghost of a sound was left. This profound and increasingly impressive stillness endured for some time--the best preparation for music, spectacle, or speech conceivable. I should think our show people would have invented or imported that simple and impressive device for securing and solidifying the attention of an audience long ago; instead of which there continue to this day to open a performance against a deadly competition in the form of noise, confusion, and a scattered interest.

Finally, out of darkness and distance and mystery soft rich notes rose upon the stillness, and from his grave the dead magician began to weave his spells about his disciples and steep their souls in his enchantments. There was something strangely impressive in the fancy which kept intruding itself that the composer was conscious in his grave of what was going on here, and that these divine souls were the clothing of thoughts which were at this moment passing through his brain, and not recognized and familiar ones which had issued from it at some former time.

The entire overture, long as it was, was played to a dark house with the curtain down. It was exquisite; it was delicious. But straightway thereafter, or course, came the singing, and it does seem to me that nothing can make a Wagner opera absolutely perfect and satisfactory to the untutored but to leave out the vocal parts. I wish I could see a Wagner opera done in pantomime once. Then one would have the lovely orchestration unvexed to listen to and bathe his spirit in, and the bewildering beautiful scenery to intoxicate his eyes with, and the dumb acting couldn't mar these pleasures, because there isn't often anything in the Wagner opera that one would call by such a violent name as acting; as a rule all you would see would be a couple of silent people, one of them standing still, the other catching flies. Of course I do not really mean that he would be catching flies; I only mean that the usual operatic gestures which consist in reaching first one hand out into the air and then the other might suggest the sport I speak of if the operator attended strictly to business and uttered no sound.

This present opera was "Parsifal." Madame Wagner does not permit its representation anywhere but in Bayreuth. The first act of the three occupied two hours, and I enjoyed that in spite of the singing.

I trust that I know as well as anybody that singing is one of the most entrancing and bewitching and moving and eloquent of all the vehicles invented by man for the conveying of feeling; but it seems to me that the chief virtue in song is melody, air, tune, rhythm, or what you please to call it, and that when this feature is absent what remains is a picture with the color left out. I was not able to detect in the vocal parts of "Parsifal" anything that might with confidence be called rhythm or tune or melody; one person performed at a time--and a long time, too-- often in a noble, and always in a high-toned, voice; but he only pulled out long notes, then some short ones, then another long one, then a sharp, quick, peremptory bark or two--and so on and so on; and when he was done you saw that the information which he had conveyed had not compensated for the disturbance. Not always, but pretty often. If two of them would but put in a duet occasionally and blend the voices; but no, they don't do that. The great master, who knew so well how to make a hundred instruments rejoice in unison and pour out their souls in mingled and melodious tides of delicious sound, deals only in barren solos when he puts in the vocal parts. It may be that he was deep, and only added the singing to his operas for the sake of the contrast it would make with the music. Singing! It does seem the wrong name to apply to it. Strictly described, it is a practicing of difficult and unpleasant intervals, mainly. An ignorant person gets tired of listening to gymnastic intervals in the long run, no matter how pleasant they may be. In "Parsifal" there is a hermit named Gurnemanz who stands on the stage in one spot and practices by the hour, while first one and then another character of the cast endures what he can of it and then retires to die.

During the evening there was an intermission of three- quarters of an hour after the first act and one an hour long after the second. In both instances the theater was totally emptied. People who had previously engaged tables in the one sole eating-house were able to put in their time very satisfactorily; the other thousand went hungry. The opera was concluded at ten in the evening or a little later. When we reached home we had been gone more than seven hours. Seven hours at five dollars a ticket is almost too much for the money.

While browsing about the front yard among the crowd between the acts I encountered twelve or fifteen friends from different parts of America, and those of them who were most familiar with Wagner said that "Parsifal" seldom pleased at first, but that after one had heard it several times it was almost sure to become a favorite. It seemed impossible, but it was true, for the statement came from people whose word was not to be doubted.

And I gathered some further information. On the ground I found part of a German musical magazine, and in it a letter written by Uhlic thirty-three years ago, in which he defends the scorned and abused Wagner against people like me, who found fault with the comprehensive absence of what our kind regards as singing. Uhlic says Wagner despised "JENE PLAPPERUDE MUSIC," and therefore "runs, trills, and SCHNORKEL are discarded by him." I don't know what a SCHNORKEL is, but now that I know it has been left out of these operas I never have missed so much in my life. And Uhlic further says that Wagner's

song is true: that it is "simply emphasized intoned speech."
That certainly describes it --in "Parsifal" and some of the operas;
and if I understand Uhlic's elaborate German he apologizes for
the beautiful airs in "Tannh:auser." Very well; now that Wagner
and I understand each other, perhaps we shall get along better,
and I shall stop calling Waggner, on the American plan, and
thereafter call him Waggner as per German custom, for I feel
entirely friendly now. The minute we get reconciled to a person,
how willing we are to throw aside little needless puctilios and
pronounce his name right!

Of course I came home wondering why people should come
from all corners of America to hear these operas, when we have
lately had a season or two of them in New York with these same
singers in the several parts, and possibly this same orchestra. I
resolved to think that out at all hazards.

TUESDAY.--Yesterday they played the only operatic favorite I
have ever had--an opera which has always driven me mad with
ignorant delight whenever I have heard it--"Tannh:auser." I
heard it first when I was a youth; I heard it last in the last
German season in New York. I was busy yesterday and I did not
intend to go, knowing I should have another "Tannh:auser"
opportunity in a few days; but after five o'clock I found myself
free and walked out to the opera-house and arrived about the
beginning of the second act. My opera ticket admitted me to
the grounds in front, past the policeman and the chain, and I
thought I would take a rest on a bench for an hour and two and
wait for the third act.

In a moment or so the first bugles blew, and the multitude
began to crumble apart and melt into the theater. I will explain
that this bugle-call is one of the pretty features here. You see,
the theater is empty, and hundreds of the audience are a good

way off in the feeding-house; the first bugle-call is blown about a quarter of an hour before time for the curtain to rise. This company of buglers, in uniform, march out with military step and send out over the landscape a few bars of the theme of the approaching act, piercing the distances with the gracious notes; then they march to the other entrance and repeat. Presently they do this over again. Yesterday only about two hundred people were still left in front of the house when the second call was blown; in another half-minute they would have been in the house, but then a thing happened which delayed them--the only solitary thing in this world which could be relied on with certainty to accomplish it, I suppose--an imperial princess appeared in the balcony above them. They stopped dead in their tracks and began to gaze in a stupor of gratitude and satisfaction. The lady presently saw that she must disappear or the doors would be closed upon these worshipers, so she returned to her box. This daughter-in-law of an emperor was pretty; she had a kind face; she was without airs; she is known to be full of common human sympathies. There are many kinds of princesses, but this kind is the most harmful of all, for wherever they go they reconcile people to monarchy and set back the clock of progress. The valuable princes, the desirable princes, are the czars and their sort. By their mere dumb presence in the world they cover with derision every argument that can be invented in favor of royalty by the most ingenious casuist. In his time the husband of this princess was valuable. He led a degraded life, he ended it with his own hand in circumstances and surroundings of a hideous sort, and was buried like a god.

In the opera-house there is a long loft back of the audience, a kind of open gallery, in which princes are displayed. It is sacred to them; it is the holy of holies. As soon as the filling of the house is about complete the standing multitude turn and fix their eyes upon the princely layout and gaze mutely and longingly and adoringly and regretfully like sinners looking into heaven. They become rapt, unconscious, steeped in worship. There is no spectacle anywhere that is more pathetic than this. It is worth crossing many oceans to see. It is somehow not the same gaze that people rivet upon a Victor Hugo, or Niagara, or the bones of the mastodon, or the guillotine of the Revolution, or the great pyramid, or distant Vesuvius smoking in the sky, or any man long celebrated to you by his genius and achievements, or thing long celebrated to you by the praises of books and pictures--no, that gaze is only the gaze of intense curiosity, interest, wonder, engaged in drinking delicious deep draughts that taste good all the way down and appease and satisfy the thirst of a lifetime. Satisfy it--that is the word. Hugo and the mastodon will still have a degree of intense interest thereafter when encountered, but never anything approaching the ecstasy of that first view. The interest of a prince is different. It may be envy, it may be worship, doubtless it is a mixture of both--and it does not satisfy its thirst with one view, or even noticeably diminish it. Perhaps the essence of the thing is the value which men attach to a valuable something which has come by luck and not been earned. A dollar picked up in the road is more satisfaction to you than the ninety-and-nine which you had to work for, and money won at faro or in stocks snuggles into your heart in the same way. A prince picks up grandeur, power, and a permanent holiday and gratis support by a pure accident, the accident of birth, and he stands always before the grieved eye of poverty and obscurity a monumental representative of luck. And then--supremest value of all-his is the only high fortune on the earth which is secure. The commercial millionaire may become a beggar; the illustrious statesman can make a vital mistake and be dropped and forgotten; the illustrious general can lose a decisive battle and with it the consideration of men; but once a prince always a prince--that is to say, an imitation god, and neither hard fortune nor an infamous character nor an addled brain nor the speech of an ass can undeify him. By common consent of all the nations and all the ages the most valuable thing in this world is the homage of men, whether deserved or undeserved. It follows without doubt or question, then, that the most desirable position possible is that of a prince. And I think it also follows that the so-called usurpations with which history is littered are the most excusable misdemeanors which men have committed. To usurp a usurpation--that is all it amounts to, isn't it?

A prince is not to us what he is to a European, of course. We have not been taught to regard him as a god, and so one good look at him is likely to so nearly appease our curiosity as to make him an object of no greater interest the next time. We want a fresh one. But it is not so with the European. I am quite sure of it. The same old one will answer; he never stales. Eighteen years ago I was in London and I called at an Englishman's house on a bleak and foggy and dismal December afternoon to visit his wife and married daughter by appointment. I waited half an hour and then they arrived, frozen. They explained that they had been delayed by an unlooked-for circumstance: while passing in the neighborhood of Marlborough House they saw a crowd gathering and were told that the Prince of Wales was about to drive out, so they stopped to get a sight of him. They had waited half an hour on the sidewalk, freezing with the crowd, but were disappointed at last--the Prince had changed his mind. I said, with a good deal of surprise, "Is it possible that you two have lived in London all your lives and have never seen the Prince of Wales?"

Apparently it was their turn to be surprised, for they exclaimed: "What an idea! Why, we have seen him hundreds of times."

They had seem him hundreds of times, yet they had waited half an hour in the gloom and the bitter cold, in the midst of a jam of patients from the same asylum, on the chance of seeing him again. It was a stupefying statement, but one is obliged to believe the English, even when they say a thing like that. I fumbled around for a remark, and got out this one:

"I can't understand it at all. If I had never seen General Grant I doubt if I would do that even to get a sight of him." With a slight emphasis on the last word.

Their blank faces showed that they wondered where the parallel came in. Then they said, blankly: "Of course not. He is only a President."

It is doubtless a fact that a prince is a permanent interest, an interest not subject to deterioration. The general who was never defeated, the general who never held a council of war, the only general who ever commanded a connected battle-front twelve hundred miles long, the smith who welded together the broken parts of a great republic and re-established it where it is quite likely to outlast all the monarchies present and to come, was really a person of no serious consequence to these people. To them, with their training, my General was only a man, after all, while their Prince was clearly much more than that--a being of a wholly unsimilar construction and constitution, and being of no more blood and kinship with men than are the serene eternal lights of the firmament with the poor dull tallow candles of commerce that sputter and die and leave nothing behind but a pinch of ashes and a stink.

I saw the last act of "Tannh:auser." I sat in the gloom and the deep stillness, waiting--one minute, two minutes, I do not know exactly how long--then the soft music of the hidden orchestra began to breathe its rich, long sighs out from under the distant stage, and by and by the drop-curtain parted in the middle and was drawn softly aside, disclosing the twilighted wood and a wayside shrine, with a white-robed girl praying and a man standing near. Presently that noble chorus of men's voices was heard approaching, and from that moment until the closing of the curtain it was music, just music--music to make one drunk with pleasure, music to make one take scrip and staff and beg his way round the globe to hear it.

To such as are intending to come here in the Wagner season next year I wish to say, bring your dinner-pail with you. If you do, you will never cease to be thankful. If you do not, you will find it a hard fight to save yourself from famishing in Bayreuth. Bayreuth is merely a large village, and has no very large hotels or eating-houses. The principal inns are the Golden Anchor and the Sun. At either of these places you can get an excellent meal--no, I mean you can go there and see other people get it. There is no charge for this. The town is littered with restaurants, but they are small and bad, and they are overdriven with custom. You must secure a table hours beforehand, and often when you arrive you will find somebody occupying it. We have had this experience. We have had a daily scramble for life; and when I say we, I include shoals of people. I have the impression that the only people who do not have to scramble are the veterans--the disciples who have been here before and know the ropes. I think they arrive about a week before the first opera, and engage all the tables for the season. My tribe had tried all kinds of places--some outside of the town, a mile or two--and have captured only nibblings and odds and ends, never in any instance a complete and satisfying meal. Digestible? No, the reverse. These odds and ends are going to serve as souvenirs of Bayreuth, and in that regard their value is not to be overestimated. Photographs fade, bric-a-brac gets lost, busts of Wagner get broken, but once you absorb a Bayreuth-restaurant meal it is your possession and your property until the time comes to embalm the rest of you. Some of these pilgrims here become, in effect, cabinets; cabinets of souvenirs of Bayreuth. It is believed among scientists that you could examine the crop of a dead Bayreuth pilgrim anywhere in the earth and tell where he came from. But I like this ballast. I think a "Hermitage" scrap-up at eight in the evening, when all the famine-breeders have been there and laid in their mementoes and gone, is the quietest thing you can lay on your keelson except gravel.

THURSDAY.--They keep two teams of singers in stock for the chief roles, and one of these is composed of the most renowned artists in the world, with Materna and Alvary in the lead. I suppose a double team is necessary; doubtless a single team would die of exhaustion in a week, for all the plays last from four in the afternoon till ten at night. Nearly all the labor falls upon the half-dozen head singers, and apparently they are required to furnish all the noise they can for the money. If they feel a soft, whispery, mysterious feeling they are required to open out and let the public know it. Operas are given only on Sundays, Mondays, Wednesdays, and Thursdays, with three days of ostensible rest per week, and two teams to do the four operas; but the ostensible rest is devoted largely to rehearsing. It is said that the off days are devoted to rehearsing from some time in the morning till ten at night. Are there two orchestras also? It is quite likely, since there are one hundred and ten names in the orchestra list.

Yesterday the opera was "Tristan and Isolde." I have seen all sorts of audiences--at theaters, operas, concerts, lectures, sermons, funerals--but none which was twin to the Wagner audience of Bayreuth for fixed and reverential attention. Absolute attention and petrified retention to the end of an act of the attitude assumed at the beginning of it. You detect no movement in the solid mass of heads and shoulders. You seem to sit with the dead in the gloom of a tomb. You know that they are being stirred to their profoundest depths; that there are times when they want to rise and wave handkerchiefs and shout their approbation, and times when tears are running down their faces, and it would be a relief to free their pent emotions in sobs or screams; yet you hear not one utterance till the curtain swings together and the closing strains have slowly faded out and died; then the dead rise with one impulse and shake the building with their applause. Every seat is full in the first act; there is not a vacant one in the last. If a man would be conspicuous, let him come here and retire from the house in the midst of an act. It would make him celebrated.

This audience reminds me of nothing I have ever seen and of nothing I have read about except the city in the Arabian tale where all the inhabitants have been turned to brass and the traveler finds them after centuries mute, motionless, and still retaining the attitudes which they last knew in life. Here the Wagner audience dress as they please, and sit in the dark and worship in silence. At the Metropolitan in New York they sit in a glare, and wear their showiest harness; they hum airs, they squeak fans, they titter, and they gabble all the time. In some of the boxes the conversation and laughter are so loud as to divide the attention of the house with the stage. In large measure the Metropolitan is a show-case for rich fashionables who are not trained in Wagnerian music and have no reverence for it, but who like to promote art and show their clothes.

Can that be an agreeable atmosphere to persons in whom this music produces a sort of divine ecstasy and to whom its creator is a very deity, his stage a temple, the works of his brain and hands consecrated things, and the partaking of them with eye and ear a sacred solemnity? Manifestly, no. Then, perhaps the temporary expatriation, the tedious traversing of seas and continents, the pilgrimage to Bayreuth stands explained. These devotees would worship in an atmosphere of devotion. It is only here that they can find it without fleck or blemish or any worldly pollution. In this remote village there are no sights to see, there is no newspaper to intrude the worries of the distant world, there is nothing going on, it is always Sunday. The pilgrim wends to his temple out of town, sits out his moving service, returns to his bed with his heart and soul and his body exhausted by long hours of tremendous emotion, and he is in no fit condition to do anything but to lie torpid and slowly gather back life and strength for the next service. This opera of "Tristan and Isolde" last night broke the hearts of all witnesses who were of the faith, and I know of some who have heard of many who could not sleep after it, but cried the night away. I feel strongly out of place here. Sometimes I feel like the sane person in a community of the mad; sometimes I feel like the one blind man where all others see; the one groping savage in the college of the learned, and always, during service, I feel like a heretic in heaven.

But by no means do I ever overlook or minify the fact that this is one of the most extraordinary experiences of my life. I have never seen anything like this before. I have never seen anything so great and fine and real as this devotion.

FRIDAY.--Yesterday's opera was "Parsifal" again. The others went and they show marked advance in appreciation; but I went hunting for relics and reminders of the Margravine Wilhelmina, she of the imperishable "Memoirs." I am properly grateful to her for her (unconscious) satire upon monarchy and nobility, and therefore nothing which her hand touched or her eye looked upon is indifferent to me. I am her pilgrim; the rest of this multitude here are Wagner's.

TUESDAY.--I have seen my last two operas; my season is ended, and we cross over into Bohemia this afternoon. I was supposing that my musical regeneration was accomplished and perfected, because I enjoyed both of these operas, singing and all, and, moreover, one of them was "Parsifal," but the experts have disenchanted me. They say:

"Singing! That wasn't singing; that was the wailing, screeching of third-rate obscurities, palmed off on us in the interest of economy."

Well, I ought to have recognized the sign--the old, sure sign that has never failed me in matters of art. Whenever I enjoy anything in art it means that it is mighty poor. The private knowledge of this fact has saved me from going to pieces with enthusiasm in front of many and many a chromo. However, my base instinct does bring me profit sometimes; I was the only man out of thirty-two hundred who got his money back on those two operas.

WILLIAM DEAN HOWELLS

I S it true that the sun of a man's mentality touches noon at forty and then begins to wane toward setting? Doctor Osler is charged with saying so. Maybe he said it, maybe he didn't; I don't know which it is. But if he said it, I can point him to a case which proves his rule. Proves it by being an exception to it. To this place I nominate Mr. Howells.

I read his VENETIAN DAYS about forty years ago. I compare it with his paper on Machiavelli in a late number of HARPER, and I cannot find that his English has suffered any impairment. For forty years his English has been to me a continual delight and astonishment.   In the sustained exhibition of certain great qualities--clearness,   compression,   verbal   exactness,   and unforced and seemingly unconscious felicity of phrasing--he is, in my belief, without his peer in the English-writing world. SUSTAINED. I entrench myself behind that protecting word. There are others who exhibit those great qualities as greatly as he does, but only by intervaled distributions of rich moonlight, with stretches of veiled and dimmer landscape between; whereas Howells's moon sails cloudless skies all night and all the nights.

In the matter of verbal exactness Mr. Howells has no superior, I suppose. He seems to be almost always able to find that elusive and shifty grain of gold, the RIGHT WORD. Others have to put up with approximations, more or less frequently; he has better luck. To me, the others are miners working with the gold-pan-- of necessity some of the gold washes over and escapes; whereas, in my fancy, he is quicksilver raiding down a riffle--no grain of the metal stands much chance of eluding him. A powerful agent is the right word: it lights the reader's way and makes it plain; a close approximation to it will answer, and much traveling is done in a well-enough fashion by its help, but we do not welcome it and applaud it and rejoice in it as we do when THE right one blazes out on us. Whenever we come upon one of those intensely right words in a book or a newspaper the resulting effect is physical as well as spiritual, and electrically prompt: it tingles exquisitely around through the walls of the mouth and tastes as tart and crisp and good as the autumn-butter that creams the sumac-berry. One has no time to examine the word and vote upon its rank and standing, the automatic recognition of its supremacy is so immediate. There is a plenty of acceptable literature which deals largely in approximations, but it may be likened to a fine landscape seen through the rain; the right word would dismiss the rain, then you would see it better. It doesn't rain when Howells is at work.

And where does he get the easy and effortless flow of his speech? and its cadenced and undulating rhythm? and its architectural felicities of construction, its graces of expression, its pemmican quality of compression, and all that? Born to him, no doubt. All in shining good order in the beginning, all extraordinary; and all just as shining, just as extraordinary today, after forty years of diligent wear and tear and use. He passed his fortieth year long and long ago; but I think his English of today--his perfect English, I wish to say -- can throw down the glove before his English of that antique time and not be afraid.

I will got back to the paper on Machiavelli now, and ask the reader to examine this passage from it which I append. I do not mean examine it in a bird's-eye way; I mean search it, study it. And, of course, read it aloud. I may be wrong, still it is my conviction that one cannot get out of finely wrought literature all that is in it by reading it mutely:

Mr. Dyer is rather of the opinion, first luminously suggested by Macaulay, that Machiavelli was in earnest, but must not be judged as a political moralist of our time and race would be judged. He thinks that Machiavelli was in earnest, as none but an idealist can be, and he is the first to imagine him an idealist immersed in realities, who involuntarily transmutes the events under his eye into something like the visionary issues of reverie. The Machiavelli whom he depicts does not cease to be politically a republican and socially a just man because he holds up an atrocious despot like Caesar Borgia as a mirror for rulers. What Machiavelli beheld round him in Italy was a civic disorder in which there was oppression without statecraft, and revolt without patriotism. When a miscreant like Borgia appeared upon the scene and reduced both tyrants and rebels to an apparent quiescence, he might very well seem to such a dreamer the savior of society whom a certain sort of dreamers are always looking for. Machiavelli was no less honest when he honored the diabolical force than Carlyle was when at different times he extolled the strong man who destroys liberty in creating order. But Carlyle has only just ceased to be mistaken for a reformer, while it is still Machiavelli's hard fate to be so trammeled in his material that his name stands for whatever is most malevolent and perfidious in human nature.

You see how easy and flowing it is; how unvexed by rugged-nesses, clumsinesses, broken meters; how simple and--so far as you or I can make out--unstudied; how clear, how limpid, how understandable, how unconfused by cross-currents, eddies, undertows; how seemingly unadorned, yet is all adornment, like the lily-of-the-valley; and how compressed, how compact, without a complacency-signal hung out anywhere to call attention to it.

There are twenty-three lines in the quoted passage. After reading it several times aloud, one perceives that a good deal of matter is crowded into that small space. I think it is a model of compactness. When I take its materials apart and work them over and put them together in my way, I find I cannot crowd the result back into the same hole, there not being room enough. I find it a case of a woman packing a man's trunk: he can get the things out, but he can't ever get them back again.

The proffered paragraph is a just and fair sample; the rest of the article is as compact as it is; there are no waste words. The sample is just in other ways: limpid, fluent, graceful, and rhythmical as it is, it holds no superiority in these respects over the rest of the essay. Also, the choice phrasing noticeable in the sample is not lonely; there is a plenty of its kin distributed through the other paragraphs. This is claiming much when that kin must face the challenge of a phrase like the one in the middle sentence: "an idealist immersed in realities who involuntarily transmutes the events under his eye into something like the visionary issues of reverie." With a hundred words to do it with, the literary artisan could catch that airy thought and tie it down and reduce it to a concrete condition, visible, substantial, understandable and all right, like a cabbage; but the artist does it with twenty, and the result is a flower.

The quoted phrase, like a thousand others that have come from the same source, has the quality of certain scraps of verse which take hold of us and stay in our memories, we do not understand why, at first: all the words being the right words, none of them is conspicuous, and so they all seem inconspicuous, therefore we wonder what it is about them that makes their message take hold.

The mossy marbles rest On the lips that he has prest In their bloom,

And the names he loved to hear Have been carved for many a year On the tomb.

It is like a dreamy strain of moving music, with no sharp notes in it. The words are all "right" words, and all the same size. We do not notice it at first. We get the effect, it goes straight home to us, but we do not know why. It is when the right words are conspicuous that they thunder:

The glory that was Greece and the grandeur that was Rome!

When I got back from Howells old to Howells young I find him arranging and clustering English words well, but not any better than now. He is not more felicitous in concreting abstractions now than he was in translating, then, the visions of the eyes of flesh into words that reproduced their forms and colors:

In Venetian streets they give the fallen snow no rest. It is at once shoveled into the canals by hundreds of half-naked FACCHINI; and now in St. Mark's Place the music of innumerable shovels smote upon my ear; and I saw the shivering legion of poverty as it engaged the elements in a struggle for the possession of the Piazza. But the snow continued to fall, and through the twilight of the descending flakes all this toil and encountered looked like that weary kind of effort in dreams, when the most determined industry seems only to renew the task. The lofty crest of the bell-tower was hidden in the folds of falling snow, and I could no longer see the golden angel upon its summit. But looked at across the Piazza, the beautiful outline of St. Mark's Church was perfectly penciled in the air, and the shifting threads of the snowfall were woven into a spell of novel enchantment around the structure that always seemed to me too exquisite in its fantastic loveliness to be anything but the creation of magic. The tender snow had compassionated the beautiful edifice for all the wrongs of time, and so hid the stains and ugliness of decay that it looked as if just from the hand of the builder--or, better said, just from the brain of the architect. There was marvelous freshness in the colors of the mosaics in the great arches of the facade, and all that gracious harmony into which the temple rises, or marble scrolls and leafy exuberance airily supporting the statues of the saints, was a hundred times etherealized by the purity and whiteness of the drifting flakes. The snow lay lightly on the golden gloves that tremble like peacocks-crests above the vast domes, and plumed them with softest white; it robed the saints in ermine; and it danced over all its works, as if exulting in its beauty--beauty which filled me with subtle, selfish yearning to keep such evanescent loveliness for the little-while-longer of my whole life, and with despair to think that even the poor lifeless shadow of it could never be fairly reflected in picture or poem.

Through the wavering snowfall, the Saint Theodore upon one of the granite pillars of the Piazzetta did not show so grim as his wont is, and the winged lion on the other might have been a winged lamb, so gentle and mild he looked by the tender light of the storm. The towers of the island churches loomed faint and far away in the dimness; the sailors in the rigging of the ships that lay in the Basin wrought like phantoms among the shrouds; the gondolas stole in and out of the opaque distance more noiselessly and dreamily than ever; and a silence, almost palpable, lay upon the mutest city in the world.

The spirit of Venice is there: of a city where Age and Decay, fagged with distributing damage and repulsiveness among the other cities of the planet in accordance with the policy and business of their profession, come for rest and play between seasons, and treat themselves to the luxury and relaxation of sinking the shop and inventing and squandering charms all about, instead of abolishing such as they find, as it their habit when not on vacation.

In the working season they do business in Boston sometimes, and a character in THE UNDISCOVERED COUNTRY takes accurate note of pathetic effects wrought by them upon the aspects of a street of once dignified and elegant homes whose occupants have moved away and left them a prey to neglect and gradual ruin and progressive degradation; a descent which reaches bottom at last, when the street becomes a roost for humble professionals of the faith-cure and fortune-telling sort.

What a queer, melancholy house, what a queer, melancholy street! I don't think I was ever in a street before when quite so many professional ladies, with English surnames, preferred Madam to Mrs. on their door-plates. And the poor old place has such a desperately conscious air of going to the deuce. Every house seems to wince as you go by, and button itself up to the chin for fear you should find out it had no shirt on--so to speak. I don't know what's the reason, but these material tokens of a social decay afflict me terribly; a tipsy woman isn't dreadfuler than a haggard old house, that's once been a home, in a street like this.

Mr. Howells's pictures are not mere stiff, hard, accurate photographs; they are photographs with feeling in them, and sentiment, photographs taken in a dream, one might say.

As concerns his humor, I will not try to say anything, yet I would try, if I had the words that might approximately reach up to its high place. I do not think any one else can play with humorous fancies so gracefully and delicately and deliciously as he does, nor has so many to play with, nor can come so near making them look as if they were doing the playing themselves and he was not aware that they were at it. For they are unobtrusive, and quiet in their ways, and well conducted. His is a humor which flows softly all around about and over and through the mesh of the page, pervasive, refreshing, health-giving, and makes no more show and no more noise than does the circulation of the blood.

There is another thing which is contentingly noticeable in Mr. Howells's books. That is his "stage directions"--those artifices which authors employ to throw a kind of human naturalness around a scene and a conversation, and help the reader to see the one and get at meanings in the other which might not be perceived if entrusted unexplained to the bare words of the talk. Some authors overdo the stage directions, they elaborate them quite beyond necessity; they spend so much time and take up so much room in telling us how a person said a thing and how he looked and acted when he said it that we get tired and vexed and wish he hadn't said it all. Other authors' directions are brief enough, but it is seldom that the brevity contains either wit or information. Writers of this school go in rags, in the matter of state directions; the majority of them having nothing in stock but a cigar, a laugh, a blush, and a bursting into tears. In their poverty they work these sorry things to the bone. They say:

". . . replied Alfred, flipping the ash from his cigar." (This explains nothing; it only wastes space.)

". . . responded Richard, with a laugh." (There was nothing to laugh about; there never is. The writer puts it in from habit--automatically; he is paying no attention to his work; or he would see that there is nothing to laugh at; often, when a remark is unusually and poignantly flat and silly, he tries to deceive the reader by enlarging the stage direction and making

Richard break into "frenzies of uncontrollable laughter." This makes the reader sad.)

". . . murmured Gladys, blushing." (This poor old shop-worn blush is a tiresome thing. We get so we would rather Gladys would fall out of the book and break her neck than do it again. She is always doing it, and usually irrelevantly. Whenever it is her turn to murmur she hangs out her blush; it is the only thing she's got. In a little while we hate her, just as we do Richard.)

". . . repeated Evelyn, bursting into tears." (This kind keep a book damp all the time. They can't say a thing without crying. They cry so much about nothing that by and by when they have something to cry ABOUT they have gone dry; they sob, and fetch nothing; we are not moved. We are only glad.)

They gavel me, these stale and overworked stage directions, these carbon films that got burnt out long ago and cannot now carry any faintest thread of light. It would be well if they could be relieved from duty and flung out in the literary back yard to rot and disappear along with the discarded and forgotten "steeds" and "halidomes" and similar stage-properties once so dear to our grandfathers. But I am friendly to Mr. Howells's stage directions; more friendly to them than to any one else's, I think. They are done with a competent and discriminating art, and are faithful to the requirements of a state direction's proper and lawful office, which is to inform. Sometimes they convey a scene and its conditions so well that I believe I could see the scene and get the spirit and meaning of the accompanying dialogue if some one would read merely the stage directions to me and leave out the talk. For instance, a scene like this, from THE UNDISCOVERED COUNTRY:

". . . and she laid her arms with a beseeching gesture on her father's shoulder."

". . . she answered, following his gesture with a glance."

". . . she said, laughing nervously."

". . . she asked, turning swiftly upon him that strange, searching glance."

". . . she answered, vaguely."

". . . she reluctantly admitted."

". . . but her voice died wearily away, and she stood looking into his face with puzzled entreaty."

Mr. Howells does not repeat his forms, and does not need to; he can invent fresh ones without limit. It is mainly the repetition over and over again, by the third-rates, of worn and commonplace and juiceless forms that makes their novels such a weariness and vexation to us, I think. We do not mind one or two deliveries of their wares, but as we turn the pages over and keep on meeting them we presently get tired of them and wish they would do other things for a change.

". . . replied Alfred, flipping the ash from his cigar."

". . . responded Richard, with a laugh."

". . . murmured Gladys, blushing."

". . . repeated Evelyn, bursting into tears."

". . . replied the Earl, flipping the ash from his cigar."

". . . responded the undertaker, with a laugh."

". . . murmured the chambermaid, blushing."

". . . repeated the burglar, bursting into tears."

". . . replied the conductor, flipping the ash from his cigar."

". . . responded Arkwright, with a laugh."

". . . murmured the chief of police, blushing."

". . . repeated the house-cat, bursting into tears."

And so on and so on; till at last it ceases to excite. I always notice stage directions, because they fret me and keep me trying to get out of their way, just as the automobiles do. At first; then by and by they become monotonous and I get run over.

Mr. Howells has done much work, and the spirit of it is as beautiful as the make of it. I have held him in admiration and affection so many years that I know by the number of those years that he is old now; but his heart isn't, nor his pen; and years do not count. Let him have plenty of them; there is profit in them for us.

ENGLISH AS SHE IS TAUGHT

IN the appendix to Croker's Boswell's Johnson one finds this anecdote:

CATO'S SOLILOQUY.--One day Mrs. Gastrel set a little girl to repeat to him [Dr. Samuel Johnson] Cato's Soliloquy, which she went through very correctly. The Doctor, after a pause, asked the child:

"What was to bring Cato to an end?"

She said it was a knife.

"No, my dear, it was not so."

"My aunt Polly said it was a knife."

"Why, Aunt Polly's knife MAY DO, but it was a DAGGER, my dear."

He then asked her the meaning of "bane and antidote," which she was unable to give. Mrs. Gastrel said:

"You cannot expect so young a child to know the meaning of such words."

He then said:

"My dear, how many pence are there in SIXPENCE?"

"I cannot tell, sir," was the half-terrified reply.

On this, addressing himself to Mrs. Gastrel, he said:

"Now, my dear lady, can anything be more ridiculous than to teach a child Cato's Soliloquy, who does not know how many pence there are in a sixpence?"

In a lecture before the Royal Geographical Society Professor Ravenstein quoted the following list of frantic questions, and said that they had been asked in an examination:

Mention all names of places in the world derived from Julius Caesar or Augustus Caesar.

Where are the following rivers: Pisuerga, Sakaria, Guadalete, Jalon, Mulde?

All you know of the following: Machacha, Pilmo, Schebulos, Crivoscia, Basces, Mancikert, Taxhem, Citeaux, Meloria, Zutphen.

The highest peaks of the Karakorum range.

The number of universities in Prussia.

Why are the tops of mountains continually covered with snow [sic]?

Name the length and breadth of the streams of lava which issued from the Skaptar Jokul in the eruption of 1783.

That list would oversize nearly anybody's geographical knowledge. Isn't it reasonably possible that in our schools many of the questions in all studies are several miles ahead of where the pupil is?--that he is set to struggle with things that are ludicrously beyond his present reach, hopelessly beyond his present strength? This remark in passing, and by way of text; now I come to what I was going to say.

I have just now fallen upon a darling literary curiosity. It is a little book, a manuscript compilation, and the compiler sent it to me with the request that I say whether I think it ought to be published or not. I said, Yes; but as I slowly grow wise I briskly grow cautious; and so, now that the publication is imminent, it has seemed to me that I should feel more comfortable if I could divide up this responsibility with the public by adding them to the court. Therefore I will print some extracts from the book, in the hope that they may make converts to my judgment that the volume has merit which entitles it to publication.

As to its character. Every one has sampled "English as She is Spoke" and "English as She is Wrote"; this little volume furnishes us an instructive array of examples of "English as She is Taught"--in the public schools of--well, this country. The collection is made by a teacher in those schools, and all the examples in it are genuine; none of them have been tampered with, or doctored in any way. From time to time, during several years, whenever a pupil has delivered himself of anything peculiarly quaint or toothsome in the course of his recitations, this teacher and her associates have privately set that thing down in a memorandum-book; strictly following the original, as to grammar, construction, spelling, and all; and the result is this literary curiosity.

The contents of the book consist mainly of answers given by the boys and girls to questions, said answers being given sometimes verbally, sometimes in writing. The subjects touched upon are fifteen in number: I. Etymology; II. Grammar; III. Mathematics;

IV. Geography; V. "Original"; VI. Analysis; VII. History; VIII. "Intellectual"; IX. Philosophy; X. Physiology; XI. Astronomy; XII. Politics; XIII. Music; XIV. Oratory; XV. Metaphysics.

You perceive that the poor little young idea has taken a shot at a good many kinds of game in the course of the book. Now as to results. Here are some quaint definitions of words. It will be noticed that in all of these instances the sound of the word, or the look of it on paper, has misled the child:

ABORIGINES, a system of mountains.

ALIAS, a good man in the Bible.

AMENABLE, anything that is mean.

AMMONIA, the food of the gods.

ASSIDUITY, state of being an acid.

AURIFEROUS, pertaining to an orifice.

CAPILLARY, a little caterpillar.

CORNIFEROUS, rocks in which fossil corn is found.

EMOLUMENT, a headstone to a grave.

EQUESTRIAN, one who asks questions.

EUCHARIST, one who plays euchre.

FRANCHISE, anything belonging to the French.

IDOLATER, a very idle person.

IPECAC, a man who likes a good dinner.

IRRIGATE, to make fun of.

MENDACIOUS, what can be mended.

MERCENARY, one who feels for another.

PARASITE, a kind of umbrella.

PARASITE, the murder of an infant.

PUBLICAN, a man who does his prayers in public.

TENACIOUS, ten acres of land.

Here is one where the phrase "publicans and sinners" has got mixed up in the child's mind with politics, and the result is a definition which takes one in a sudden and unexpected way:

REPUBLICAN, a sinner mentioned in the Bible.

Also in Democratic newspapers now and then. Here are two where the mistake has resulted from sound assisted by remote fact:

PLAGIARIST, a writer of plays.

DEMAGOGUE, a vessel containing beer and other liquids.

I cannot quite make out what it was that misled the pupil in the following instances; it would not seem to have been the sound of the word, nor the look of it in print:

ASPHYXIA, a grumbling, fussy temper.

QUARTERNIONS, a bird with a flat beak and no bill, living in New Zealand.

QUARTERNIONS, the name given to a style of art practiced by the Phoenicians.

QUARTERNIONS, a religious convention held every hundred years.

SIBILANT, the state of being idiotic.

CROSIER, a staff carried by the Deity.

In the following sentences the pupil's ear has been deceiving him again:

The marriage was illegible.

He was totally dismasted with the whole performance.

He enjoys riding on a philosopher.

She was very quick at repertoire.

He prayed for the waters to subsidize.

The leopard is watching his sheep.

They had a strawberry vestibule.

Here is one which--well, now, how often we do slam right into the truth without ever suspecting it:

The men employed by the Gas Company go around and speculate the meter.

Indeed they do, dear; and when you grow up, many and many's the time you will notice it in the gas bill. In the following sentences the little people have some information to convey, every time; but in my case they fail to connect: the light always went out on the keystone word:

The coercion of some things is remarkable; as bread and molasses.

Her hat is contiguous because she wears it on one side.

He preached to an egregious congregation.

The captain eliminated a bullet through the man's heart.

You should take caution and be precarious.

The supercilious girl acted with vicissitude when the perennial time came.

The last is a curiously plausible sentence; one seems to know what it means, and yet he knows all the time that he doesn't. Here is an odd (but entirely proper) use of a word, and a most sudden descent from a lofty philosophical altitude to a very practical and homely illustration:

We should endeavor to avoid extremes--like those of wasps and bees.

And here--with "zoological" and "geological" in his mind, but not ready to his tongue--the small scholar has innocently gone and let out a couple of secrets which ought never to have been divulged in any circumstances:

There are a good many donkeys in theological gardens.

Some of the best fossils are found in theological gardens.

Under the head of "Grammar" the little scholars furnish the following information:

Gender is the distinguishing nouns without regard to sex.

A verb is something to eat.

Adverbs should always be used as adjectives and adjectives as adverbs.

Every sentence and name of God must begin with a caterpillar.

"Caterpillar" is well enough, but capital letter would have been stricter. The following is a brave attempt at a solution, but it failed to liquify:

When they are going to say some prose or poetry before they say the poetry or prose they must put a semicolon just after the introduction of the prose or poetry.

The chapter on "Mathematics" is full of fruit. From it I take a few samples--mainly in an unripe state:

A straight line is any distance between two places.

Parallel lines are lines that can never meet until they run together.

A circle is a round straight line with a hole in the middle.

Things which are equal to each other are equal to anything else.

To find the number of square feet in a room you multiply the room by the number of the feet. The product is the result.

Right you are. In the matter of geography this little book is unspeakably rich. The questions do not appear to have applied the microscope to the subject, as did those quoted by Professor Ravenstein; still, they proved plenty difficult enough without that. These pupils did not hunt with a microscope, they hunted with a shot-gun; this is shown by the crippled condition of the game they brought in:

America is divided into the Passiffic slope and the Mississippi valey.

North America is separated by Spain.

America consists from north to south about five hundred miles.

The United States is quite a small country compared with some other countrys, but it about as industrious.

The capital of the United States is Long Island.

The five seaports of the U.S. are Newfunlan and Sanfrancisco.

The principal products of the U.S. is earthquakes and volcanoes.

The Alaginnies are mountains in Philadelphia.

The Rocky Mountains are on the western side of Philadelphia.

Cape Hateras is a vast body of water surrounded by land and flowing into the Gulf of Mexico.

Mason and Dixon's line is the Equator.

One of the leading industries of the United States is mollasses, book-covers, numbers, gas, teaching, lumber, manufacturers, paper-making, publishers, coal.

In Austria the principal occupation is gathering Austrich feathers.

Gibraltar is an island built on a rock.

Russia is very cold and tyrannical.

Sicily is one of the Sandwich Islands.

Hindoostan flows through the Ganges and empties into the Mediterranean Sea.

Ireland is called the Emigrant Isle because it is so beautiful and green.

The width of the different zones Europe lies in depend upon the surrounding country.

The imports of a country are the things that are paid for, the exports are the things that are not.

Climate lasts all the time and weather only a few days.

The two most famous volcanoes of Europe are Sodom and Gomorrah.

The chapter headed "Analysis" shows us that the pupils in our public schools are not merely loaded up with those showy facts about geography, mathematics, and so on, and left in that incomplete state; no, there's machinery for clarifying and expanding their minds. They are required to take poems and analyze them, dig out their common sense, reduce them to statistics, and reproduce them in a luminous prose translation which shall tell you at a glance what the poet was trying to get at. One sample will do. Here is a stanza from "The Lady of the Lake," followed by the pupil's impressive explanation of it:

Alone, but with unbated zeal, The horseman plied with scourge and steel; For jaded now and spent with toil, Embossed with foam and dark with soil, While every gasp with sobs he drew, The laboring stag strained full in view.

The man who rode on the horse performed the whip and an instrument made of steel alone with strong ardor not diminishing, for, being tired from the time passed with hard labor overworked with anger and ignorant with weariness, while every breath for labor he drew with cries full or sorrow, the young deer made imperfect who worked hard filtered in sight.

I see, now, that I never understood that poem before. I have had glimpses of its meaning, it moments when I was not as ignorant with weariness as usual, but this is the first time the whole spacious idea of it ever filtered in sight. If I were a public-school pupil I would put those other studies aside and stick to analysis; for, after all, it is the thing to spread your mind.

We come now to historical matters, historical remains, one might say. As one turns the pages he is impressed with the depth to which one date has been driven into the American child's head --1492. The date is there, and it is there to stay. And it is always at hand, always deliverable at a moment's notice. But the Fact that belongs with it? That is quite another matter. Only the date itself is familiar and sure: its vast Fact has failed of lodgment. It would appear that whenever you ask a public- school pupil when a thing--anything, no matter what-- happened, and he is in doubt, he always rips out his 1492. He applies it to everything, from the landing of the ark to the introduction of the horse-car. Well, after all, it is our first date, and so it is right enough to honor it, and pay the public schools to teach our children to honor it:

George Washington was born in 1492.

Washington wrote the Declaration of Independence in 1492.

St. Bartholemew was massacred in 1492.

The Brittains were the Saxons who entered England in 1492 under Julius Caesar.

The earth is 1492 miles in circumference.

To proceed with "History"

Christopher Columbus was called the Father of his Country.

Queen Isabella of Spain sold her watch and chain and other millinery so that Columbus could discover America.

The Indian wars were very desecrating to the country.

The Indians pursued their warfare by hiding in the bushes and then scalping them.

Captain John Smith has been styled the father of his country. His life was saved by his daughter Pochahantas.

The Puritans found an insane asylum in the wilds of America.

The Stamp Act was to make everybody stamp all materials so they should be null and void.

Washington died in Spain almost broken-hearted. His remains were taken to the cathedral in Havana.

Gorilla warfare was where men rode on gorillas.

John Brown was a very good insane man who tried to get fugitives slaves into Virginia. He captured all the inhabitants, but was finally conquered and condemned to his death. The confederasy was formed by the fugitive slaves.

Alfred the Great reigned 872 years. He was distinguished for letting some buckwheat cakes burn, and the lady scolded him.

Henry Eight was famous for being a great widower haveing lost several wives.

Lady Jane Grey studied Greek and Latin and was beheaded after a few days.

John Bright is noted for an incurable disease.

Lord James Gordon Bennet instigated the Gordon Riots.

The Middle Ages come in between antiquity and posterity.

Luther introduced Christianity into England a good many thousand years ago. His birthday was November 1883. He was once a Pope. He lived at the time of the Rebellion of Worms.

Julius Caesar is noted for his famous telegram dispatch I came I saw I conquered.

Julius Caesar was really a very great man. He was a very great soldier and wrote a book for beginners in the Latin.

Cleopatra was caused by the death of an asp which she dissolved in a wine cup.

The only form of government in Greece was a limited monkey.

The Persian war lasted about 500 years.

Greece had only 7 wise men.

Socrates . . . destroyed some statues and had to drink Shamrock.

Here is a fact correctly stated; and yet it is phrased with such ingenious infelicity that it can be depended upon to convey misinformation every time it is uncarefully unread:

By the Salic law no woman or descendant of a woman could occupy the throne.

To show how far a child can travel in history with judicious and diligent boosting in the public school, we select the following mosaic:

Abraham Lincoln was born in Wales in 1599.

In the chapter headed "Intellectual" I find a great number of most interesting statements. A sample or two may be found not amiss:

Bracebridge Hall was written by Henry Irving.

Show Bound was written by Peter Cooper.

The House of the Seven Gables was written by Lord Bryant.

Edgar A. Poe was a very curdling writer.

Cotton Mather was a writer who invented the cotten gin and wrote histories.

Beowulf wrote the Scriptures.

Ben Johnson survived Shakspeare in some respects.

In the Canterbury Tale it gives account of King Alfred on his way to the shrine of Thomas Bucket.

Chaucer was the father of English pottery.

Chaucer was a bland verse writer of the third century.

Chaucer was succeeded by H. Wads. Longfellow an American Writer. His writings were chiefly prose and nearly one hundred years elapsed.

Shakspere translated the Scriptures and it was called St. James because he did it.

In the middle of the chapter I find many pages of information concerning Shakespeare's plays, Milton's works, and those of Bacon, Addison, Samuel Johnson, Fielding, Richardson, Sterne, Smollett, De Foe, Locke, Pope, Swift, Goldsmith, Burns, Cowper, Wordsworth, Gibbon, Byron, Coleridge, Hood, Scott, Macaulay, George Eliot, Dickens, Bulwer, Thackeray, Browning, Mrs. Browning, Tennyson, and Disraeli--a fact which shows that into the restricted stomach of the public-school pupil is shoveled every year the blood, bone, and viscera of a gigantic literature, and the same is there digested and disposed of in a most successful and characteristic and gratifying public-school way. I have space for but a trifling few of the results:

Lord Byron was the son of an heiress and a drunken man.

Wm. Wordsworth wrote the Barefoot Boy and Imitations on Immortality.

Gibbon wrote a history of his travels in Italy. This was original.

George Eliot left a wife and children who mourned greatly for his genius.

George Eliot Miss Mary Evans Mrs. Cross Mrs. Lewis was the greatest female poet unless George Sands is made an exception of.

Bulwell is considered a good writer.

Sir Walter Scott Charles Bronte Alfred the Great and Johnson were the first great novelists.

Thomas Babington Makorlay graduated at Harvard and then studied law, he was raised to the peerage as baron in 1557 and died in 1776.

Here are two or three miscellaneous facts that may be of value, if taken in moderation:

Homer's writings are Homer's Essays Virgil the Aenid and Paradise lost some people say that these poems were not written by Homer but by another man of the same name.

A sort of sadness kind of shone in Bryant's poems.

Holmes is a very profligate and amusing writer.

When the public-school pupil wrestles with the political features of the Great Republic, they throw him sometimes:

A bill becomes a law when the President vetoes it.

The three departments of the government is the President rules the world, the governor rules the State, the mayor rules the city.

The first conscientious Congress met in Philadelphia.

The Constitution of the United States was established to ensure domestic hostility.

Truth crushed to earth will rise again. As follows:

The Constitution of the United States is that part of the book at the end which nobody reads.

And here she rises once more and untimely. There should be a limit to public-school instruction; it cannot be wise or well to let the young find out everything:

Congress is divided into civilized half civilized and savage.

Here are some results of study in music and oratory:

An interval in music is the distance on the keyboard from one piano to the next.

A rest means you are not to sing it.

Emphasis is putting more distress on one word than another.

The chapter on "Physiology" contains much that ought not to be lost to science:

Physillogigy is to study about your bones stummick and vertebry.

Occupations which are injurious to health are cabolic acid gas which is impure blood.

We have an upper and lower skin. The lower skin moves all the time and the upper skin moves when we do.

The body is mostly composed of water and about one half is avaricious tissue.

The stomach is a small pear-shaped bone situated in the body.

The gastric juice keeps the bones from creaking.

The Chyle flows up the middle of the backbone and reaches the heart where it meets the oxygen and is purified.

The salivary glands are used to salivate the body.

In the stomach starch is changed to cane sugar and cane sugar to sugar cane.

The olfactory nerve enters the cavity of the orbit and is developed into the special sense of hearing.

The growth of a tooth begins in the back of the mouth and extends to the stomach.

If we were on a railroad track and a train was coming the train would deafen our ears so that we couldn't see to get off the track.

If, up to this point, none of my quotations have added flavor to the Johnsonian anecdote at the head of this article, let us make another attempt:

The theory that intuitive truths are discovered by the light of nature originated from St. John's interpretation of a passage in the Gospel of Plato.

The weight of the earth is found by comparing a mass of known lead with that of a mass of unknown lead.

To find the weight of the earth take the length of a degree on a meridian and multiply by 6 1/2 pounds.

The spheres are to each other as the squares of their homologous sides.

A body will go just as far in the first second as the body will go plus the force of gravity and that's equal to twice what the body will go.

Specific gravity is the weight to be compared weight of an equal volume of or that is the weight of a body compared with the weight of an equal volume.

The law of fluid pressure divide the different forms of organized bodies by the form of attraction and the number increased will be the form.

Inertia is that property of bodies by virtue of which it cannot change its own condition of rest or motion. In other words it is the negative quality of passiveness either in recoverable latency or insipient latescence.

If a laugh is fair here, not the struggling child, nor the unintelligent teacher--or rather the unintelligent Boards, Committees, and Trustees--are the proper target for it. All through this little book one detects the signs of a certain probable fact--that a large part of the pupil's "instruction" consists in cramming him with obscure and wordy "rules" which he does not understand and has no time to understand. It would be as useful to cram him with brickbats; they would at least stay. In a town in the interior of New York, a few years ago, a gentleman set forth a mathematical problem and proposed to give a prize to every public-school pupil who should furnish the correct solution of it. Twenty-two of the brightest boys in the public schools entered the contest. The problem was not a very difficult one for pupils of their mathematical rank and standing, yet they all failed--by a hair--through one trifling mistake or another. Some searching questions were asked, when it turned out that these lads were as glib as parrots with the "rules," but could not reason out a single rule or explain the principle underlying it. Their memories had been stocked, but not their understandings. It was a case of brickbat culture, pure and simple.

There are several curious "compositions" in the little book, and we must make room for one. It is full of naivete, brutal truth, and unembarrassed directness, and is the funniest (genuine) boy's composition I think I have ever seen:

ON GIRLS

Girls are very stuck up and dignefied in their maner and be have your. They think more of dress than anything and like to play with dowls and rags. They cry if they see a cow in a far distance and are afraid of guns. They stay at home all the time and go to church on Sunday. They are al-ways sick. They are al- ways funy and making fun of boy's hands and they say how dirty. They cant play marbels. I pity them poor things. They make fun of boys and then turn round and love them. I dont beleave they ever kiled a cat or anything. They look out every nite and say oh ant the moon lovely. Thir is one thing I have not told and that is they al-ways now their lessons bettern boys.

From Mr. Edward Channing's recent article in SCIENCE:

The marked difference between the books now being produced by French, English, and American travelers, on the one hand, and German explorers, on the other, is too great to escape attention. That difference is due entirely to the fact that in school and university the German is taught, in the first place to see, and in the second place to understand what he does see.

A SIMPLIFIED ALPHABET

(This article, written during the autumn of 1899, was about the last writing done by Mark Twain on any impersonal subject.)

I have had a kindly feeling, a friendly feeling, a cousinly feeling toward Simplified Spelling, from the beginning of the movement three years ago, but nothing more inflamed than that. It seemed to me to merely propose to substitute one inadequacy for another; a sort of patching and plugging poor old dental relics with cement and gold and porcelain paste; what was really needed was a new set of teeth. That is to say, a new ALPHABET.

The heart of our trouble is with our foolish alphabet. It doesn't know how to spell, and can't be taught. In this it is like all other alphabets except one--the phonographic. This is the only competent alphabet in the world. It can spell and correctly pronounce any word in our language.

That admirable alphabet, that brilliant alphabet, that inspired alphabet, can be learned in an hour or two. In a week the student can learn to write it with some little facility, and to read it with considerable ease. I know, for I saw it tried in a public school in Nevada forty-five years ago, and was so impressed by the incident that it has remained in my memory ever since.

I wish we could adopt it in place of our present written (and printed) character. I mean SIMPLY the alphabet; simply the consonants and the vowels--I don't mean any REDUCTIONS or abbreviations of them, such as the shorthand writer uses in order to get compression and speed. No, I would SPELL EVERY WORD OUT.

I will insert the alphabet here as I find it in Burnz's PHONIC SHORTHAND. [Figure 1] It is arranged on the basis of Isaac Pitman's PHONOGRAPHY. Isaac Pitman was the originator and father of scientific phonography. It is used throughout the globe. It was a memorable invention. He made it public seventy- three years ago. The firm of Isaac Pitman & Sons, New York, still exists, and they continue the master's work.

What should we gain?

First of all, we could spell DEFINITELY--and correctly--any word you please, just by the SOUND of it. We can't do that with our present alphabet. For instance, take a simple, every-day word PHTHISIS. If we tried to spell it by the sound of it, we should make it TYSIS, and be laughed at by every educated person.

Secondly, we should gain in REDUCTION OF LABOR in writing.

Simplified Spelling makes valuable reductions in the case of several hundred words, but the new spelling must be LEARNED. You can't spell them by the sound; you must get them out of the book.

But even if we knew the simplified form for every word in the language, the phonographic alphabet would still beat the Simplified Speller "hands down" in the important matter of economy of labor. I will illustrate:

PRESENT FORM: through, laugh, highland.

SIMPLIFIED FORM: thru, laff, hyland.

PHONOGRAPHIC FORM: [Figure 2]

To write the word "through," the pen has to make twenty-one strokes.

To write the word "thru," then pen has to make twelve strokes-- a good saving.

To write that same word with the phonographic alphabet, the pen has to make only THREE strokes.

To write the word "laugh," the pen has to make FOURTEEN strokes.

To write "laff," the pen has to make the SAME NUMBER of strokes--no labor is saved to the penman.

To write the same word with the phonographic alphabet, the pen has to make only THREE strokes.

To write the word "highland," the pen has to make twenty-two strokes.

To write "hyland," the pen has to make eighteen strokes.

To write that word with the phonographic alphabet, the pen has to make only FIVE strokes. [Figure 3]

To write the words "phonographic alphabet," the pen has to make fifty-three strokes.

To write "fonografic alfabet," the pen has to make fifty strokes. To the penman, the saving in labor is insignificant.

To write that word (with vowels) with the phonographic alphabet, the pen has to make only SEVENTEEN strokes.

Without the vowels, only THIRTEEN strokes. [Figure 4] The vowels are hardly necessary, this time.

We make five pen-strokes in writing an m. Thus: [Figure 5] a stroke down; a stroke up; a second stroke down; a second stroke up; a final stroke down. Total, five. The phonographic alphabet accomplishes the m with a single stroke--a curve, like a parenthesis that has come home drunk and has fallen face down right at the front door where everybody that goes along will see him and say, Alas!

When our written m is not the end of a word, but is otherwise located, it has to be connected with the next letter, and that requires another pen-stroke, making six in all, before you get rid of that m. But never mind about the connecting strokes--let them go. Without counting them, the twenty-six letters of our alphabet consumed about eighty pen-strokes for their construction--about three pen-strokes per letter.

It is THREE TIMES THE NUMBER required by the phonographic alphabet. It requires but ONE stroke for each letter.

My writing-gait is--well, I don't know what it is, but I will time myself and see. Result: it is twenty-four words per minute. I don't mean composing; I mean COPYING. There isn't any definite composing-gait.

Very well, my copying-gait is 1,440 words per hour--say 1,500. If I could use the phonographic character with facility I could do the 1,500 in twenty minutes. I could do nine hours' copying in three hours; I could do three years' copying in one year. Also, if

I had a typewriting machine with the phonographic alphabet on it--oh, the miracles I could do!

I am not pretending to write that character well. I have never had a lesson, and I am copying the letters from the book. But I can accomplish my desire, at any rate, which is, to make the reader get a good and clear idea of the advantage it would be to us if we could discard our present alphabet and put this better one in its place--using it in books, newspapers, with the typewriter, and with the pen.

[Figure 6] --MAN DOG HORSE. I think it is graceful and would look comely in print. And consider--once more, I beg--what a labor-saver it is! Ten pen-strokes with the one system to convey those three words above, and thirty-three by the other! [Figure 6] I mean, in SOME ways, not in all. I suppose I might go so far as to say in most ways, and be within the facts, but never mind; let it go at SOME. One of the ways in which it exercises this birthright is--as I think--continuing to use our laughable alphabet these seventy-three years while there was a rational one at hand, to be had for the taking.

It has taken five hundred years to simplify some of Chaucer's rotten spelling--if I may be allowed to use to frank a term as that--and it will take five hundred years more to get our exasperating new Simplified Corruptions accepted and running smoothly. And we sha'n't be any better off then than we are now; for in that day we shall still have the privilege the Simplifiers are exercising now: ANYBODY can change the spelling that wants to.

BUT YOU CAN'T CHANGE THE PHONOGRAPHIC SPELLING; THERE ISN'T ANY WAY. It will always follow the SOUND. If you want to change the spelling, you have to change the sound first.

Mind, I myself am a Simplified Speller; I belong to that unhappy guild that is patiently and hopefully trying to reform our drunken old alphabet by reducing his whiskey. Well, it will improve him. When they get through and have reformed him all they can by their system he will be only HALF drunk. Above that condition their system can never lift him. There is no competent, and lasting, and real reform for him but to take away his whiskey entirely, and fill up his jug with Pitman's wholesome and undiseased alphabet.

One great drawback to Simplified Spelling is, that in print a simplified word looks so like the very nation! and when you bunch a whole squadron of the Simplified together the spectacle is very nearly unendurable.

The da ma ov koars kum when the publik ma be expektd to get rekonsyled to the bezair asspekt of the Simplified Kombyna-shuns, but--if I may be allowed the expression--is it worth the wasted time? [Figure 7]

To see our letters put together in ways to which we are not accustomed offends the eye, and also takes the EXPRESSION out of the words.

La on, Makduf, and damd be he hoo furst krys hold, enuf!

It doesn't thrill you as it used to do. The simplifications have sucked the thrill all out of it.

But a written character with which we are NOT ACQUAINTED does not offend us--Greek, Hebrew, Russian, Arabic, and the others--they have an interesting look, and we see beauty in them, too. And this is true of hieroglyphics, as well. There is something pleasant and engaging about the mathematical signs when we do not understand them. The mystery hidden in these things has a fascination for us: we can't come across a printed page of shorthand without being impressed by it and wishing we could read it.

Very well, what I am offering for acceptance and adopting is not shorthand, but longhand, written with the SHORTHAND ALPHABET UNREACHED. You can write three times as many words in a minute with it as you can write with our alphabet. And so, in a way, it IS properly a shorthand. It has a pleasant look, too; a beguiling look, an inviting look. I will write something in it, in my rude and untaught way: [Figure 8]

Even when _I_ do it it comes out prettier than it does in Simplified Spelling. Yes, and in the Simplified it costs one hundred and twenty-three pen-strokes to write it, whereas in the phonographic it costs only twenty-nine.

[Figure 9] is probably [Figure 10].

Let us hope so, anyway.

AS CONCERNS INTERPRETING THE DEITY

I

THIS line of hieroglyphics was for fourteen years the despair of all the scholars who labored over the mysteries of the Rosetta stone: [Figure 1]

After five years of study Champollion translated it thus:

Therefore let the worship of Epiphanes be maintained in all the temples, this upon pain of death.

That was the twenty-forth translation that had been furnished by scholars. For a time it stood. But only for a time. Then doubts began to assail it and undermine it, and the scholars resumed their labors. Three years of patient work produced eleven new translations; among them, this, by Gr:unfeldt, was received with considerable favor:

The horse of Epiphanes shall be maintained at the public expense; this upon pain of death.

But the following rendering, by Gospodin, was received by the learned world with yet greater favor:

The priest shall explain the wisdom of Epiphanes to all these people, and these shall listen with reverence, upon pain of death.

Seven years followed, in which twenty-one fresh and widely varying renderings were scored--none of them quite convincing. But now, at last, came Rawlinson, the youngest of all the scholars, with a translation which was immediately and universally recognized as being the correct version, and his name became famous in a day. So famous, indeed, that even the children were familiar with it; and such a noise did the achievement itself make that not even the noise of the monumental political event of that same year--the flight from Elba--was able to smother it to silence. Rawlinson's version reads as follows:

Therefore, walk not away from the wisdom of Epiphanes, but turn and follow it; so shall it conduct thee to the temple's peace, and soften for thee the sorrows of life and the pains of death.

Here is another difficult text: [Figure 2]

It is demotic--a style of Egyptian writing and a phase of the language which has perished from the knowledge of all men twenty-five hundred years before the Christian era.

Our red Indians have left many records, in the form of pictures, upon our crags and boulders. It has taken our most gifted and painstaking students two centuries to get at the meanings hidden in these pictures; yet there are still two little lines of hieroglyphics among the figures grouped upon the Dighton Rocks which they have not succeeds in interpreting to their satisfaction. These: [Figure 3]

The suggested solutions are practically innumerable; they would fill a book.

Thus we have infinite trouble in solving man-made mysteries; it is only when we set out to discover the secret of God that our difficulties disappear. It was always so. In antique Roman times it was the custom of the Deity to try to conceal His intentions in the entrails of birds, and this was patiently and hopefully continued century after century, although the attempted concealment never succeeded, in a single recorded instance. The augurs could read entrails as easily as a modern child can read coarse print. Roman history is full of the marvels of interpretation which these extraordinary men performed. These strange and wonderful achievements move our awe and compel our admiration. Those men could pierce to the marrow of a mystery instantly. If the Rosetta-stone idea had been introduced it would have defeated them, but entrails had no embarrassments for them. Entrails have gone out, now-- entrails and dreams. It was at last found out that as hiding-places for the divine intentions they were inadequate.

A part of the wall of Valletri in former times been struck with thunder, the response of the soothsayers was, that a native of that town would some time or other arrive at supreme power.-- BOHN'S SUETONIUS, p. 138.

"Some time or other." It looks indefinite, but no matter, it happened, all the same; one needed only to wait, and be patient, and keep watch, then he would find out that the thunder- stroke had Caesar Augustus in mind, and had come to give notice.

There were other advance-advertisements. One of them appeared just before Caesar Augustus was born, and was most poetic and touching and romantic in its feelings and aspects. It was a dream. It was dreamed by Caesar Augustus's mother, and interpreted at the usual rates:

Atia, before her delivery, dreamed that her bowels stretched to the stars and expanded through the whole circuit of heaven and earth.--SUETONIUS, p. 139.

That was in the augur's line, and furnished him no difficulties, but it would have taken Rawlinson and Champollion fourteen years to make sure of what it meant, because they would have been surprised and dizzy. It would have been too late to be valuable, then, and the bill for service would have been barred by the statute of limitation.

In those old Roman days a gentleman's education was not complete until he had taken a theological course at the seminary and learned how to translate entrails. Caesar Augustus's education received this final polish. All through his life, whenever he had poultry on the menu he saved the interiors and kept himself informed of the Deity's plans by exercising upon those interiors the arts of augury.

In his first consulship, while he was observing the auguries, twelve vultures presented themselves, as they had done to Romulus. And when he offered sacrifice, the livers of all the victims were folded inward in the lower part; a circumstance which was regarded by those present who had skill in things of that nature, as an indubitable prognostic of great and wonderful fortune.--SUETONIUS, p. 141.

"Indubitable" is a strong word, but no doubt it was justified, if the livers were really turned that way. In those days chicken livers were strangely and delicately sensitive to coming events, no matter how far off they might be; and they could never keep still, but would curl and squirm like that, particularly when vultures came and showed interest in that approaching great event and in breakfast.

II

We may now skip eleven hundred and thirty or forty years, which brings us down to enlightened Christian times and the troubled days of King Stephen of England. The augur has had his day and has been long ago forgotten; the priest had fallen heir to his trade.

King Henry is dead; Stephen, that bold and outrageous person, comes flying over from Normandy to steal the throne from Henry's daughter. He accomplished his crime, and Henry of Huntington, a priest of high degree, mourns over it in his Chronicle. The Archbishop of Canterbury consecrated Stephen: "wherefore the Lord visited the Archbishop with the same judgment which he had inflicted upon him who struck Jeremiah the great priest: he died with a year."

Stephen's was the greater offense, but Stephen could wait; not so the Archbishop, apparently.

The kingdom was a prey to intestine wars; slaughter, fire, and rapine spread ruin throughout the land; cries of distress, horror, and woe rose in every quarter.

That was the result of Stephen's crime. These unspeakable conditions continued during nineteen years. Then Stephen died as comfortably as any man ever did, and was honorably buried. It makes one pity the poor Archbishop, and with that he, too, could have been let off as leniently. How did Henry of Huntington know that the Archbishop was sent to his grave by judgment of God for consecrating Stephen? He does not explain. Neither does he explain why Stephen was awarded a pleasanter death than he was entitled to, while the aged King Henry, his predecessor, who had ruled England thirty-five years to the people's strongly worded satisfaction, was condemned to close his life in circumstances most distinctly unpleasant, inconvenient, and disagreeable. His was probably the most uninspiring funeral that is set down in history. There is not a detail about it that is attractive. It seems to have been just the funeral for Stephen, and even at this far-distant day it is matter of just regret that by an indiscretion the wrong man got it.

Whenever God punishes a man, Henry of Huntington knows why it was done, and tells us; and his pen is eloquent with admiration; but when a man has earned punishment, and escapes, he does not explain. He is evidently puzzled, but he does not say anything. I think it is often apparent that he is pained by these discrepancies, but loyally tries his best not to show it. When he cannot praise, he delivers himself of a silence so marked that a suspicious person could mistake it for suppressed criticism. However, he has plenty of opportunities to feel contented with the way things go--his book is full of them.

King David of Scotland . . . under color of religion caused his followers to deal most barbarously with the English. They ripped open women, tossed children on the points of spears, butchered priests at the altars, and, cutting off the heads from the images on crucifixes, placed them on the bodies of the slain, while in exchange they fixed on the crucifixes the heads of their victims. Wherever the Scots came, there was the same scene of horror and cruelty: women shrieking, old men lamenting, amid the groans of the dying and the despair of the living.

But the English got the victory.

Then the chief of the men of Lothian fell, pierced by an arrow, and all his followers were put to flight. For the Almighty was offended at them and their strength was rent like a cobweb.

Offended at them for what? For committing those fearful butcheries? No, for that was the common custom on both sides, and not open to criticism. Then was it for doing the butcheries "under cover of religion"? No, that was not it; religious feeling was often expressed in that fervent way all through those old centuries. The truth is, He was not offended at "them" at all; He was only offended at their king, who had been false to an oath. Then why did not He put the punishment upon the king instead of upon "them"? It is a difficult question. One can see by the Chronicle that the "judgments" fell rather customarily upon the wrong person, but Henry of Huntington does not explain why. Here is one that went true; the chronic-ler's satisfaction in it is not hidden:

In the month of August, Providence displayed its justice in a remarkable manner; for two of the nobles who had converted monasteries into fortifications, expelling the monks, their sin being the same, met with a similar punishment. Robert Marmion was one, Godfrey de Mandeville the other. Robert Marmion, issuing forth against the enemy, was slain under the walls of the monastery, being the only one who fell, though he was surrounded by his troops. Dying excommunicated, he became subject to death everlasting. In like manner Earl Godfrey was singled out among his followers, and shot with an arrow by a common foot-soldier. He made light of the wound, but he died of it in a few days, under excommunication. See here the like judgment of God, memorable through all ages!

The exaltation jars upon me; not because of the death of the men, for they deserved that, but because it is death eternal, in white-hot fire and flame. It makes my flesh crawl. I have not known more than three men, or perhaps four, in my whole lifetime, *whom I would rejoice to see writhing in those fires for even a year, let alone forever. I believe I would relent before the year was up, and get them out if I could. I think that in the long run, if a man's wife and babies, who had not harmed me, should come crying and pleading, I couldn't stand it; I know I should forgive him and let him go, even if he had violated a monastery. Henry of Huntington has been watching Godfrey and Marmion for nearly seven hundred and fifty years, now, but I couldn't do it, I know I couldn't. I am soft and gentle in my nature, and I should have forgiven them seventy-and-seven times, long ago. And I think God has; but this is only an opinion, and not authoritative, like Henry of Huntington's interpretations. I could learn to interpret, but I have never tried; I get so little time.

All through his book Henry exhibits his familiarity with the intentions of God, and with the reasons for his intentions. Sometimes--very often, in fact--the act follows the intention after such a wide interval of time that one wonders how Henry could fit one act out of a hundred to one intention out of a hundred and get the thing right every time when there was such abundant choice among acts and intentions. Sometimes a man offends the Deity with a crime, and is punished for it thirty years later; meantime he was committed a million other crimes: no matter, Henry can pick out the one that brought the worms. Worms were generally used in those days for the slaying of particularly wicked people. This has gone out, now, but in old times it was a favorite. It always indicated a case of "wrath." For instance:

. . . the just God avenging Robert Fitzhilderbrand's perfidy, a worm grew in his vitals, which gradually gnawing its way through his intestines fattened on the abandoned man till, tortured with excruciating sufferings and venting himself in bitter moans, he was by a fitting punishment brought to his end. --(P. 400.)

It was probably an alligator, but we cannot tell; we only know it was a particular breed, and only used to convey wrath. Some authorities think it was an ichthyosaurus, but there is much doubt.

However, one thing we do know; and that is that that worm had been due years and years. Robert F. had violated a monastery once; he had committed unprintable crimes since, and they had been permitted--under disapproval--but the ravishment of the monastery had not been forgotten nor forgiven, and the worm came at last.

Why were these reforms put off in this strange way? What was to be gained by it? Did Henry of Huntington really know his facts, or was he only guessing? Sometimes I am half persuaded that he is only a guesser, and not a good one. The divine wisdom must surely be of the better quality than he makes it out to be.

Five hundred years before Henry's time some forecasts of the Lord's purposes were furnished by a pope, who perceived, by certain perfectly trustworthy signs furnished by the Deity for the information of His familiars, that the end of the world was

. . . about to come. But as this end of the world draws near many things are at hand which have not before happened, as changes in the air, terrible signs in the heavens, tempests out of the common order of the seasons, wars, famines, pestilences, earthquakes in various places; all which will not happen in our days, but after our days all will come to pass.

Still, the end was so near that these signs were "sent before that we may be careful for our souls and be found prepared to meet the impending judgment."

That was thirteen hundred years ago. This is really no improvement on the work of the Roman augurs.

CONCERNING TOBACCO

A S concerns tobacco, there are many superstitions. And the chiefest is this--that there is a STANDARD governing the matter, whereas there is nothing of the kind. Each man's own preference is the only standard for him, the only one which he can accept, the only one which can command him. A congress of all the tobacco-lovers in the world could not elect a standard which would be binding upon you or me, or would even much influence us.

The next superstition is that a man has a standard of his own. He hasn't. He thinks he has, but he hasn't. He thinks he can tell what he regards as a good cigar from what he regards as a bad one--but he can't. He goes by the brand, yet imagines he goes by the flavor. One may palm off the worst counterfeit upon him; if it bears his brand he will smoke it contentedly and never suspect.

Children of twenty-five, who have seven years experience, try to tell me what is a good cigar and what isn't. Me, who never learned to smoke, but always smoked; me, who came into the world asking for a light.

No one can tell me what is a good cigar--for me. I am the only judge. People who claim to know say that I smoke the worst cigars in the world. They bring their own cigars when they come to my house. They betray an unmanly terror when I offer them a cigar; they tell lies and hurry away to meet engagements which they have not made when they are threatened with the hospitalities of my box. Now then, observe what superstition, assisted by a man's reputation, can do. I was to have twelve personal friends to supper one night. One of them was as notorious for costly and elegant cigars as I was for cheap and devilish ones. I called at his house and when no one was looking borrowed a double handful of his very choicest; cigars which cost him forty cents apiece and bore red-and-gold labels in sign of their nobility. I removed the labels and put the cigars into a box with my favorite brand on it--a brand which those people all knew, and which cowed them as men are cowed by an epidemic. They took these cigars when offered at the end of the supper, and lit them and sternly struggled with them--in dreary silence, for hilarity died when the fell brand came into view and started around--but their fortitude held for a short time only; then they made excuses and filed out, treading on one another's heels with indecent eagerness; and in the morning when I went out to observe results the cigars lay all between the front door and the gate. All except one--that one lay in the plate of the man from whom I had cabbaged the lot. One or two whiffs was all he could stand. He told me afterward that some day I would get shot for giving people that kind of cigars to smoke.

Am I certain of my own standard? Perfectly; yes, absolutely -- unless somebody fools me by putting my brand on some other kind of cigar; for no doubt I am like the rest, and know my cigar by the brand instead of by the flavor. However, my standard is a pretty wide one and covers a good deal of territory. To me, almost any cigar is good that nobody else will smoke, and to me almost all cigars are bad that other people consider good. Nearly any cigar will do me, except a Havana. People think they hurt my feelings when then come to my house with their life preservers on--I mean, with their own cigars in their pockets. It is an error; I take care of myself in a similar way. When I go into danger--that is, into rich people's houses, where, in the nature of things, they will have high-tariff cigars, red-and-gilt girded and nested in a rosewood box along with a damp sponge, cigars which develop a dismal black ash and burn down the side and smell, and will grow hot to the fingers, and will go on growing hotter and hotter, and go on smelling more and more infamously and unendurably the deeper the fire tunnels down inside below the thimbleful of honest tobacco that is in the front end, the furnisher of it praising it all the time and telling you how much the deadly thing cost--yes, when I go into that sort of peril I carry my own defense along; I carry my own brand--twenty-seven cents a barrel--and I live to see my family again. I may seem to light his red-gartered cigar, but that is only for courtesy's sake; I smuggle it into my pocket for the poor, of whom I know many, and light one of my own; and while he praises it I join in, but when he says it cost forty-five cents I say nothing, for I know better.

However, to say true, my tastes are so catholic that I have never seen any cigars that I really could not smoke, except those that cost a dollar apiece. I have examined those and know that they are made of dog-hair, and not good dog-hair at that.

I have a thoroughly satisfactory time in Europe, for all over the Continent one finds cigars which not even the most hardened newsboys in New York would smoke. I brought cigars with me, the last time; I will not do that any more. In Italy, as in France, the Government is the only cigar-peddler. Italy has three or four domestic brands: the Minghetti, the Trabuco, the Virginia, and a very coarse one which is a modification of the Virginia. The Minghettis are large and comely, and cost three dollars and sixty cents a hundred; I can smoke a hundred in seven days and enjoy every one of them. The Trabucos suit me, too; I don't remember the price. But one has to learn to like the Virginia, nobody is born friendly to it. It looks like a rat- tail file, but smokes better, some think. It has a straw through it; you pull this out, and it leaves a flue, otherwise there would be no draught, not even as much as there is to a nail. Some prefer a nail at first. However, I like all the French, Swiss, German, and Italian domestic cigars, and have never cared to inquire what they are made of; and nobody would know, anyhow, perhaps. There is even a brand of European smoking-tobacco that I like. It is a brand used by the Italian peasants. It is loose and dry and black, and looks like tea-grounds. When the fire is applied it expands, and climbs up and towers above the pipe, and presently tumbles off inside of one's vest. The tobacco itself is cheap, but it raises the insurance. It is as I remarked in the beginning--the taste for tobacco is a matter of superstition. There are no standards--no real standards. Each man's preference is the only standard for him, the only one which he can accept, the only one which can command him.

THE BEE

I T was Maeterlinck who introduced me to the bee. I mean, in the psychical and in the poetical way. I had had a business introduction earlier. It was when I was a boy. It is strange that I should remember a formality like that so long; it must be nearly sixty years.

Bee scientists always speak of the bee as she. It is because all the important bees are of that sex. In the hive there is one married bee, called the queen; she has fifty thousand children; of these, about one hundred are sons; the rest are daughters. Some of the daughters are young maids, some are old maids, and all are virgins and remain so.

Every spring the queen comes out of the hive and flies away with one of her sons and marries him. The honeymoon lasts only an hour or two; then the queen divorces her husband and returns home competent to lay two million eggs. This will be enough to last the year, but not more than enough, because hundreds of bees are drowned every day, and other hundreds are eaten by birds, and it is the queen's business to keep the population up to standard --say, fifty thousand. She must always have that many children on hand and efficient during the busy season, which is summer, or winter would catch the community short of food. She lays from two thousand to three thousand eggs a day, according to the demand; and she must exercise judgment, and not lay more than are needed in a slim flower-harvest, nor fewer than are required in a prodigal one, or the board of directors will dethrone her and elect a queen that has more sense.

There are always a few royal heirs in stock and ready to take her place--ready and more than anxious to do it, although she is their own mother. These girls are kept by themselves, and are regally fed and tended from birth. No other bees get such fine food as they get, or live such a high and luxurious life. By consequence they are larger and longer and sleeker than their working sisters. And they have a curved sting, shaped like a scimitar, while the others have a straight one.

A common bee will sting any one or anybody, but a royalty stings royalties only. A common bee will sting and kill another common bee, for cause, but when it is necessary to kill the queen other ways are employed. When a queen has grown old and slack and does not lay eggs enough one of her royal daughters is allowed to come to attack her, the rest of the bees looking on at the duel and seeing fair play. It is a duel with the curved stings. If one of the fighters gets hard pressed and gives it up and runs, she is brought back and must try again--once, maybe twice; then, if she runs yet once more for her life, judicial death is her portion; her children pack themselves into a ball around her person and hold her in that compact grip two or three days, until she starves to death or is suffocated. Meantime the victor bee is receiving royal honors and performing the one royal function--laying eggs.

As regards the ethics of the judicial assassination of the queen, that is a matter of politics, and will be discussed later, in its proper place.

During substantially the whole of her short life of five or six years the queen lives in Egyptian darkness and stately seclusion of the royal apartments, with none about her but plebeian servants, who give her empty lip-affection in place of the love which her heart hungers for; who spy upon her in the interest of her waiting heirs, and report and exaggerate her defects and deficiencies to them; who fawn upon her and flatter her to her face and slander her behind her back; who grovel before her in the day of her power and forsake her in her age and weakness. There she sits, friendless, upon her throne through the long night of her life, cut off from the consoling sympathies and sweet companionship and loving endearments which she craves, by the gilded barriers of her awful rank; a forlorn exile in her own house and home, weary object of formal ceremonies and machine-made worship, winged child of the sun, native to the free air and the blue skies and the flowery fields, doomed by the splendid accident of her birth to trade this priceless heritage for a black captivity, a tinsel grandeur, and a loveless life, with shame and insult at the end and a cruel death--and condemned by the human instinct in her to hold the bargain valuable!

Huber, Lubbock, Maeterlinck--in fact, all the great authorities-- are agreed in denying that the bee is a member of the human family. I do not know why they have done this, but I think it is from dishonest motives. Why, the innumerable facts brought to light by their own painstaking and exhaustive experiments prove that if there is a master fool in the world, it is the bee. That seems to settle it.

But that is the way of the scientist. He will spend thirty years in building up a mountain range of facts with the intent to prove a certain theory; then he is so happy in his achievement that as a rule he overlooks the main chief fact of all--that his accumulation proves an entirely different thing. When you point out this miscarriage to him he does not answer your letters; when you call to convince him, the servant prevaricates and you do not get in. Scientists have odious manners, except when you prop up their theory; then you can borrow money of them.

To be strictly fair, I will concede that now and then one of them will answer your letter, but when they do they avoid the issue-- you cannot pin them down. When I discovered that the bee was human I wrote about it to all those scientists whom I have just mentioned. For evasions, I have seen nothing to equal the answers I got.

After the queen, the personage next in importance in the hive is the virgin. The virgins are fifty thousand or one hundred thousand in number, and they are the workers, the laborers. No work is done, in the hive or out of it, save by them. The males do not work, the queen does no work, unless laying eggs is work, but it does not seem so to me. There are only two million of them, anyway, and all of five months to finish the contract in. The distribution of work in a hive is as cleverly and elaborately specialized as it is in a vast American machine-shop or factory. A bee that has been trained to one of the many and various industries of the concern doesn't know how to exercise any other, and would be offended if asked to take a hand in anything outside of her profession. She is as human as a cook; and if you should ask the cook to wait on the table, you know what will happen. Cooks will play the piano if you like, but they draw the line there. In my time I have asked a cook to chop wood, and I know about these things. Even the hired girl has her frontiers; true, they are vague, they are ill-defined, even flexible, but they are there. This is not conjecture; it is founded on the absolute. And then the butler. You ask the butler to wash the dog. It is just as I say; there is much to be learned in these ways, without going to books. Books are very well, but books do not cover the whole domain of esthetic human culture. Pride of profession is one of the boniest bones in existence, if not the boniest. Without doubt it is so in the hive.

TAMING THE BICYCLE

IN the early eighties Mark Twain learned to ride one of the old high-wheel bicycles of that period. He wrote an account of his experience, but did not offer it for publication. The form of bicycle he rode long ago became antiquated, but in the humor of his pleasantry is a quality which does not grow old.

A. B. P.

I

I thought the matter over, and concluded I could do it. So I went down a bought a barrel of Pond's Extract and a bicycle. The Expert came home with me to instruct me. We chose the back yard, for the sake of privacy, and went to work.

Mine was not a full-grown bicycle, but only a colt--a fifty-inch, with the pedals shortened up to forty-eight--and skittish, like any other colt. The Expert explained the thing's points briefly, then he got on its back and rode around a little, to show me how easy it was to do. He said that the dismounting was perhaps the hardest thing to learn, and so we would leave that to the last. But he was in error there. He found, to his surprise and joy, that all that he needed to do was to get me on to the machine and stand out of the way; I could get off, myself. Although I was wholly inexperienced, I dismounted in the best time on record. He was on that side, shoving up the machine; we all came down with a crash, he at the bottom, I next, and the machine on top.

We examined the machine, but it was not in the least injured. This was hardly believable. Yet the Expert assured me that it was true; in fact, the examination proved it. I was partly to realize, then, how admirably these things are constructed. We applied some Pond's Extract, and resumed. The Expert got on the OTHER side to shove up this time, but I dismounted on that side; so the result was as before.

The machine was not hurt. We oiled ourselves again, and resumed. This time the Expert took up a sheltered position behind, but somehow or other we landed on him again.

He was full of admiration; said it was abnormal. She was all right, not a scratch on her, not a timber started anywhere. I said it was wonderful, while we were greasing up, but he said that when I came to know these steel spider-webs I would realize that nothing but dynamite could cripple them. Then he limped out to position, and we resumed once more. This time the Expert took up the position of short-stop, and got a man to shove up behind. We got up a handsome speed, and presently traversed a brick, and I went out over the top of the tiller and landed, head down, on the instructor's back, and saw the machine fluttering in the air between me and the sun. It was well it came down on us, for that broke the fall, and it was not injured.

Five days later I got out and was carried down to the hospital, and found the Expert doing pretty fairly. In a few more days I was quite sound. I attribute this to my prudence in always dismounting on something soft. Some recommend a feather bed, but I think an Expert is better.

The Expert got out at last, brought four assistants with him. It was a good idea. These four held the graceful cobweb upright while I climbed into the saddle; then they formed in column and marched on either side of me while the Expert pushed behind; all hands assisted at the dismount.

The bicycle had what is called the "wabbles," and had them very badly. In order to keep my position, a good many things were required of me, and in every instance the thing required was against nature. That is to say, that whatever the needed thing might be, my nature, habit, and breeding moved me to attempt it in one way, while some immutable and unsuspected law of physics required that it be done in just the other way. I perceived by this how radically and grotesquely wrong had been the life-long education of my body and members. They were steeped in ignorance; they knew nothing--nothing which it could profit them to know. For instance, if I found myself falling to the right, I put the tiller hard down the other way, by a quite natural impulse, and so violated a law, and kept on going down. The law required the opposite thing--the big wheel must be turned in the direction in which you are falling. It is hard to believe this, when you are told it. And not merely hard to believe it, but impossible; it is opposed to all your notions. And it is just as hard to do it, after you do come to believe it. Believing it, and knowing by the most convincing proof that it is true, does not help it: you can't any more DO it than you could before; you can neither force nor persuade yourself to do it at first. The intellect has to come to the front, now. It has to teach the limbs to discard their old education and adopt the new.

The steps of one's progress are distinctly marked. At the end of each lesson he knows he has acquired something, and he also knows what that something is, and likewise that it will stay with him. It is not like studying German, where you mull along, in a groping, uncertain way, for thirty years; and at last, just as you think you've got it, they spring the subjunctive on you, and there you are. No--and I see now, plainly enough, that the great pity about the German language is, that you can't fall off it and hurt yourself. There is nothing like that feature to make you attend strictly to business. But I also see, by what I have learned of bicycling, that the right and only sure way to learn German is by the bicycling method. That is to say, take a grip on one villainy of it at a time, leaving that one half learned.

When you have reached the point in bicycling where you can balance the machine tolerably fairly and propel it and steer it, then comes your next task--how to mount it. You do it in this way: you hop along behind it on your right foot, resting the other on the mounting-peg, and grasping the tiller with your hands. At the word, you rise on the peg, stiffen your left leg, hang your other one around in the air in a general in indefinite way, lean your stomach against the rear of the saddle, and then fall off, maybe on one side, maybe on the other; but you fall off. You get up and do it again; and once more; and then several times.

By this time you have learned to keep your balance; and also to steer without wrenching the tiller out by the roots (I say tiller because it IS a tiller; "handle-bar" is a lamely descriptive phrase). So you steer along, straight ahead, a little while, then you rise forward, with a steady strain, bringing your right leg, and then your body, into the saddle, catch your breath, fetch a violent hitch this way and then that, and down you go again.

But you have ceased to mind the going down by this time; you are getting to light on one foot or the other with considerable certainty. Six more attempts and six more falls make you perfect. You land in the saddle comfortably, next time, and stay there--that is, if you can be content to let your legs dangle, and leave the pedals alone a while; but if you grab at once for the pedals, you are gone again. You soon learn to wait a little and perfect your balance before reaching for the pedals; then the mounting-art is acquired, is complete, and a little practice will make it simple and easy to you, though spectators ought to keep off a rod or two to one side, along at first, if you have nothing against them.

And now you come to the voluntary dismount; you learned the other kind first of all. It is quite easy to tell one how to do the voluntary dismount; the words are few, the requirement simple, and apparently undifficult; let your left pedal go down till your left leg is nearly straight, turn your wheel to the left, and get off as you would from a horse. It certainly does sound exceedingly easy; but it isn't. I don't know why it isn't but it isn't. Try as you may, you don't get down as you would from a horse, you get down as you would from a house afire. You make a spectacle of yourself every time.

II

During the eight days I took a daily lesson an hour and a half. At the end of this twelve working-hours' appreticeship I was graduated--in the rough. I was pronounced competent to paddle my own bicycle without outside help. It seems incredible, this celerity of acquirement. It takes considerably longer than that to learn horseback-riding in the rough.

Now it is true that I could have learned without a teacher, but it would have been risky for me, because of my natural clumsi-ness. The self-taught man seldom knows anything accurately, and he does not know a tenth as much as he could have known if he had worked under teachers; and, besides, he brags, and is the means of fooling other thoughtless people into going and doing as he himself has done. There are those who imagine that the unlucky accidents of life--life's "experiences"--are in some way useful to us. I wish I could find out how. I never knew one of them to happen twice. They always change off and swap around and catch you on your inexperienced side. If personal experience can be worth anything as an education, it wouldn't seem likely that you could trip Methuselah; and yet if that old person could come back here it is more that likely that one of the first things he would do would be to take hold of one of these electric wires and tie himself all up in a knot. Now the surer thing and the wiser thing would be for him to ask somebody whether it was a good thing to take hold of. But that would not suit him; he would be one of the self-taught kind that go by experience; he would want to examine for himself. And he would find, for his instruction, that the coiled patriarch shuns the electric wire; and it would be useful to him, too, and would leave his education in quite a complete and rounded-out condition, till he should come again, some day, and go to bouncing a dynamite-can around to find out what was in it.

But we wander from the point. However, get a teacher; it saves much time and Pond's Extract.

Before taking final leave of me, my instructor inquired concerning my physical strength, and I was able to inform him that I hadn't any. He said that that was a defect which would make up-hill wheeling pretty difficult for me at first; but he also said the bicycle would soon remove it. The contrast between his muscles and mine was quite marked. He wanted to test mine, so I offered my biceps--which was my best. It almost made him smile. He said, "It is pulpy, and soft, and yielding, and rounded; it evades pressure, and glides from under the fingers; in the dark a body might think it was an oyster in a rag." Perhaps this made me look grieved, for he added, briskly: "Oh, that's all right, you needn't worry about that; in a little while you can't tell it from a petrified kidney. Just go right along with your practice; you're all right."

Then he left me, and I started out alone to seek adventures. You don't really have to seek them--that is nothing but a phrase -- they come to you.

I chose a reposeful Sabbath-day sort of a back street which was about thirty yards wide between the curbstones. I knew it was not wide enough; still, I thought that by keeping strict watch and wasting no space unnecessarily I could crowd through.

Of course I had trouble mounting the machine, entirely on my own responsibility, with no encouraging moral support from the outside, no sympathetic instructor to say, "Good! now you're doing well--good again--don't hurry--there, now, you're all right --brace up, go ahead." In place of this I had some other support. This was a boy, who was perched on a gate-post munching a hunk of maple sugar.

He was full of interest and comment. The first time I failed and went down he said that if he was me he would dress up in pillows, that's what he would do. The next time I went down he advised me to go and learn to ride a tricycle first. The third time I collapsed he said he didn't believe I could stay on a horse-car. But the next time I succeeded, and got clumsily under way in a weaving, tottering, uncertain fashion, and occupying pretty much all of the street. My slow and lumbering gait filled the boy to the chin with scorn, and he sung out, "My, but don't he rip along!" Then he got down from his post and loafed along the sidewalk, still observing and occasionally commenting. Presently he dropped into my wake and followed along behind. A little girl passed by, balancing a wash-board on her head, and giggled, and seemed about to make a remark, but the boy said, rebukingly, "Let him alone, he's going to a funeral."

I have been familiar with that street for years, and had always supposed it was a dead level; but it was not, as the bicycle now informed me, to my surprise. The bicycle, in the hands of a novice, is as alert and acute as a spirit-level in the detecting the delicate and vanishing shades of difference in these matters. It notices a rise where your untrained eye would not observe that one existed; it notices any decline which water will run down. I was toiling up a slight rise, but was not aware of it. It made me tug and pant and perspire; and still, labor as I might, the machine came almost to a standstill every little while. At such times the boy would say: "That's it! take a rest-- there ain't no hurry. They can't hold the funeral without YOU."

Stones were a bother to me. Even the smallest ones gave me a panic when I went over them. I could hit any kind of a stone, no matter how small, if I tried to miss it; and of course at first I couldn't help trying to do that. It is but natural. It is part of the ass that is put in us all, for some inscrutable reason.

It was at the end of my course, at last, and it was necessary for me to round to. This is not a pleasant thing, when you undertake it for the first time on your own responsibility, and neither is it likely to succeed. Your confidence oozes away, you fill steadily up with nameless apprehensions, every fiber of you is tense with a watchful strain, you start a cautious and gradual curve, but your squirmy nerves are all full of electric anxieties, so the curve is quickly demoralized into a jerky and perilous zigzag; then suddenly the nickel-clad horse takes the bit in its mouth and goes slanting for the curbstone, defying all prayers and all your powers to change its mind--your heart stands still, your breath hangs fire, your legs forget to work, straight on you go, and there are but a couple of feet between you and the curb now. And now is the desperate moment, the last chance to save yourself; of course all your instructions fly out of your head, and you whirl your wheel AWAY from the curb instead of TOWARD it, and so you go sprawling on that granite-bound inhospitable shore. That was my luck; that was my experience. I dragged myself out from under the indestructible bicycle and sat down on the curb to examine.

I started on the return trip. It was now that I saw a farmer's wagon poking along down toward me, loaded with cabbages. If I needed anything to perfect the precariousness of my steering, it was just that. The farmer was occupying the middle of the road with his wagon, leaving barely fourteen or fifteen yards of space on either side. I couldn't shout at him--a beginner can't shout; if he opens his mouth he is gone; he must keep all his attention on his business. But in this grisly emergency, the boy came to the rescue, and for once I had to be grateful to him. He kept a sharp lookout on the swiftly varying impulses and inspirations of my bicycle, and shouted to the man accordingly:

"To the left! Turn to the left, or this jackass 'll run over you!" The man started to do it. "No, to the right, to the right! Hold on! THAT won't do!--to the left!--to the right!--to the LEFT--right! left--ri-- Stay where you ARE, or you're a goner!"

And just then I caught the off horse in the starboard and went down in a pile. I said, "Hang it! Couldn't you SEE I was coming?"

"Yes, I see you was coming, but I couldn't tell which WAY you was coming. Nobody could--now, COULD they? You couldn't yourself--now, COULD you? So what could _I_ do?

There was something in that, and so I had the magnanimity to say so. I said I was no doubt as much to blame as he was.

Within the next five days I achieved so much progress that the boy couldn't keep up with me. He had to go back to his gate-post, and content himself with watching me fall at long range.

There was a row of low stepping-stones across one end of the street, a measured yard apart. Even after I got so I could steer pretty fairly I was so afraid of those stones that I always hit them. They gave me the worst falls I ever got in that street, except those which I got from dogs. I have seen it stated that no expert is quick enough to run over a dog; that a dog is always able to skip out of his way. I think that that may be true: but I think that the reason he couldn't run over the dog was because he was trying to. I did not try to run over any dog. But I ran over every dog that came along. I think it makes a great deal of difference. If you try to run over the dog he knows how to calculate, but if you are trying to miss him he does not know how to calculate, and is liable to jump the wrong way every time. It was always so in my experience. Even when I could not hit a wagon I could hit a dog that came to see me practice. They all liked to see me practice, and they all came, for there was very little going on in our neighborhood to entertain a dog. It took time to learn to miss a dog, but I achieved even that.

I can steer as well as I want to, now, and I will catch that boy one of these days and run over HIM if he doesn't reform.

Get a bicycle. You will not regret it, if you live.

IS SHAKESPEARE DEAD?

(from My Autobiography)

SCATTERED here and there through the stacks of unpub-
lished manuscript which constitute this formidable
Autobiography and Diary of mine, certain chapters will in
some distant future be found which deal with "Claimants"--
claimants historically notorious: Satan, Claimant; the Golden
Calf, Claimant; the Veiled Prophet of Khorassan, Claimant; Louis
XVII., Claimant; William Shakespeare, Claimant; Arthur Orton,
Claimant; Mary Baker G. Eddy, Claimant--and the rest of them.
Eminent Claimants, successful Claimants, defeated Claimants,
royal Claimants, pleb Claimants, showy Claimants, shabby
Claimants, revered Claimants, despised Claimants, twinkle star-
like here and there and yonder through the mists of history and
legend and tradition--and, oh, all the darling tribe are clothed in
mystery and romance, and we read about them with deep
interest and discuss them with loving sympathy or with
rancorous resentment, according to which side we hitch
ourselves to. It has always been so with the human race. There
was never a Claimant that couldn't get a hearing, nor one that
couldn't accumulate a rapturous following, no matter how
flimsy and apparently unauthentic his claim might be. Arthur
Orton's claim that he was the lost Tichborne baronet come to
life again was as flimsy as Mrs. Eddy's that she wrote SCIENCE
AND HEALTH from the direct dictation of the Deity; yet in
England nearly forty years ago Orton had a huge army of
devotees and incorrigible adherents, many of whom remained
stubbornly unconvinced after their fat god had been proven an
impostor and jailed as a perjurer, and today Mrs. Eddy's

following is not only immense, but is daily augmenting in numbers and enthusiasm. Orton had many fine and educated minds among his adherents, Mrs. Eddy has had the like among hers from the beginning. Her Church is as well equipped in those particulars as is any other Church. Claimants can always count upon a following, it doesn't matter who they are, nor what they claim, nor whether they come with documents or without. It was always so. Down out of the long- vanished past, across the abyss of the ages, if you listen, you can still hear the believing multitudes shouting for Perkin Warbeck and Lambert Simnel.

A friend has sent me a new book, from England--THE SHAKES-PEARE PROBLEM RESTATED--well restated and closely reasoned; and my fifty years' interest in that matter--asleep for the last three years--is excited once more. It is an interest which was born of Delia Bacon's book--away back in the ancient day--1857, or maybe 1856. About a year later my pilot-master, Bixby, transferred me from his own steamboat to the PENNSYLVANIA, and placed me under the orders and instructions of George Ealer--dead now, these many, many years. I steered for him a good many months--as was the humble duty of the pilot-apprentice: stood a daylight watch and spun the wheel under the severe superintendence and correction of the master. He was a prime chess-player and an idolater of Shakespeare. He would play chess with anybody; even with me, and it cost his official dignity something to do that. Also--quite uninvited--he would read Shakespeare to me; not just casually, but by the hour, when it was his watch and I was steering. He read well, but not profitably for me, because he constantly injected commands into the text. That broke it all up, mixed it all up, tangled it all up--to that degree, in fact, that if we were in a risky and difficult piece of river an ignorant person couldn't have told, sometimes, which observations were Shakespeare's and which were Ealer's. For instance:

What man dare, _I_ dare!

Approach thou WHAT are you laying in the leads for? what a hell of an idea! like the rugged ease her off a little, ease her off! rugged Russian bear, the armed rhinoceros or the THERE she goes! meet her, meet her! didn't you KNOW she'd smell the reef if you crowded in like that? Hyrcan tiger; take any ship but that and my firm nerves she'll be in the WOODS the first you know! stop he starboard! come ahead strong on the larboard! back the starboard! . . . NOW then, you're all right; come ahead on the starboard; straighten up and go 'long, never tremble: or be alive again, and dare me to the desert DAMNATION can't you keep away from that greasy water? pull her down! snatch her! snatch her baldheaded! with thy sword; if trembling I inhabit then, lay in the leads!--no, only with the starboard one, leave the other alone, protest me the baby of a girl. Hence horrible shadow! eight bells--that watchman's asleep again, I reckon, go down and call Brown yourself, unreal mockery, hence!

He certainly was a good reader, and splendidly thrilling and stormy and tragic, but it was a damage to me, because I have never since been able to read Shakespeare in a calm and sane way. I cannot rid it of his explosive interlardings, they break in everywhere with their irrelevant, "What in hell are you up to NOW! pull her down! more! MORE!--there now, steady as you go," and the other disorganizing interruptions that were always leaping from his mouth. When I read Shakespeare now I can hear them as plainly as I did in that long-departed time--fifty-one years ago. I never regarded Ealer's readings as educational. Indeed, they were a detriment to me.

His contributions to the text seldom improved it, but barring that detail he was a good reader; I can say that much for him. He did not use the book, and did not need to; he knew his Shakespeare as well as Euclid ever knew his multiplication table.

Did he have something to say--this Shakespeare-adoring Mississippi pilot--anent Delia Bacon's book?

Yes. And he said it; said it all the time, for months--in the morning watch, the middle watch, and dog watch; and probably kept it going in his sleep. He bought the literature of the dispute as fast as it appeared, and we discussed it all through thirteen hundred miles of river four times traversed in every thirty-five days--the time required by that swift boat to achieve two round trips. We discussed, and discussed, and discussed, and disputed and disputed and disputed; at any rate, HE did, and I got in a word now and then when he slipped a cog and there was a vacancy. He did his arguing with heat, with energy, with violence; and I did mine with the reverse and moderation of a subordinate who does not like to be flung out of a pilot-house and is perched forty feet above the water. He was fiercely loyal to Shakespeare and cordially scornful of Bacon and of all the pretensions of the Baconians. So was I--at first. And at first he was glad that that was my attitude. There were even indications that he admired it; indications dimmed, it is true, by the distance that lay between the lofty boss-pilotical altitude and my lowly one, yet perceptible to me; perceptible, and translatable into a compliment--compliment coming down from about the snow-line and not well thawed in the transit, and not likely to set anything afire, not even a cub-pilot's self- conceit; still a detectable complement, and precious.

Naturally it flattered me into being more loyal to Shakespeare--if possible--than I was before, and more prejudiced against

Bacon--if possible--that I was before. And so we discussed and discussed, both on the same side, and were happy. For a while. Only for a while. Only for a very little while, a very, very, very little while. Then the atmosphere began to change; began to cool off.

A brighter person would have seen what the trouble was, earlier than I did, perhaps, but I saw it early enough for all practical purposes. You see, he was of an argumentative disposition. Therefore it took him but a little time to get tired of arguing with a person who agreed with everything he said and consequently never furnished him a provocative to flare up and show what he could do when it came to clear, cold, hard, rose-cut, hundred-faceted, diamond-flashing REASONING. That was his name for it. It has been applied since, with complacency, as many as several times, in the Bacon-Shakespeare scuffle. On the Shakespeare side.

Then the thing happened which has happened to more persons than to me when principle and personal interest found themselves in opposition to each other and a choice had to be made: I let principle go, and went over to the other side. Not the entire way, but far enough to answer the requirements of the case. That is to say, I took this attitude--to wit, I only BELIEVED Bacon wrote Shakespeare, whereas I KNEW Shakespeare didn't. Ealer was satisfied with that, and the war broke loose. Study, practice, experience in handling my end of the matter presently enabled me to take my new position almost seriously; a little bit later, utterly seriously; a little later still, lovingly, gratefully, devotedly; finally: fiercely, rabidly, uncompromisingly. After that I was welded to my faith, I was theoretically ready to die for it, and I looked down with compassion not unmixed with scorn upon everybody else's faith that didn't tally with mine. That faith, imposed upon me by self-interest in that ancient day, remains my faith today, and in it I find comfort, solace, peace, and never-failing joy. You see how curiously theological it is. The "rice Christian" of the Orient goes through the very same steps, when he is after rice and the missionary is after HIM; he goes for rice, and remains to worship.

Ealer did a lot of our "reasoning"--not to say substantially all of it. The slaves of his cult have a passion for calling it by that large name. We others do not call our inductions and deductions and reductions by any name at all. They show for themselves what they are, and we can with tranquil confidence leave the world to ennoble them with a title of its own choosing.

Now and then when Ealer had to stop to cough, I pulled my induction-talents together and hove the controversial lead myself: always getting eight feet, eight and a half, often nine, sometimes even quarter-less-twain--as _I_ believed; but always "no bottom," as HE said.

I got the best of him only once. I prepared myself. I wrote out a passage from Shakespeare--it may have been the very one I quoted awhile ago, I don't remember--and riddled it with his wild steamboatful interlardings. When an unrisky opportunity offered, one lovely summer day, when we had sounded and buoyed a tangled patch of crossings known as Hell's Half Acre, and were aboard again and he had sneaked the PENNSYLVANIA triumphantly through it without once scraping sand, and the A. T. LACEY had followed in our wake and got stuck, and he was feeling good, I showed it to him. It amused him. I asked him to fire it off-- READ it; read it, I diplomatically added, as only HE could read dramatic poetry. The compliment touched him where he lived. He did read it; read it with surpassing fire and spirit; read it as it will never be read again; for HE know how to put the right music into those thunderous interlardings and make them seem a part of the text, make them sound as if they were bursting from Shakespeare's own soul, each one of them a golden inspiration and not to be left out without damage to the massed and magnificent whole.

I waited a week, to let the incident fade; waited longer; waited until he brought up for reasonings and vituperation my pet position, my pet argument, the one which I was fondest of, the one which I prized far above all others in my ammunition-wagon-- to wit, that Shakespeare couldn't have written Shakespeare's words, for the reason that the man who wrote them was limitlessly familiar with the laws, and the law-courts, and law-proceedings, and lawyer-talk, and lawyer-ways--and if Shakespeare was possessed of the infinitely divided star-dust that constituted this vast wealth, HOW did he get it, and WHERE and WHEN?

"From books."

From books! That was always the idea. I answered as my readings of the champions of my side of the great controversy had taught me to answer: that a man can't handle glibly and easily and comfortably and successfully the argot of a trade at which he has not personally served. He will make mistakes; he will not, and cannot, get the trade-phrasings precisely and exactly right; and the moment he departs, by even a shade, from a common trade- form, the reader who has served that trade will know the writer HASN'T. Ealer would not be convinced; he said a man could learn how to correctly handle the subtleties and mysteries and free- masonries of ANY trade by careful reading and studying. But when I got him to read again the passage from Shakespeare with the interlardings, he perceived, himself, that books couldn't teach a student a bewildering multitude of pilot-phrases so thoroughly and perfectly that he could talk them off in book and play or conversation and make no mistake that a pilot would not immediately discover. It was a triumph for me. He was silent awhile, and I knew what was happening--he was losing his temper. And I knew he would presently close the session with the same old argument that was always his stay and his support in time of need; the same old argument, the one I couldn't answer, because I dasn't--the argument that I was an ass, and better shut up. He delivered it, and I obeyed.

O dear, how long ago it was--how pathetically long ago! And here am I, old, forsaken, forlorn, and alone, arranging to get that argument out of somebody again.

When a man has a passion for Shakespeare, it goes without saying that he keeps company with other standard authors. Ealer always had several high-class books in the pilot-house, and he read the same ones over and over again, and did not care to change to newer and fresher ones. He played well on the flute, and greatly enjoyed hearing himself play. So did I. He had a notion that a flute would keep its health better if you took it apart when it was not standing a watch; and so, when it was not on duty it took its rest, disjointed, on the compass-shelf under the breastboard.   When the PENNSYLVANIA blew up and became a drifting rack-heap freighted with wounded and dying poor souls (my young brother Henry among them), pilot Brown had the watch below, and was probably asleep and never knew what killed him; but Ealer escaped unhurt. He and his pilot-house were shot up into the air; then they fell, and Ealer sank through the ragged cavern where the hurricane-deck and the boiler-deck had been, and landed in a nest of ruins on the main deck, on top of one of the unexploded boilers, where he lay prone in a fog of scald and deadly steam. But not for long. He did not lose his head--long familiarity with danger had taught him to keep it, in any and all emergencies. He held his coat-lapels to his nose with one hand, to keep out the steam, and scrabbled around with the other till he found the joints of his flute, then he took measures to save himself alive, and was successful. I was not on board. I had been put ashore in New Orleans by Captain Klinenfelter. The reason--however, I have told all about it in the book called OLD TIMES ON THE MISSIS-SIPPI, and it isn't important, anyway, it is so long ago.

II

When I was a Sunday-school scholar, something more than sixty years ago, I became interested in Satan, and wanted to find out all I could about him. I began to ask questions, but my class-teacher, Mr. Barclay, the stone-mason, was reluctant about answering them, it seemed to me. I was anxious to be praised for turning my thoughts to serious subjects when there wasn't another boy in the village who could be hired to do such a thing. I was greatly interested in the incident of Eve and the serpent, and thought Eve's calmness was perfectly noble. I asked Mr. Barclay if he had ever heard of another woman who, being approached by a serpeant, would not excuse herself and break for the nearest timber. He did not answer my question, but rebuked me for inquiring into matters above my age and comprehension. I will say for Mr. Barclay that he was willing to tell me the facts of Satan's history, but he stopped there: he wouldn't allow any discussion of them.

In the course of time we exhausted the facts. There were only five or six of them; you could set them all down on a visiting-card. I was disappointed. I had been meditating a biography, and was grieved to find that there were no materials. I said as much, with the tears running down. Mr. Barclay's sympathy and compassion were aroused, for he was a most kind and gentle-spirited man, and he patted me on the head and cheered me up by saying there was a whole vast ocean of materials! I can still feel the happy thrill which these blessed words shot through me.

Then he began to bail out that ocean's riches for my encouragement and joy. Like this: it was "conjectured"--though not established--that Satan was originally an angel in Heaven; that he fell; that he rebelled, and brought on a war; that he was defeated, and banished to perdition. Also, "we have reason to believe" that later he did so and so; that "we are warranted in supposing" that at a subsequent time he traveled extensively, seeking whom he might devour; that a couple of centuries afterward, "as tradition instructs us," he took up the cruel trade of tempting people to their ruin, with vast and fearful results; that by and by, "as the probabilities seem to indicate," he may have done certain things, he might have done certain other things, he must have done still other things.

And so on and so on. We set down the five known facts by themselves on a piece of paper, and numbered it "page 1"; then on fifteen hundred other pieces of paper we set down the "conjectures," and "suppositions," and "maybes," and "perhapses," and "doubtlesses," and "rumors," and guesses," and "probabilities," and "likelihoods," and "we are permitted to thinks," and "we are warranted in believings," and "might have beens," and "could have beens," and "must have beens," and "unquestionablys," and "without a shadow of doubt"--and behold!

MATERIALS? Why, we had enough to build a biography of Shakespeare!

Yet he made me put away my pen; he would not let me write the history of Satan. Why? Because, as he said, he had suspicions--suspicions that my attitude in the matter was not reverent, and that a person must be reverent when writing about the sacred characters. He said any one who spoke flippantly of Satan would be frowned upon by the religious world and also be brought to account.

I assured him, in earnest and sincere words, that he had wholly misconceived my attitude; that I had the highest respect for Satan, and that my reverence for him equaled, and possibly even exceeded, that of any member of the church. I said it wounded me deeply to perceive by his words that he thought I would make fun of Satan, and deride him, laugh at him, scoff at him; whereas in truth I had never thought of such a thing, but had only a warm desire to make fun of those others and laugh at THEM. "What others? "Why, the Supposers, the Perhapsers, the Might-Have-Beeners, the Could-Have-Beeners, the Must-Have-Beeners, the Without-a-Shadow-of-Doubters, the We-Are-Warranted-in-Believingers, and all that funny crop of solemn architects who have taken a good solid foundation of five indisputable and unimportant facts and built upon it a Conjectural Satan thirty miles high."

What did Mr. Barclay do then? Was he disarmed? Was he silenced? No. He was shocked. He was so shocked that he visibly shuddered. He said the Satanic Traditioners and Perhapsers and Conjecturers were THEMSELVES sacred! As sacred as their work. So sacred that whoso ventured to mock them or make fun of their work, could not afterward enter any respectable house, even by the back door.

How true were his words, and how wise! How fortunate it would have been for me if I had heeded them. But I was young, I was but seven years of age, and vain, foolish, and anxious to attract attention. I wrote the biography, and have never been in a respectable house since.

III

How curious and interesting is the parallel--as far as poverty of biographical details is concerned--between Satan and Shakespeare. It is wonderful, it is unique, it stands quite alone, there is nothing resembling it in history, nothing resembling it in romance, nothing approaching it even in tradition.   How sublime is their position, and how over-topping, how sky-reaching, how supreme--the two Great Unknowns, the two Illustrious Conjecturabilities!   They are the best-known unknown persons that have ever drawn breath upon the planet.

For the instruction of the ignorant I will make a list, now, of those details of Shakespeare's history which are FACTS-- verified facts, established facts, undisputed facts.

Facts

He was born on the 23d of April, 1564.

Of good farmer-class parents who could not read, could not write, could not sign their names.

At Stratford, a small back settlement which in that day was shabby and unclean, and densely illiterate. Of the nineteen important men charged with the government of the town, thirteen had to "make their mark" in attesting important documents, because they could not write their names.

Of the first eighteen years of his life NOTHING is known. They are a blank.

On the 27th of November (1582) William Shakespeare took out a license to marry Anne Whateley.

Next day William Shakespeare took out a license to marry Anne Hathaway. She was eight years his senior.

William Shakespeare married Anne Hathaway. In a hurry. By grace of a reluctantly granted dispensation there was but one publication of the banns.

Within six months the first child was born.

About two (blank) years followed, during which period NOTHING AT ALL HAPPENED TO SHAKESPEARE, so far as anybody knows.

Then came twins--1585. February.

Two blank years follow.

Then--1587--he makes a ten-year visit to London, leaving the family behind.

Five blank years follow. During this period NOTHING HAPPENED TO HIM, as far as anybody actually knows.

Then--1592--there is mention of him as an actor.

Next year--1593--his name appears in the official list of players.

Next year--1594--he played before the queen. A detail of no consequence: other obscurities did it every year of the forty-five of her reign. And remained obscure.

Three pretty full years follow. Full of play-acting. Then*

In 1597 he bought New Place, Stratford.

Thirteen or fourteen busy years follow; years in which he accumulated money, and also reputation as actor and manager.

Meantime his name, liberally and variously spelt, had become associated with a number of great plays and poems, as (ostensibly) author of the same.

Some of these, in these years and later, were pirated, but he made no protest.

Then--1610-11--he returned to Stratford and settled down for good and all, and busied himself in lending money, trading in tithes, trading in land and houses; shirking a debt of forty-one shillings, borrowed by his wife during his long desertion of his family; suing debtors for shillings and coppers; being sued himself for shillings and coppers; and acting as confederate to a neighbor who tried to rob the town of its rights in a certain common, and did not succeed.

He lived five or six years--till 1616--in the joy of these elevated pursuits. Then he made a will, and signed each of its three pages with his name.

A thoroughgoing business man's will. It named in minute detail every item of property he owned in the world--houses, lands, sword, silver-gilt bowl, and so on--all the way down to his "second-best bed" and its furniture.

It carefully and calculatingly distributed his riches among the members of his family, overlooking no individual of it. Not even his wife: the wife he had been enabled to marry in a hurry by urgent grace of a special dispensation before he was nineteen; the wife whom he had left husbandless so many years; the wife who had had to borrow forty-one shillings in her need, and which the lender was never able to collect of the prosperous husband, but died at last with the money still lacking. No, even this wife was remembered in Shakespeare's will.

He left her that "second-best bed."

And NOT ANOTHER THING; not even a penny to bless her lucky widowhood with.

It was eminently and conspicuously a business man's will, not a poet's.

It mentioned NOT A SINGLE BOOK.

Books were much more precious than swords and silver-gilt bowls and second-best beds in those days, and when a departing person owned one he gave it a high place in his will.

The will mentioned NOT A PLAY, NOT A POEM, NOT AN UNFINISHED

LITERARY WORK, NOT A SCRAP OF MANUSCRIPT OF ANY KIND.

Many poets have died poor, but this is the only one in history that has died THIS poor; the others all left literary remains behind. Also a book. Maybe two.

If Shakespeare had owned a dog--but we not go into that: we know he would have mentioned it in his will. If a good dog, Susanna would have got it; if an inferior one his wife would have got a downer interest in it. I wish he had had a dog, just so we could see how painstakingly he would have divided that dog among the family, in his careful business way.

He signed the will in three places.

In earlier years he signed two other official documents.

These five signatures still exist.

There are NO OTHER SPECIMENS OF HIS PENMANSHIP IN EXISTENCE. Not a line.

Was he prejudiced against the art? His granddaughter, whom he loved, was eight years old when he died, yet she had had no teaching, he left no provision for her education, although he was rich, and in her mature womanhood she couldn't write and couldn't tell her husband's manuscript from anybody else's--she thought it was Shakespeare's.

When Shakespeare died in Stratford, IT WAS NOT AN EVENT. It made no more stir in England than the death of any other forgotten theater-actor would have made. Nobody came down from London; there were no lamenting poems, no eulogies, no national tears--there was merely silence, and nothing more. A striking contrast with what happened when Ben Jonson, and Francis Bacon, and Spenser, and Raleigh, and the other distinguished literary folk of Shakespeare's time passed from life! No praiseful voice was lifted for the lost Bard of Avon; even Ben Jonson waited seven years before he lifted his.

SO FAR AS ANYBODY ACTUALLY KNOWS AND CAN PROVE, Shakespeare of Stratford-on-Avon never wrote a play in his life.

SO FAR AS ANY ONE KNOWS, HE RECEIVED ONLY ONE LETTER DURING HIS LIFE.

So far as any one KNOWS AND CAN PROVE, Shakespeare of Stratford wrote only one poem during his life. This one is authentic. He did write that one--a fact which stands undisputed; he wrote the whole of it; he wrote the whole of it out of his own head. He commanded that this work of art be engraved upon his tomb, and he was obeyed. There it abides to this day. This is it:

Good friend for Iesus sake forbeare To digg the dust encloased heare: Blest be ye man yt spares thes stones And curst be he yt moves my bones.

In the list as above set down will be found EVERY POSITIVELY KNOWN fact of Shakespeare's life, lean and meager as the invoice is. Beyond these details we know NOT A THING about him. All the rest of his vast history, as furnished by the biographers, is built up, course upon course, of guesses, inferences, theories, conjectures--an Eiffel Tower of artificialities rising sky-high from a very flat and very thin foundation of inconsequential facts.

IV

Conjectures

The historians "suppose" that Shakespeare attended the Free School in Stratford from the time he was seven years old till he was thirteen. There is no EVIDENCE in existence that he ever went to school at all.

The historians "infer" that he got his Latin in that school --the school which they "suppose" he attended.

They "suppose" his father's declining fortunes made it necessary for him to leave the school they supposed he attended, and get to work and help support his parents and their ten children. But there is no evidence that he ever entered or returned from the school they suppose he attended.

They "suppose" he assisted his father in the butchering business; and that, being only a boy, he didn't have to do full-grown butchering, but only slaughtering calves. Also, that whenever he killed a calf he made a high-flown speech over it. This supposition rests upon the testimony of a man who wasn't there at the time; a man who got it from a man who could have been there, but did not say whether he was nor not; and neither of them thought to mention it for decades, and decades, and decades, and two more decades after Shakespeare's death (until old age and mental decay had refreshed and vivified their memories). They hadn't two facts in stock about the long-dead distinguished citizen, but only just the one: he slaughtered calves and broke into oratory while he was at it. Curious. They had only one fact, yet the distinguished citizen had spent twenty-six years in that little town--just half his lifetime. However, rightly viewed, it was the most important fact, indeed almost the only important fact, of Shakespeare's life in Stratford. Rightly viewed. For experience is an author's most valuable asset; experience is the thing that puts the muscle and the breath and the warm blood into the book he writes. Rightly viewed, calf-butchering accounts for "Titus Andronicus," the only play--ain't it?--that the Stratford Shakespeare ever wrote; and yet it is the only one everybody tried to chouse him out of, the Baconians included.

The historians find themselves "justified in believing" that the young Shakespeare poached upon Sir Thomas Lucy's deer preserves and got haled before that magistrate for it. But there is no shred of respectworthy evidence that anything of the kind happened.

The historians, having argued the thing that MIGHT have happened into the thing that DID happen, found no trouble in turning Sir Thomas Lucy into Mr. Justice Shallow. They have long ago convinced the world--on surmise and without trustworthy evidence--that Shallow IS Sir Thomas.

The next addition to the young Shakespeare's Stratford history comes easy. The historian builds it out of the surmised deer-steeling, and the surmised trial before the magistrate, and the surmised vengeance-prompted satire upon the magistrate in the play: result, the young Shakespeare was a wild, wild, wild, oh, SUCH a wild young scamp, and that gratuitous slander is established for all time! It is the very way Professor Osborn and I built the colossal skeleton brontosaur that stands fifty- seven feet long and sixteen feet high in the Natural History Museum, the awe and admiration of all the world, the stateliest skeleton that exists on the planet. We had nine bones, and we built the rest of him out of plaster of Paris. We ran short of plaster of Paris, or we'd have built a brontosaur that could sit down beside the Stratford Shakespeare and none but an expert could tell which was biggest or contained the most plaster.

Shakespeare pronounced "Venus and Adonis" "the first heir of his invention," apparently implying that it was his first effort at literary composition. He should not have said it. It has been an embarrassment to his historians these many, many years. They have to make him write that graceful and polished and flawless and beautiful poem before he escaped from Stratford and his family--1586 or '87--age, twenty-two, or along there; because within the next five years he wrote five great plays, and could not have found time to write another line.

It is sorely embarrassing. If he began to slaughter calves, and poach deer, and rollick around, and learn English, at the earliest likely moment--say at thirteen, when he was supposably wretched from that school where he was supposably storing up Latin for future literary use--he had his youthful hands full, and much more than full. He must have had to put aside his Warwickshire dialect, which wouldn't be understood in London, and study English very hard. Very hard indeed; incredibly hard, almost, if the result of that labor was to be the smooth and rounded and flexible and letter-perfect English of the "Venus and Adonis" in the space of ten years; and at the same time learn great and fine and unsurpassable literary FORM.

However, it is "conjectured" that he accomplished all this and more, much more: learned law and its intricacies; and the complex procedure of the law-courts; and all about soldiering, and sailoring, and the manners and customs and ways of royal courts and aristocratic society; and likewise accumulated in his one head every kind of knowledge the learned then possessed, and every kind of humble knowledge possessed by the lowly and the ignorant; and added thereto a wider and more intimate knowledge of the world's great literatures, ancient and modern, than was possessed by any other man of his time--for he was going to make brilliant and easy and admiration-compelling use of these splendid treasures the moment he got to London. And according to the surmisers, that is what he did. Yes, although there was no one in Stratford able to teach him these things, and no library in the little village to dig them out of. His father could not read, and even the surmisers surmise that he did not keep a library.

It is surmised by the biographers that the young Shakespeare got his vast knowledge of the law and his familiar and accurate acquaintance with the manners and customs and shop-talk of lawyers through being for a time the CLERK OF A STRATFORD COURT; just as a bright lad like me, reared in a village on the banks of the Mississippi, might become perfect in knowledge of the Bering Strait whale-fishery and the shop-talk of the veteran exercises of that adventure-bristling trade through catching catfish with a "trot-line" Sundays. But the surmise is damaged by the fact that there is no evidence--and not even tradition-- that the young Shakespeare was ever clerk of a law-court.

It is further surmised that the young Shakespeare accumulated his law-treasures in the first years of his sojourn in London, through "amusing himself" by learning book-law in his garret and by picking up lawyer-talk and the rest of it through loitering about the law-courts and listening. But it is only surmise; there is no EVIDENCE that he ever did either of those things. They are merely a couple of chunks of plaster of Paris.

There is a legend that he got his bread and butter by holding horses in front of the London theaters, mornings and after- noons. Maybe he did. If he did, it seriously shortened his law- study hours and his recreation-time in the courts. In those very days he was writing great plays, and needed all the time he could get. The horse-holding legend ought to be strangled; it too formidably increases the historian's difficulty in accounting for the young Shakespeare's erudition--an erudition which he was acquiring, hunk by hunk and chunk by chunk, every day in those strenuous times, and emptying each day's catch into next day's imperishable drama.

He had to acquire a knowledge of war at the same time; and a knowledge of soldier-people and sailor-people and their ways and talk; also a knowledge of some foreign lands and their languages: for he was daily emptying fluent streams of these various knowledges, too, into his dramas. How did he acquire these rich assets?

In the usual way: by surmise. It is SURMISED that he traveled in Italy and Germany and around, and qualified himself to put their scenic and social aspects upon paper; that he perfected himself in French, Italian, and Spanish on the road; that he went in Leicester's expedition to the Low Countries, as soldier or sutler or something, for several months or years--or whatever length of time a surmiser needs in his business--and thus became familiar with soldiership and soldier-ways and soldier-talk and generalship and general-ways and general-talk, and seamanship and sailor-ways and sailor-talk.

Maybe he did all these things, but I would like to know who held the horses in the mean time; and who studied the books in the garret; and who frolicked in the law-courts for recreation. Also, who did the call-boying and the play-acting.

For he became a call-boy; and as early as '93 he became a "vagabond"--the law's ungentle term for an unlisted actor; and in '94 a "regular" and properly and officially listed member of that (in those days) lightly valued and not much respected profession.

Right soon thereafter he became a stockholder in two theaters, and manager of them. Thenceforward he was a busy and flourishing business man, and was raking in money with both hands for twenty years. Then in a noble frenzy of poetic inspiration he wrote his one poem--his only poem, his darling--and laid him down and died:

Good friend for Iesus sake forbeare To digg the dust encloased heare: Blest be ye man yt spares thes stones And curst be he yt moves my bones.

He was probably dead when he wrote it. Still, this is only conjecture. We have only circumstantial evidence. Internal evidence.

Shall I set down the rest of the Conjectures which constitute the giant Biography of William Shakespeare? It would strain the Unabridged Dictionary to hold them. He is a brontosaur: nine bones and six hundred barrels of plaster of Paris.

V

"We May Assume"

In the Assuming trade three separate and independent cults are transacting business. Two of these cults are known as the Shakespearites and the Baconians, and I am the other one--the Brontosaurian.

The Shakespearite knows that Shakespeare wrote Shakespeare's Works; the Baconian knows that Francis Bacon wrote them; the Brontosaurian doesn't really know which of them did it, but is quite composedly and contentedly sure that Shakespeare DIDN'T, and strongly suspects that Bacon DID. We all have to do a good deal of assuming, but I am fairly certain that in every case I can call to mind the Baconian assumers have come out ahead of the Shakespearites. Both parties handle the same materials, but the Baconians seem to me to get much more reasonable and rational and persuasive results out of them than is the case with the Shakespearites. The Shakespearite conducts his assuming upon a definite principle, an unchanging and immutable law: which is: 2 and 8 and 7 and 14, added together, make 165. I believe this to be an error. No matter, you cannot get a habit-sodden Shakespearite to cipher-up his materials upon any other basis. With the Baconian it is different. If you place before him the above figures and set him to adding them up, he will never in any case get more than 45 out of them, and in nine cases out of ten he will get just the proper 31.

Let me try to illustrate the two systems in a simple and homely way calculated to bring the idea within the grasp of the ignorant and unintelligent. We will suppose a case: take a lap- bred, house-fed, uneducated, inexperienced kitten; take a rugged old Tom that's scarred from stem to rudder-post with the memorials of strenuous experience, and is so cultured, so educated, so limitlessly erudite that one may say of him "all cat-knowledge is his province"; also, take a mouse. Lock the three up in a holeless, crackless, exitless prison-cell. Wait half an hour, then open the cell, introduce a Shakespearite and a Baconian, and let them cipher and assume. The mouse is missing: the question to be decided is, where is it? You can guess both verdicts beforehand. One verdict will say the kitten contains the mouse; the other will as certainly say the mouse is in the tom-cat.

The Shakespearite will Reason like this--(that is not my word, it is his). He will say the kitten MAY HAVE BEEN attending school when nobody was noticing; therefore WE ARE WARRANTED IN ASSUMING that it did so; also, it COULD HAVE BEEN training in a court-clerk's office when no one was noticing; since that could have happened, WE ARE JUSTIFIED IN ASSUMING that it did happen; it COULD HAVE STUDIED CATOLOGY IN A GARRET when no one was noticing--therefore it DID; it COULD HAVE attended cat-assizes on the shed-roof nights, for recreation, when no one was noticing, and have harvested a knowledge of cat court-forms and cat lawyer- talk in that way: it COULD have done it, therefore without a doubt it DID; it COULD HAVE gone soldiering with a war-tribe when no one was noticing, and learned soldier-wiles and soldier-ways, and what to do with a mouse when opportunity offers; the plain inference, therefore, is that that is what it DID. Since all these manifold things COULD have occurred, we have EVERY RIGHT TO BELIEVE they did occur. These patiently and painstakingly accumulated vast acquirements and competences needed but one thing more-- opportunity--to convert themselves into triumphal action. The opportunity came, we have the result; BEYOND SHADOW OF QUESTION the mouse is in the kitten.

It is proper to remark that when we of the three cults plant a "WE THINK WE MAY ASSUME," we expect it, under careful watering and fertilizing and tending, to grow up into a strong and hardy and weather-defying "THERE ISN'T A SHADOW OF A DOUBT" at last-- and it usually happens.

We know what the Baconian's verdict would be: "THERE IS NOT A RAG OF EVIDENCE THAT THE KITTEN HAS HAD ANY TRAINING, ANY EDUCATION, ANY EXPERIENCE QUALIFYING IT FOR THE PRESENT OCCASION, OR IS INDEED EQUIPPED FOR ANY ACHIEVEMENT ABOVE LIFTING SUCH UNCLAIMED MILK AS COMES ITS WAY; BUT THERE IS ABUNDANT EVIDENCE-- UNASSAILABLE PROOF, IN FACT--THAT THE OTHER ANIMAL IS EQUIPPED, TO THE LAST DETAIL, WITH EVERY QUALIFICATION NECESSARY FOR THE EVENT. WITHOUT SHADOW OF DOUBT THE TOM-CAT CONTAINS THE MOUSE."

VI

When Shakespeare died, in 1616, great literary productions attributed to him as author had been before the London world and in high favor for twenty-four years. Yet his death was not an event. It made no stir, it attracted no attention. Apparently his eminent literary contemporaries did not realize that a celebrated poet had passed from their midst. Perhaps they knew a play-actor of minor rank had disappeared, but did not regard him as the author of his Works. "We are justified in assuming" this.

His death was not even an event in the little town of Stratford. Does this mean that in Stratford he was not regarded as a celebrity of ANY kind?

"We are privileged to assume"--no, we are indeed OBLIGED to assume--that such was the case. He had spent the first twenty-two or twenty-three years of his life there, and of course knew everybody and was known by everybody of that day in the town, including the dogs and the cats and the horses. He had spent the last five or six years of his life there, diligently trading in every big and little thing that had money in it; so we are compelled to assume that many of the folk there in those said latter days knew him personally, and the rest by sight and hearsay. But not as a CELEBRITY? Apparently not. For everybody soon forgot to remember any contact with him or any incident connected with him. The dozens of townspeople, still alive, who had known of him or known about him in the first twenty-three years of his life were in the same unremem-bering condition: if they knew of any incident connected with that period of his life they didn't tell about it. Would the if they had been asked? It is most likely. Were they asked? It is pretty apparent that they were not. Why weren't they? It is a very plausible guess that nobody there or elsewhere was interested to know.

For seven years after Shakespeare's death nobody seems to have been interested in him. Then the quarto was published, and Ben Jonson awoke out of his long indifference and sang a song of praise and put it in the front of the book. Then silence fell AGAIN.

For sixty years. Then inquiries into Shakespeare's Stratford life began to be made, of Stratfordians. Of Stratfordians who had known Shakespeare or had seen him? No. Then of Stratfordians who had seen people who had known or seen people who had seen Shakespeare? No. Apparently the inquires were only made of Stratfordians who were not Stratfordians of Shakespeare's day, but later comers; and what they had learned had come to them from persons who had not seen Shakespeare; and what they had learned was not claimed as FACT, but only as legend-- dim and fading and indefinite legend; legend of the calf-slaughtering rank, and not worth remembering either as history or fiction.

Has it ever happened before--or since--that a celebrated person who had spent exactly half of a fairly long life in the village where he was born and reared, was able to slip out of this world and leave that village voiceless and gossipless behind him-- utterly voiceless., utterly gossipless? And permanently so? I don't believe it has happened in any case except Shakespeare's. And couldn't and wouldn't have happened in his case if he had been regarded as a celebrity at the time of his death.

When I examine my own case--but let us do that, and see if it will not be recognizable as exhibiting a condition of things quite likely to result, most likely to result, indeed substantially SURE to result in the case of a celebrated person, a benefactor of the human race. Like me.

My parents brought me to the village of Hannibal, Missouri, on the banks of the Mississippi, when I was two and a half years old. I entered school at five years of age, and drifted from one school to another in the village during nine and a half years. Then my father died, leaving his family in exceedingly straitened circumstances; wherefore my book-education came to a standstill forever, and I became a printer's apprentice, on board and clothes, and when the clothes failed I got a hymn-book in place of them. This for summer wear, probably. I lived in Hannibal fifteen and a half years, altogether, then ran away, according to the custom of persons who are intending to become celebrated. I never lived there afterward. Four years later I became a "cub" on a Mississippi steamboat in the St. Louis and New Orleans trade, and after a year and a half of hard study and hard work the U.S. inspectors rigorously examined me through a couple of long sittings and decided that I knew every inch of the Mississippi--thirteen hundred miles--in the dark and in the day-- as well as a baby knows the way to its mother's paps day or night. So they licensed me as a pilot-- knighted me, so to speak --and I rose up clothed with authority, a responsible servant of the United States Government.

Now then. Shakespeare died young--he was only fifty-two. He had lived in his native village twenty-six years, or about that. He died celebrated (if you believe everything you read in the books). Yet when he died nobody there or elsewhere took any notice of it; and for sixty years afterward no townsman remembered to say anything about him or about his life in Stratford. When the inquirer came at last he got but one fact-- no, LEGEND--and got that one at second hand, from a person who had only heard it as a rumor and didn't claim copyright in it as a production of his own. He couldn't, very well, for its date antedated his own birth-date. But necessarily a number of persons were still alive in Stratford who, in the days of their youth, had seen Shakespeare nearly every day in the last five years of his life, and they would have been able to tell that inquirer some first-hand things about him if he had in those last days been a celebrity and therefore a person of interest to the villagers. Why did not the inquirer hunt them up and interview them? Wasn't it worth while? Wasn't the matter of sufficient consequence? Had the inquirer an engagement to see a dog-fight and couldn't spare the time?

It all seems to mean that he never had any literary celebrity, there or elsewhere, and no considerable repute as actor and manager.

Now then, I am away along in life--my seventy-third year being already well behind me--yet SIXTEEN of my Hannibal school-mates are still alive today, and can tell--and do tell-- inquirers dozens and dozens of incidents of their young lives and mine together; things that happened to us in the morning of life, in the blossom of our youth, in the good days, the dear days, "the days when we went gipsying, a long time ago." Most of them creditable to me, too. One child to whom I paid court when she was five years old and I eight still lives in Hannibal, and she visited me last summer, traversing the necessary ten or twelve hundred miles of railroad without damage to her patience or to her old-young vigor. Another little lassie to whom I paid attention in Hannibal when she was nine years old and I the same, is still alive--in London--and hale and hearty, just as I am. And on the few surviving steamboats--those lingering ghosts and remembrancers of great fleets that plied the big river in the beginning of my water-career--which is exactly as long ago as the whole invoice of the life-years of Shakespeare numbers-- there are still findable two or three river-pilots who saw me do creditable things in those ancient days; and several white-headed engineers; and several roustabouts and mates; and several deck-hands who used to heave the lead for me and send up on the still night the "Six--feet--SCANT!" that made me shudder, and the "M-a-r-k-- TWAIN!" that took the shudder away, and presently the darling "By the d-e-e-p--FOUR!" that lifted me to heaven for joy. [1] They know about me, and can tell. And so do printers, from St. Louis to New York; and so do newspaper reporters, from Nevada to San Francisco. And so do the police   If Shakespeare had really been celebrated, like me, Stratford could have told things about him; and if my experience goes for anything, they'd have done it.

------

1. Four fathoms--twenty-four feet.

VII

If I had under my superintendence a controversy appointed to decide whether Shakespeare wrote Shakespeare or not, I believe I would place before the debaters only the one question, WAS SHAKESPEARE EVER A PRACTICING LAWYER? and leave everything else out.

It is maintained that the man who wrote the plays was not merely myriad-minded, but also myriad-accomplished: that he not only knew some thousands of things about human life in all its shades and grades, and about the hundred arts and trades and crafts and professions which men busy themselves in, but that he could TALK about the men and their grades and trades accurately, making no mistakes. Maybe it is so, but have the experts spoken, or is it only Tom, Dick, and Harry? Does the exhibit stand upon wide, and loose, and eloquent generalizing-- which is not evidence, and not proof--or upon details, particulars, statistics, illustrations, demonstrations?

Experts of unchallengeable authority have testified definitely as to only one of Shakespeare's multifarious craft- equipments, so far as my recollections of Shakespeare-Bacon talk abide with me--his law-equipment. I do not remember that Wellington or Napoleon ever examined Shakespeare's battles and sieges and strategies, and then decided and established for good and all that they were militarily flawless; I do not remember that any Nelson, or Drake, or Cook ever examined his seamanship and said it showed profound and accurate familiarity with that art; I don't remember that any king or prince or duke has ever testified that Shakespeare was letter-perfect in his handling of royal court-manners and the talk and manners of aristocracies; I don't remember that any illustrious Latinist or Grecian or Frenchman or Spaniard or Italian has proclaimed him a past-master in those languages; I don't remember--well, I don't remember that there is TESTIMONY--great testimony--imposing testimony-- unanswerable and unattackable testimony as to any of Shakespeare's hundred specialties, except one--the law.

Other things change, with time, and the student cannot trace back with certainty the changes that various trades and their processes and technicalities have undergone in the long stretch of a century or two and find out what their processes and technicalities were in those early days, but with the law it is different: it is mile-stoned and documented all the way back, and the master of that wonderful trade, that complex and intricate trade, that awe-compelling trade, has competent ways of knowing whether Shakespeare-law is good law or not; and whether his law-court procedure is correct or not, and whether his legal shop-talk is the shop-talk of a veteran practitioner or only a machine-made counterfeit of it gathered from books and from occasional loiterings in Westminster.

Richard H. Dana served two years before the mast, and had every experience that falls to the lot of the sailor before the mast of our day. His sailor-talk flows from his pen with the sure touch and the ease and confidence of a person who has LIVED what he is talking about, not gathered it from books and random listenings. Hear him:

Having hove short, cast off the gaskets, and made the bunt of each sail fast by the jigger, with a man on each yard, at the word the whole canvas of the ship was loosed, and with the greatest rapidity possible everything was sheeted home and hoisted up, the anchor tripped and cat-headed, and the ship under headway.

Again:

The royal yards were all crossed at once, and royals and sky-sails set, and, as we had the wind free, the booms were run out, and all were aloft, active as cats, laying out on the yards and booms, reeving the studding-sail gear; and sail after sail the captain piled upon her, until she was covered with canvas, her sails looking like a great white cloud resting upon a black speck.

Once more. A race in the Pacific:

Our antagonist was in her best trim. Being clear of the point, the breeze became stiff, and the royal-masts bent under our sails, but we would not take them in until we saw three boys spring into the rigging of the CALIFORNIA; then they were all furled at once, but with orders to our boys to stay aloft at the top-gallant mast-heads and loose them again at the word. It was my duty to furl the fore-royal; and while standing by to loose it again, I had a fine view of the scene. From where I stood, the two vessels seemed nothing but spars and sails, while their narrow decks, far below, slanting over by the force of the wind aloft, appeared hardly capable of supporting the great fabrics raised upon them. The CALIFORNIA was to windward of us, and had every advantage; yet, while the breeze was stiff we held our own. As soon as it began to slacken she ranged a little ahead, and the order was given to loose the royals. In an instant the gaskets were off and the bunt dropped. "Sheet home the fore-royal!"-- "Weather sheet's home!"--"Lee sheet's home!"--"Hoist away, sir!" is bawled from aloft. "Overhaul your clew-lines!" shouts the mate. "Aye-aye, sir, all clear!"--"Taut leech! belay! Well the lee brace; haul taut to windward!" and the royals are set.

What would the captain of any sailing-vessel of our time say to that? He would say, "The man that wrote that didn't learn his trade out of a book, he has BEEN there!" But would this same captain be competent to sit in judgment upon Shakespeare's seamanship--considering the changes in ships and ship-talk that have necessarily taken place, unrecorded, unremembered, and lost to history in the last three hundred years? It is my conviction that Shakespeare's sailor-talk would be Choctaw to him. For instance--from "The Tempest":

MASTER. Boatswain!

BOATSWAIN. Here, master; what cheer?

MASTER. Good, speak to the mariners: fall to 't, yarely, or we run ourselves to ground; bestir, bestir! (ENTER MARINERS.)

BOATSWAIN. Heigh, my hearts! cheerly, cheerly, my hearts! yare, yare! Take in the topsail. Tend to the master's whistle. . . . Down with the topmast! yare! lower, lower! Bring her to try wi' the main course. . . . Lay her a-hold, a-hold! Set her two courses. Off to sea again; lay her off.

That will do, for the present; let us yare a little, now, for a change.

If a man should write a book and in it make one of his charac-ters say, "Here, devil, empty the quoins into the standing galley and the imposing-stone into the hell-box; assemble the comps around the frisket and let them jeff for takes and be quick about it," I should recognize a mistake or two in the phrasing, and would know that the writer was only a printer theoretically, not practically.

I have been a quartz miner in the silver regions--a pretty hard life; I know all the palaver of that business: I know all about discovery claims and the subordinate claims; I know all about lodes, ledges, outcroppings, dips, spurs, angles, shafts, drifts, inclines, levels, tunnels, air-shafts, "horses," clay casings, granite casings; quartz mills and their batteries; arastras, and how to charge them with quicksilver and sulphate of copper; and how to clean them up, and how to reduce the resulting amalgam in the retorts, and how to cast the bullion into pigs; and finally I know how to screen tailings, and also how to hunt for something less robust to do, and find it. I know the argot and the quartz-mining and milling industry familiarly; and so whenever Bret Harte introduces that industry into a story, the first time one of his miners opens his mouth I recognize from his phrasing that Harte got the phrasing by listening--like Shakespeare--I mean the Stratford one--not by experience. No one can talk the quartz dialect correctly without learning it with pick and shovel and drill and fuse.

I have been a surface miner--gold--and I know all its mysteries, and the dialects that belongs with them; and whenever Harte introduces that industry into a story I know by the phrasing of his characters that neither he nor they have ever served that trade.

I have been a "pocket" miner--a sort of gold mining not findable in any but one little spot in the world, so far as I know. I know how, with horn and water, to find the trail of a pocket and trace it step by step and stage by stage up the mountain to its source, and find the compact little nest of yellow metal reposing in its secret home under the ground. I know the language of that trade, that capricious trade, that fascinating buried-treasure trade, and can catch any writer who tries to use it without having learned it by the sweat of his brow and the labor of his hands.

I know several other trades and the argot that goes with them; and whenever a person tries to talk the talk peculiar to any of them without having learned it at its source I can trap him always before he gets far on his road.

And so, as I have already remarked, if I were required to superintend a Bacon-Shakespeare controversy, I would narrow the matter down to a single question--the only one, so far as the previous controversies have informed me, concerning which illustrious experts of unimpeachable competency have testified: WAS THE AUTHOR OF SHAKESPEARE'S WORKS A LAWYER?--a lawyer deeply read and of limitless experience? I would put aside the guesses and surmises, and perhapes, and might-have-beens, and could-have- beens, and must-have-beens, and we-are-justified-in-presumings, and the rest of those vague specters and shadows and indefintenesses, and stand or fall, win or lose, by the verdict rendered by the jury upon that single question. If the verdict was Yes, I should feel quite convinced that the Stratford Shakespeare, the actor, manager, and trader who died so obscure, so forgotten, so destitute of even village consequence, that sixty years afterward no fellow-citizen and friend of his later days remembered to tell anything about him, did not write the Works.

Chapter XIII of THE SHAKESPEARE PROBLEM RESTATED bears the heading "Shakespeare as a Lawyer," and comprises some fifty pages of expert testimony, with comments thereon, and I will copy the first nine, as being sufficient all by themselves, as it seems to me, to settle the question which I have conceived to be the master-key to the Shakespeare-Bacon puzzle.

VIII

Shakespeare as a Lawyer [1]

The Plays and Poems of Shakespeare supply ample evidence that their author not only had a very extensive and accurate knowledge of law, but that he was well acquainted with the manners and customs of members of the Inns of Court and with legal life generally.

"While novelists and dramatists are constantly making mistakes as to the laws of marriage, of wills, of inheritance, to Shakespeare's law, lavishly as he expounds it, there can neither be demurrer, nor bill of exceptions, nor writ of error." Such was the testimony borne by one of the most distinguished lawyers of the nineteenth century who was raised to the high office of Lord Chief Justice in 1850, and subsequently became Lord Chancellor. Its weight will, doubtless, be more appreciated by lawyers than by laymen, for only lawyers know how impossible it is for those who have not served an apprenticeship to the law to avoid displaying their ignorance if they venture to employ legal terms and to discuss legal doctrines. "There is nothing so dangerous," wrote Lord Campbell, "as for one not of the craft to tamper with our freemasonry." A layman is certain to betray himself by using some expression which a lawyer would never employ. Mr. Sidney Lee himself supplies us with an example of this. He writes (p. 164): "On February 15, 1609, Shakespeare . . . obtained judgment from a jury against Addenbroke for the payment of No. 6, and No. 1, 5s. 0d. costs." Now a lawyer would never have spoken of obtaining "judgment from a jury," for it is the function of a jury not to deliver judgment (which is the prerogative of the court), but to find a verdict on the facts. The error is, indeed, a venial one, but it is just one of those little things which at once enable a lawyer to know if the writer is a layman or "one of the craft."

But when a layman ventures to plunge deeply into legal subjects, he is naturally apt to make an exhibition of his incompetence. "Let a non-professional man, however acute," writes Lord Campbell again, "presume to talk law, or to draw illustrations from legal science in discussing other subjects, and he will speedily fall into laughable absurdity."

And what does the same high authority say about Shakespeare? He had "a deep technical knowledge of the law," and an easy familiarity with "some of the most abstruse proceedings in English jurisprudence." And again: "Whenever he indulges this propensity he uniformly lays down good law." Of "Henry IV.," Part 2, he says: "If Lord Eldon could be supposed to have written the play, I do not see how he could be chargeable with having forgotten any of his law while writing it." Charles and Mary Cowden Clarke speak of "the marvelous intimacy which he displays with legal terms, his frequent adoption of them in illustration, and his curiously technical knowledge of their form and force." Malone, himself a lawyer, wrote: "His knowledge of legal terms is not merely such as might be acquired by the casual observation of even his all-comprehending mind; it has the appearance of technical skill." Another lawyer and well-known Shakespearean, Richard Grant White, says: "No dramatist of the time, not even Beaumont, who was the younger son of a judge of the Common Pleas, and who after studying in the Inns of Court abandoned law for the drama, used legal phrases with Shakespeare's readiness and exactness. And the significance of this fact is heightened by another, that is only to the language of the law that he exhibits this inclination. The phrases peculiar to other occupations serve him on rare occasions by way of description, comparison, or illustration, generally when something in the scene suggests them, but legal phrases flow from his pen as part of his vocabulary and parcel of his thought. Take the word 'purchase' for instance, which, in ordinary use, means to acquire by giving value, but applies in law to all legal modes of obtaining property except by inheritance or descent, and in this peculiar sense the word occurs five times in Shakespeare's thirty-four plays, and only in one single instance in the fifty-four plays of Beaumont and Fletcher. It has been suggested that it was in attendance upon the courts in London that he picked up his legal vocabulary. But this supposition not only fails to account for Shakespeare's peculiar freedom and exactness in the use of that phraseology, it does not even place him in the way of learning those terms his use of which is most remarkable, which are not such as he would have heard at ordinary proceedings at NISI PRIUS, but such as refer to the tenure or transfer of real property, 'fine and recovery,' 'statutes merchant,' 'purchase,' 'indenture,' 'tenure,' 'double voucher,' 'fee simple,' 'fee farm,' 'remainder,' 'reversion,' 'forfeiture,' etc. This conveyancer's jargon could not have been picked up by hanging round the courts of law in London two hundred and fifty years ago, when suits as to the title of real property were comparatively rare. And besides, Shakespeare uses his law just as freely in his first plays, written in his first London years, as in those produced at a later period. Just as exactly, too; for the correctness and propriety with which these terms are introduced have compelled the admiration of a Chief Justice and a Lord Chancellor."

Senator Davis wrote: "We seem to have something more than a sciolist's temerity of indulgence in the terms of an unfamiliar art. No legal solecisms will be found. The abstrusest elements of the common law are impressed into a disciplined service. Over and over again, where such knowledge is unexampled in writers unlearned in the law, Shakespeare appears in perfect possession of it. In the law of real property, its rules of tenure and descents, its entails, its fines and recoveries, their vouchers and double vouchers, in the procedure of the Courts, the method of bringing writs and arrests, the nature of actions, the rules of pleading, the law of escapes and of contempt of court, in the principles of evidence, both technical and philosophical, in the distinction between the temporal and spiritual tribunals, in the law of attainder and forfeiture, in the requisites of a valid marriage, in the presumption of legitimacy, in the learning of the law of prerogative, in the inalienable character of the Crown, this mastership appears with surprising authority."

To all this testimony (and there is much more which I have not cited) may now be added that of a great lawyer of our own times, VIZ.: Sir James Plaisted Wilde, Q.C. 1855, created a Baron of the Exchequer in 1860, promoted to the post of Judge-Ordinary and Judge of the Courts of Probate and Divorce in 1863, and better known to the world as Lord Penzance, to which dignity he was raised in 1869. Lord Penzance, as all lawyers know, and as the late Mr. Inderwick, K.C., has testified, was one of the first legal authorities of his day, famous for his "remarkable grasp of legal principles," and "endowed by nature with a remarkable facility for marshaling facts, and for a clear expression of his views."

Lord Penzance speaks of Shakespeare's "perfect familiarity with not only the principles, axioms, and maxims, but the technicalities of English law, a knowledge so perfect and intimate that he was never incorrect and never at fault. . . . The mode in which this knowledge was pressed into service on all occasions to express his meaning and illustrate his thoughts was quite unexampled. He seems to have had a special pleasure in his complete and ready mastership of it in all its branches. As manifested in the plays, this legal knowledge and learning had therefore a special character which places it on a wholly different footing from the rest of the multifarious knowledge which is exhibited in page after page of the plays. At every turn and point at which the author required a metaphor, simile, or illustration, his mind ever turned FIRST to the law. He seems almost to have THOUGHT in legal phrases, the commonest of legal expressions were ever at the end of his pen in description or illustration. That he should have descanted in lawyer language when he had a forensic subject in hand, such as Shylock's bond, was to be expected, but the knowledge of law in 'Shakespeare' was exhibited in a far different manner: it protruded itself on all occasions, appropriate or inappropriate, and mingled itself with strains of thought widely divergent from forensic subjects." Again: "To acquire a perfect familiarity with legal principles, and an accurate and ready use of the technical terms and phrases not only of the conveyancer's office, but of the pleader's chambers and the Courts at Westminster, nothing short of employment in some career involving constant contact with legal questions and general legal work would be requisite. But a continuous employment involves the element of time, and time was just what the manager of two theaters had not at his disposal. In what portion of Shakespeare's (i.e., Shakspere's) career would it be possible to point out that time could be found for the interposition of a legal employment in the chambers or offices of practicing lawyers?"

Stratfordians, as is well known, casting about for some possible explanation of Shakespeare's extraordinary knowledge of law, have made the suggestion that Shakespeare might, conceivably, have been a clerk in an attorney's office before he came to London. Mr. Collier wrote to Lord Campbell to ask his opinion as to the probability of this being true. His answer was as follows: "You require us to believe implicitly a fact, of which, if true, positive and irrefragable evidence in his own handwriting might have been forthcoming to establish it. Not having been actually enrolled as an attorney, neither the records of the local court at Stratford nor of the superior Court at Westminster would present his name as being concerned in any suit as an attorney, but it might reasonably have been expected that there would be deeds or wills witnessed by him still extant, and after a very diligent search none such can be discovered."

Upon this Lord Penzance commends: "It cannot be doubted that Lord Campbell was right in this. No young man could have been at work in an attorney's office without being called upon continually to act as a witness, and in many other ways leaving traces of his work and name." There is not a single fact or incident in all that is known of Shakespeare, even by rumor or tradition, which supports this notion of a clerkship. And after much argument and surmise which has been indulged in on this subject, we may, I think, safely put the notion on one side, for no less an authority than Mr. Grant White says finally that the idea of his having been clerk to an attorney has been "blown to pieces."

It is altogether characteristic of Mr. Churton Collins that he, nevertheless, adopts this exploded myth. "That Shakespeare was in early life employed as a clerk in an attorney's office may be correct. At Stratford there was by royal charter a Court of Record sitting every fortnight, with six attorneys, besides the town clerk, belonging to it, and it is certainly not straining probability to suppose that the young Shakespeare may have had employment in one of them. There is, it is true, no tradition to this effect, but such traditions as we have about Shakespeare's occupation between the time of leaving school and going to London are so loose and baseless that no confidence can be placed in them. It is, to say the least, more probable that he was in an attorney's office than that he was a butcher killing calves 'in a high style,' and making speeches over them."

This is a charming specimen of Stratfordian argument. There is, as we have seen, a very old tradition that Shakespeare was a butcher's apprentice. John Dowdall, who made a tour of Warwickshire in 1693, testifies to it as coming from the old clerk who showed him over the church, and it is unhesitatingly accepted as true by Mr. Halliwell-Phillipps. (Vol. I, p. 11, and Vol. II, pp. 71, 72.) Mr. Sidney Lee sees nothing improbable in it, and it is supported by Aubrey, who must have written his account some time before 1680, when his manuscript was completed. Of the attorney's clerk hypothesis, on the other hand, there is not the faintest vestige of a tradition. It has been evolved out of the fertile imaginations of embarrassed Stratfordians, seeking for some explanation of the Stratford rustic's marvelous acquaintance with law and legal terms and legal life. But Mr. Churton Collins has not the least hesitation in throwing over the tradition which has the warrant of antiquity and setting up in its stead this ridiculous invention, for which not only is there no shred of positive evidence, but which, as Lord Campbell and Lord Penzance pointed out, is really put out of court by the negative evidence, since "no young man could have been at work in an attorney's office without being called upon continually to act as a witness, and in many other ways leaving traces of his work and name." And as Mr. Edwards further points out, since the day when Lord Campbell's book was published (between forty and fifty years ago), "every old deed or will, to say nothing of other legal papers, dated during the period of William Shakespeare's youth, has been scrutinized over half a dozen shires, and not one signature of the young man has been found."

Moreover, if Shakespeare had served as clerk in an attorney's office it is clear that he must have served for a considerable period in order to have gained (if, indeed, it is credible that he could have so gained) his remarkable knowledge of the law. Can we then for a moment believe that, if this had been so, tradition would have been absolutely silent on the matter? That Dowdall's old clerk, over eighty years of age, should have never heard of it (though he was sure enough about the butcher's apprentice) and that all the other ancient witnesses should be in similar ignorance!

But such are the methods of Stratfordian controversy. Tradition is to be scouted when it is found inconvenient, but cited as irrefragable truth when it suits the case. Shakespeare of Stratford was the author of the Plays and Poems, but the author of the Plays and Poems could not have been a butcher's apprentice. Anyway, therefore, with tradition. But the author of the Plays and Poems MUST have had a very large and a very accurate knowledge of the law. Therefore, Shakespeare of Stratford must have been an attorney's clerk! The method is simplicity itself. By similar reasoning Shakespeare has been made a country schoolmaster, a soldier, a physician, a printer, and a good many other things besides, according to the inclination and the exigencies of the commentator. It would not be in the least surprising to find that he was studying Latin as a schoolmaster and law in an attorney's office at the same time.

However, we must do Mr. Collins the justice of saying that he has fully recognized, what is indeed tolerable obvious, that Shakespeare must have had a sound legal training. "It may, of course, be urged," he writes, "that Shakespeare's knowledge of medicine, and particularly that branch of it which related to morbid psychology, is equally remarkable, and that no one has ever contended that he was a physician. (Here Mr. Collins is wrong; that contention also has been put forward.) It may be urged that his acquaintance with the technicalities of other crafts and callings, notably of marine and military affairs, was also extraordinary, and yet no one has suspected him of being a sailor or a soldier. (Wrong again. Why, even Messrs. Garnett and Gosse "suspect" that he was a soldier!) This may be conceded, but the concession hardly furnishes an analogy. To these and all other subjects he recurs occasionally, and in season, but with reminiscences of the law his memory, as is abundantly clear, was simply saturated. In season and out of season now in manifest, now in recondite application, he presses it into the service of expression and illustration. At least a third of his myriad metaphors are derived from it. It would indeed be difficult to find a single act in any of his dramas, nay, in some of them, a single scene, the diction and imagery of which are not colored by it. Much of his law may have been acquired from three books easily accessible to him--namely, Tottell's PRECEDENTS (1572), Pulton's STATUTES (1578), and Fraunce's LAWIER'S LOGIKE (1588), works with which he certainly seems to have been familiar; but much of it could only have come from one who had an intimate acquaintance with legal proceedings. We quite agree with Mr. Castle that Shakespeare's legal knowledge is not what could have been picked up in an attorney's office, but could only have been learned by an actual attendance at the Courts, at a Pleader's Chambers, and on circuit, or by associating intimately with members of the Bench and Bar."

This is excellent. But what is Mr. Collins's explanation? "Perhaps the simplest solution of the problem is to accept the hypothesis that in early life he was in an attorney's office (!), that he there contracted a love for the law which never left him, that as a young man in London he continued to study or dabble in it for his amusement, to stroll in leisure hours into the Courts, and to frequent the society of lawyers. On no other supposition is it possible to explain the attraction which the law evidently had for him, and his minute and undeviating accuracy in a subject where no layman who has indulged in such copious and ostentatious display of legal technicalities has ever yet succeeded in keeping himself from tripping."

A lame conclusion. "No other supposition" indeed! Yes, there is another, and a very obvious supposition--namely, that Shakespeare was himself a lawyer, well versed in his trade, versed in all the ways of the courts, and living in close intimacy with judges and members of the Inns of Court.

One is, of course, thankful that Mr. Collins has appreciated the fact that Shakespeare must have had a sound legal training, but I may be forgiven if I do not attach quite so much importance to his pronouncements on this branch of the subject as to those of Malone, Lord Campbell, Judge Holmes, Mr. Castle, K.C., Lord Penzance, Mr. Grant White, and other lawyers, who have expressed their opinion on the matter of Shakespeare's legal acquirements.

. . .

Here it may, perhaps, be worth while to quote again from Lord Penzance's book as to the suggestion that Shakespeare had somehow or other managed "to acquire a perfect familiarity with legal principles, and an accurate and ready use of the technical terms and phrases, not only of the conveyancer's office, but of the pleader's chambers and the Courts at Westminster." This, as Lord Penzance points out, "would require nothing short of employment in some career involving CONSTANT CONTACT with legal questions and general legal work." But "in what portion of Shakespeare's career would it be possible to point out that time could be found for the interposition of a legal employment in the chambers or offices of practicing lawyers? . . . It is beyond doubt that at an early period he was called upon to abandon his attendance at school and assist his father, and was soon after, at the age of sixteen,

bound apprentice to a trade. While under the obligation of this
bond he could not have pursued any other employment. Then
he leaves Stratford and comes to London. He has to provide
himself with the means of a livelihood, and this he did in some
capacity at the theater. No one doubt that. The holding of
horses is scouted by many, and perhaps with justice, as being
unlikely and certainly unproved; but whatever the nature of his
employment was at the theater, there is hardly room for the
belief that it could have been other than continuous, for his
progress there was so rapid. Ere long he had been taken into
the company as an actor, and was soon spoken of as a "Jo-
hannes Factotum.' His rapid accumulation of wealth speaks
volumes for the constancy and activity of his services. One fails
to see when there could be a break in the current of his life at
this period of it, giving room or opportunity for legal or indeed
any other employment. 'In 1589,' says Knight, 'we have
undeniable evidence that he had not only a casual engagement,
was not only a salaried servant, as may players were, but was a
shareholder in the company of the Queen's players with other
shareholders below him on the list.' This (1589) would be
within two years after his arrival in London, which is placed by
White and Halliwell- Phillipps about the year 1587. The
difficulty in supposing that, starting with a state of ignorance in
1587, when he is supposed to have come to London, he was
induced to enter upon a course of most extended study and
mental culture, is almost insuperable. Still it was physically
possible, provided always that he could have had access to the
needful books. But this legal training seems to me to stand on a
different footing. It is not only unaccountable and incredible,
but it is actually negatived by the known facts of his career."
Lord Penzance then refers to the fact that "by 1592 (according
to the best authority, Mr. Grant White) several of the plays had
been written. 'The Comedy of Errors' in 1589, 'Love's Labour's
Lost' in 1589, 'Two Gentlemen of Verona' in 1589 or 1590," and

so forth, and then asks, "with this catalogue of dramatic work on hand . . . was it possible that he could have taken a leading part in the management and conduct of two theaters, and if Mr. Phillipps is to be relied upon, taken his share in the performances of the provincial tours of his company--and at the same time devoted himself to the study of the law in all its branches so efficiently as to make himself complete master of its principles and practice, and saturate his mind with all its most technical terms?"

I have cited this passage from Lord Penzance's book, because it lay before me, and I had already quoted from it on the matter of Shakespeare's legal knowledge; but other writers have still better set forth the insuperable difficulties, as they seem to me, which beset the idea that Shakespeare might have found them in some unknown period of early life, amid multifarious other occupations, for the study of classics, literature, and law, to say nothing of languages and a few other matters. Lord Penzance further asks his readers: "Did you ever meet with or hear of an instance in which a young man in this country gave himself up to legal studies and engaged in legal employments, which is the only way of becoming familiar with the technicalities of practice, unless with the view of practicing in that profession? I do not believe that it would be easy, or indeed possible, to produce an instance in which the law has been seriously studied in all its branches, except as a qualification for practice in the legal profession."

This testimony is so strong, so direct, so authoritative; and so uncheapened, unwatered by guesses, and surmises, and maybe-so's, and might-have-beens, and could-have-beens, and must-have-beens, and the rest of that ton of plaster of Paris out of which the biographers have built the colossal brontosaur which goes by the Stratford actor's name, that it quite convinces me that the man who wrote Shakespeare's Works knew all about law and lawyers. Also, that that man could not have been the Stratford Shakespeare--and WASN'T.

Who did write these Works, then?

I wish I knew.

-----

1. From Chapter XIII of THE SHAKESPEARE PROBLEM RESTATED. By George G. Greenwood, M.P. John Lane Company, publishers.

IX

Did Francis Bacon write Shakespeare's Works? Nobody knows.

We cannot say we KNOW a thing when that thing has not been proved. KNOW is too strong a word to use when the evidence is not final and absolutely conclusive. We can infer, if we want to, like those slaves. . . . No, I will not write that word, it is not kind, it is not courteous. The upholders of the Stratford-Shakespeare superstition call US the hardest names they can think of, and they keep doing it all the time; very well, if they like to descend to that level, let them do it, but I will not so undignify myself as to follow them. I cannot call them harsh names; the most I can do is to indicate them by terms reflecting my disapproval; and this without malice, without venom.

To resume. What I was about to say was, those thugs have built their entire superstition upon INFERENCES, not upon known and established facts. It is a weak method, and poor, and I am glad to be able to say our side never resorts to it while there is anything else to resort to.

But when we must, we must; and we have now arrived at a place of that sort. . . . Since the Stratford Shakespeare couldn't have written the Works, we infer that somebody did. Who was it, then? This requires some more inferring.

Ordinarily when an unsigned poem sweeps across the continent like a tidal wave whose roar and boom and thunder are made up of admiration, delight, and applause, a dozen obscure people rise up and claim the authorship. Why a dozen, instead of only one or two? One reason is, because there are a dozen that are recognizably competent to do that poem. Do you remember "Beautiful Snow"? Do you remember "Rock Me to Sleep, Mother, Rock Me to Sleep"? Do you remember "Backward, turn, backward, O Time, in thy flight! Make me a child again just for tonight"? I remember them very well. Their authorship was claimed by most of the grown-up people who were alive at the time, and every claimant had one plausible argument in his favor, at least--to wit, he could have done the authoring; he was competent.

Have the Works been claimed by a dozen? They haven't. There was good reason. The world knows there was but one man on the planet at the time who was competent--not a dozen, and not two. A long time ago the dwellers in a far country used now and then to find a procession of prodigious footprints stretching across the plain--footprints that were three miles apart, each footprint a third of a mile long and a furlong deep, and with forests and villages mashed to mush in it. Was there any doubt as to who made that mighty trail? Were there a dozen claimants? Where there two? No--the people knew who it was that had been along there: there was only one Hercules.

There has been only one Shakespeare. There couldn't be two; certainly there couldn't be two at the same time. It takes ages to bring forth a Shakespeare, and some more ages to match him. This one was not matched before his time; nor during his time; and hasn't been matched since. The prospect of matching him in our time is not bright.

The Baconians claim that the Stratford Shakespeare was not qualified to write the Works, and that Francis Bacon was. They claim that Bacon possessed the stupendous equipment--both natural and acquired--for the miracle; and that no other Englishman of his day possessed the like; or, indeed, anything closely approaching it.

Macaulay, in his Essay, has much to say about the splendor and horizonless magnitude of that equipment. Also, he has synopsized Bacon's history--a thing which cannot be done for the Stratford Shakespeare, for he hasn't any history to synopsize. Bacon's history is open to the world, from his boyhood to his death in old age--a history consisting of known facts, displayed in minute and multitudinous detail; FACTS, not guesses and conjectures and might-have-beens.

Whereby it appears that he was born of a race of statesmen, and had a Lord Chancellor for his father, and a mother who was "distinguished both as a linguist and a theologian: she corresponded in Greek with Bishop Jewell, and translated his APOLOGIA from the Latin so correctly that neither he nor Archbishop Parker could suggest a single alteration." It is the atmosphere we are reared in that determines how our inclinations and aspirations shall tend. The atmosphere furnished by the parents to the son in this present case was an atmosphere saturated with learning; with thinkings and ponderings upon deep subjects; and with polite culture. It had its natural effect. Shakespeare of Stratford was reared in a house which had no use for books, since its owners, his parents, were without education. This may have had an effect upon the son, but we do not know, because we have no history of him of an informing sort. There were but few books anywhere, in that day, and only the well-to-do and highly educated possessed them, they being almost confined to the dead languages. "All the valuable books then extant in all the vernacular dialects of Europe would hardly have filled a single shelf"--imagine it! The few existing books were in the Latin tongue mainly. "A person who was ignorant of it was shut out from all acquaintance--not merely with Cicero and Virgil, but with the most interesting memoirs, state papers, and pamphlets of his own time"--a literature necessary to the Stratford lad, for his fictitious reputation's sake, since the writer of his Works would begin to use it wholesale and in a most masterly way before the lad was hardly more than out of his teens and into his twenties.

At fifteen Bacon was sent to the university, and he spent three years there. Thence he went to Paris in the train of the English Ambassador, and there he mingled daily with the wise, the cultured, the great, and the aristocracy of fashion, during another three years. A total of six years spent at the sources of knowledge; knowledge both of books and of men. The three spent at the university were coeval with the second and last three spent by the little Stratford lad at Stratford school supposedly, and perhapsedly, and maybe, and by inference-- with nothing to infer from. The second three of the Baconian six were "presumably" spent by the Stratford lad as apprentice to a butcher. That is, the thugs presume it--on no evidence of any kind. Which is their way, when they want a historical fact. Fact and presumption are, for business purposes, all the same to them. They know the difference, but they also know how to blink it. They know, too, that while in history-building a fact is better than a presumption, it doesn't take a presumption long to bloom into a fact when THEY have the handling of it. They know by old experience that when they get hold of a presump-tion- tadpole he is not going to STAY tadpole in their history-tank; no, they know how to develop him into the giant four-legged bullfrog of FACT, and make him sit up on his hams, and puff out his chin, and look important and insolent and come-to-stay; and assert his genuine simon-pure authenticity with a thundering bellow that will convince everybody because it is so loud. The thug is aware that loudness convinces sixty persons where reasoning convinces but one. I wouldn't be a thug, not even if-- but never mind about that, it has nothing to do with the argument, and it is not noble in spirit besides. If I am better than a thug, is the merit mine? No, it is His. Then to Him be the praise. That is the right spirit.

They "presume" the lad severed his "presumed" connection with the Stratford school to become apprentice to a butcher. They also "presume" that the butcher was his father. They don't know. There is no written record of it, nor any other actual evidence. If it would have helped their case any, they would have apprenticed him to thirty butchers, to fifty butchers, to a wilderness of butchers--all by their patented method "presumption." If it will help their case they will do it yet; and if it will further help it, they will "presume" that all those butchers were his father. And the week after, they will SAY it. Why, it is just like being the past tense of the compound reflexive adverbial incandescent hypodermic irregular accusative Noun of Multitude; which is father to the expression which the grammarians call Verb. It is like a whole ancestry, with only one posterity.

To resume. Next, the young Bacon took up the study of law, and mastered that abstruse science. From that day to the end of his life he was daily in close contact with lawyers and judges; not as a casual onlooker in intervals between holding horses in front of a theater, but as a practicing lawyer--a great and successful one, a renowned one, a Launcelot of the bar, the most formidable lance in the high brotherhood of the legal Table Round; he lived in the law's atmosphere thenceforth, all his years, and by sheer ability forced his way up its difficult steeps to its supremest summit, the Lord-Chancellorship, leaving behind him no fellow-craftsman qualified to challenge his divine right to that majestic place.

When we read the praises bestowed by Lord Penzance and the other illustrious experts upon the legal condition and legal aptnesses, brilliances, profundities, and felicities so prodigally displayed in the Plays, and try to fit them to the historyless Stratford stage-manager, they sound wild, strange, incredible, ludicrous; but when we put them in the mouth of Bacon they do not sound strange, they seem in their natural and rightful place, they seem at home there. Please turn back and read them again. Attributed to Shakespeare of Stratford they are meaningless, they are inebriate extravagancies--intemperate admirations of the dark side of the moon, so to speak; attributed to Bacon, they are admirations of the golden glories of the moon's front side, the moon at the full--and not intemperate, not overwrought, but sane and right, and justified. "At ever turn and point at which the author required a metaphor, simile, or illustration, his mind ever turned FIRST to the law; he seems almost to have THOUGHT in legal phrases; the commonest legal phrases, the commonest of legal expressions, were ever at the end of his pen." That could happen to no one but a person whose TRADE was the law; it could not happen to a dabbler in it. Veteran mariners fill their conversation with sailor-phrases and draw all their similes from the ship and the sea and the storm, but no mere PASSENGER ever does it, be he of Stratford or elsewhere; or could do it with anything resembling accuracy, if he were hardy enough to try. Please read again what Lord Campbell and the other great authorities have said about Bacon when they thought they were saying it about Shakespeare of Stratford.

X

The Rest of the Equipment

The author of the Plays was equipped, beyond every other man of his time, with wisdom, erudition, imagination, capaciousness of mind, grace, and majesty of expression. Everyone one had said it, no one doubts it. Also, he had humor, humor in rich abundance, and always wanting to break out. We have no evidence of any kind that Shakespeare of Stratford possessed any of these gifts or any of these acquirements. The only lines he ever wrote, so far as we know, are substantially barren of them-- barren of all of them.

Good friend for Iesus sake forbeare To digg the dust encloased heare: Blest be ye man yt spares thes stones And curst be he yt moves my bones. Ben Jonson says of Bacon, as orator:

His language, WHERE HE COULD SPARE AND PASS BY A JEST, was nobly censorious. No man ever spoke more neatly, more pressly, more weightily, or suffered less emptiness, less idleness, in what he uttered. No member of his speech but consisted of his (its) own graces. . . . The fear of every man that heard him was lest he should make an end.

From Macaulay:

He continued to distinguish himself in Parliament, particularly by his exertions in favor of one excellent measure on which the King's heart was set--the union of England and Scotland. It was not difficult for such an intellect to discover many irresistible arguments in favor of such a scheme. He conducted the great case of the POST NATI in the Exchequer Chamber; and the decision of the judges--a decision the legality of which may be questioned, but the beneficial effect of which must be acknowledged--was in a great measure attributed to his dexterous management.

Again:

While actively engaged in the House of Commons and in the courts of law, he still found leisure for letters and philosophy. The noble treatise on the ADVANCEMENT OF LEARNING, which at a later period was expanded into the DE AUGMENTIS, appeared in 1605.

The WISDOM OF THE ANCIENTS, a work which, if it had proceeded from any other writer, would have been considered as a masterpiece of wit and learning, was printed in 1609.

In the mean time the NOVUM ORGANUM was slowly proceeding. Several distinguished men of learning had been permitted to see portions of that extraordinary book, and they spoke with the greatest admiration of his genius.

Even Sir Thomas Bodley, after perusing the COGITATA ET VISA, one of the most precious of those scattered leaves out of which the great oracular volume was afterward made up, acknowledged that "in all proposals and plots in that book, Bacon showed himself a master workman"; and that "it could not be gainsaid but all the treatise over did abound with choice conceits of the present state of learning, and with worthy contemplations of the means to procure it."

In 1612 a new edition of the ESSAYS appeared, with additions surpassing the original collection both in bulk and quality.

Nor did these pursuits distract Bacon's attention from a work the most arduous, the most glorious, and the most useful that even his mighty powers could have achieved, "the reducing and recompiling," to use his own phrase, "of the laws of England."

To serve the exacting and laborious offices of Attorney-General and Solicitor-General would have satisfied the appetite of any other man for hard work, but Bacon had to add the vast literary industries just described, to satisfy his. He was a born worker.

The service which he rendered to letters during the last five years of his life, amid ten thousand distractions and vexations, increase the regret with which we think on the many years which he had wasted, to use the words of Sir Thomas Bodley, "on such study as was not worthy such a student."

He commenced a digest of the laws of England, a History of England under the Princes of the House of Tudor, a body of National History, a Philosophical Romance. He made extensive and valuable additions to his Essays. He published the inestimable TREATISE DE AUGMENTIS SCIENTIARUM.

Did these labors of Hercules fill up his time to his contentment, and quiet his appetite for work? Not entirely:

The trifles with which he amused himself in hours of pain and languor bore the mark of his mind. THE BEST JEST-BOOK IN THE WORLD is that which he dictated from memory, without referring to any book, on a day on which illness had rendered him incapable of serious study.

Here are some scattered remarks (from Macaulay) which throw light upon Bacon, and seem to indicate--and maybe demon-strate-- that he was competent to write the Plays and Poems:

With great minuteness of observation he had an amplitude of comprehension such as has never yet been vouchsafed to any other human being.

The ESSAYS contain abundant proofs that no nice feature of character, no peculiarity in the ordering of a house, a garden, or a court-masque, could escape the notice of one whose mind was capable of taking in the whole world of knowledge.

His understanding resembled the tent which the fairy Paribanou gave to Prince Ahmed: fold it, and it seemed a toy for the hand of a lady; spread it, and the armies of the powerful Sultans might repose beneath its shade.

The knowledge in which Bacon excelled all men was a knowledge of the mutual relations of all departments of knowledge.

In a letter written when he was only thirty-one, to his uncle, Lord Burleigh, he said, "I have taken all knowledge to be my province."

Though Bacon did not arm his philosophy with the weapons of logic, he adorned her profusely with all the richest decorations of rhetoric.

The practical faculty was powerful in Bacon; but not, like his wit, so powerful as occasionally to usurp the place of his reason and to tyrannize over the whole man.

There are too many places in the Plays where this happens. Poor old dying John of Gaunt volleying second-rate puns at his own name, is a pathetic instance of it. "We may assume" that it is Bacon's fault, but the Stratford Shakespeare has to bear the blame.

No imagination was ever at once so strong and so thoroughly subjugated. It stopped at the first check from good sense.

In truth, much of Bacon's life was passed in a visionary world-- amid things as strange as any that are described in the ARABIAN TALES . . . amid buildings more sumptuous than the palace of Aladdin, fountains more wonderful than the golden water of Parizade, conveyances more rapid than the hippogryph of Ruggiero, arms more formidable than the lance of Astolfo, remedies more effacious than the balsam of Fierabras. Yet in his magnificent day-dreams there was nothing wild--nothing but what sober reason sanctioned.

Bacon's greatest performance is the first book of the NOVUM ORGANUM. . . . Every part of it blazes with wit, but with wit which is employed only to illustrate and decorate truth. No book ever made so great a revolution in the mode of thinking, overthrew so may prejudices, introduced so many new opinions.

But what we most admire is the vast capacity of that intellect which, without effort, takes in at once all the domains of science--all the past, the present and the future, all the errors of two thousand years, all the encouraging signs of the passing times, all the bright hopes of the coming age.

He had a wonderful talent for packing thought close and rendering it portable.

His eloquence would alone have entitled him to a high rank in literature.

It is evident that he had each and every one of the mental gifts and each and every one of the acquirements that are so prodigally displayed in the Plays and Poems, and in much higher and richer degree than any other man of his time or of any previous time. He was a genius without a mate, a prodigy not matable. There was only one of him; the planet could not produce two of him at one birth, nor in one age. He could have written anything that is in the Plays and Poems. He could have written this:

The cloud-cap'd towers, the gorgeous palaces, The solemn temples, the great globe itself, Yea, all which it inherit, shall dissolve, And, like an insubstantial pageant faded, Leave not a rack behind. We are such stuff As dreams are made of, and our little life Is rounded with a sleep.

Also, he could have written this, but he refrained:

Good friend for Iesus sake forbeare To digg the dust encloased heare: Blest be ye man yt spares thes stones And curst be he yt moves my bones.

When a person reads the noble verses about the cloud-cap'd towers, he ought not to follow it immediately with Good friend for Iesus sake forbeare, because he will find the transition from great poetry to poor prose too violent for comfort. It will give him a shock. You never notice how commonplace and unpoetic gravel is until you bite into a layer of it in a pie.

XI

Am I trying to convince anybody that Shakespeare did not write Shakespeare's Works? Ah, now, what do you take me for? Would I be so soft as that, after having known the human race familiarly for nearly seventy-four years? It would grieve me to know that any one could think so injuriously of me, so uncomplimentarily, so unadmiringly of me. No, no, I am aware that when even the brightest mind in our world has been trained up from childhood in a superstition of any kind, it will never be possible for that mind, in its maturity, to examine sincerely, dispassionately, and conscientiously any evidence or any circumstance which shall seem to cast a doubt upon the validity of that superstition. I doubt if I could do it myself. We always get at second hand our notions about systems of government; and high tariff and low tariff; and prohibition and anti-prohibition; and the holiness of peace and the glories of war; and codes of honor and codes of morals; and approval of the duel and disapproval of it; and our beliefs concerning the nature of cats; and our ideas as to whether the murder of helpless wild animals is base or is heroic; and our preferences in the matter of religious and political parties; and our acceptance or rejection of the Shakespeares and the Author Ortons and the Mrs. Eddys. We get them all at second hand, we reason none of them out for ourselves. It is the way we are made. It is the way we are all made, and we can't help it, we can't change it. And whenever we have been furnished a fetish, and have been taught to believe in it, and love it and worship it, and refrain from examining it, there is no evidence, howsoever clear and strong, that can persuade us to withdraw from it our loyalty and our devotion. In morals, conduct, and beliefs we take the color of our environment and associations, and it is a color that can safely be warranted to wash. Whenever we have been furnished with a tar baby ostensibly stuffed with jewels, and warned that it will be dishonorable and irreverent to disembowel it and test the jewels, we keep our sacrilegious hands off it. We submit, not reluctantly, but rather gladly, for we are privately afraid we should find, upon examination that the jewels are of the sort that are manufactured at North Adams, Mass.

I haven't any idea that Shakespeare will have to vacate his pedestal this side of the year 2209. Disbelief in him cannot come swiftly, disbelief in a healthy and deeply-loved tar baby has never been known to disintegrate swiftly; it is a very slow process. It took several thousand years to convince our fine race--including every splendid intellect in it--that there is no such thing as a witch; it has taken several thousand years to convince the same fine race--including every splendid intellect in it--that there is no such person as Satan; it has taken several centuries to remove perdition from the Protestant Church's program of post-mortem entertainments; it has taken a weary long time to persuade American Presbyterians to give up infant damnation and try to bear it the best they can; and it looks as if their Scotch brethren will still be burning babies in the everlasting fires when Shakespeare comes down from his perch.

We are The Reasoning Race. We can't prove it by the above examples, and we can't prove it by the miraculous "histories" built by those Stratfordolaters out of a hatful of rags and a barrel of sawdust, but there is a plenty of other things we can prove it by, if I could think of them. We are The Reasoning Race, and when we find a vague file of chipmunk-tracks stringing through the dust of Stratford village, we know by our reasoning bowers that Hercules has been along there. I feel that our fetish is safe for three centuries yet. The bust, too--there in the Stratford Church. The precious bust, the priceless bust, the calm bust, the serene bust, the emotionless bust, with the dandy mustache, and the putty face, unseamed of care--that face which has looked passionlessly down upon the awed pilgrim for a hundred and fifty years and will still look down upon the awed pilgrim three hundred more, with the deep, deep, deep, subtle, subtle, subtle expression of a bladder.

XII

Irreverence

One of the most trying defects which I find in these--these -- what shall I call them? for I will not apply injurious epithets to them, the way they do to us, such violations of courtesy being repugnant to my nature and my dignity. The farthest I can go in that direction is to call them by names of limited reverence-- names merely descriptive, never unkind, never offensive, never tainted by harsh feeling. If THEY would do like this, they would feel better in their hearts. Very well, then--to proceed. One of the most trying defects which I find in these Stratfordolaters, these Shakesperiods, these thugs, these bangalores, these troglodytes, these herumfrodites, these blatherskites, these buccaneers, these bandoleers, is their spirit of irreverence. It is detectable in every utterance of theirs when they are talking about us. I am thankful that in me there is nothing of that spirit. When a thing is sacred to me it is impossible for me to be irreverent toward it. I cannot call to mind a single instance where I have ever been irreverent, except towards the things which were sacred to other people. Am I in the right? I think so. But I ask no one to take my unsupported word; no, look at the dictionary; let the dictionary decide. Here is the definition:

IRREVERENCE. The quality or condition of irreverence toward God and sacred things.

What does the Hindu say? He says it is correct. He says irreverence is lack of respect for Vishnu, and Brahma, and Chrishna, and his other gods, and for his sacred cattle, and for his temples and the things within them. He endorses the definition, you see; and there are 300,000,000 Hindus or their equivalents back of him.

The dictionary had the acute idea that by using the capital G it could restrict irreverence to lack of reverence for OUR Deity and our sacred things, but that ingenious and rather sly idea miscarried: for by the simple process of spelling HIS deities with capitals the Hindu confiscates the definition and restricts it to his own sects, thus making it clearly compulsory upon us to revere HIS gods and HIS sacred things, and nobody's else. We can't say a word, for he had our own dictionary at his back, and its decision is final.

This law, reduced to its simplest terms, is this: 1. Whatever is sacred to the Christian must be held in reverence by everybody else; 2. whatever is sacred to the Hindu must be held in reverence by everybody else; 3. therefore, by consequence, logically, and indisputably, whatever is sacred to ME must be held in reverence by everybody else.

Now then, what aggravates me is that these troglodytes and muscovites and bandoleers and buccaneers are ALSO trying to crowd in and share the benefit of the law, and compel everybody to revere their Shakespeare and hold him sacred. We can't have that: there's enough of us already. If you go on widening and spreading and inflating the privilege, it will presently come to be conceded that each man's sacred things are the ONLY ones, and the rest of the human race will have to be humbly reverent toward them or suffer for it. That can surely happen, and when it happens, the word Irreverence will be regarded as the most meaningless, and foolish, and self-conceited, and insolent, and impudent, and dictatorial word in the language. And people will say, "Whose business is it what gods I worship and what things hold sacred? Who has the right to dictate to my conscience, and where did he get that right?"

We cannot afford to let that calamity come upon us. We must save the word from this destruction. There is but one way to do it, and that is to stop the spread of the privilege and strictly confine it to its present limits--that is, to all the Christian sects, to all the Hindu sects, and me. We do not need any more, the stock is watered enough, just as it is.

It would be better if the privilege were limited to me alone. I think so because I am the only sect that knows how to employ it gently, kindly, charitably, dispassionately. The other sects lack the quality of self-restraint. The Catholic Church says the most irreverent things about matters which are sacred to the Protestants, and the Protestant Church retorts in kind about the confessional and other matters which Catholics hold sacred; then both of these irreverencers turn upon Thomas Paine and charge HIM with irreverence. This is all unfortunate, because it makes it difficult for students equipped with only a low grade of mentality to find out what Irreverence really IS.

It will surely be much better all around if the privilege of regulating the irreverent and keeping them in order shall eventually be withdrawn from all the sects but me. Then there will be no more quarreling, no more bandying of disrespectful epithets, no more heartburnings.

There will then be nothing sacred involved in this Bacon-Shakespeare controversy except what is sacred to me. That will simplify the whole matter, and trouble will cease. There will be irreverence no longer, because I will not allow it. The first time those criminals charge me with irreverence for calling their Stratford myth an Arthur-Orton-Mary-Baker-Thompson-Eddy-Louis- the-Seventeenth-Veiled-Prophet-of-Khorassan will be the last. Taught by the methods found effective in extinguishing earlier offenders by the Inquisition, of holy memory, I shall know how to quiet them.

XIII

Isn't it odd, when you think of it, that you may list all the celebrated Englishmen, Irishmen, and Scotchmen of modern times, clear back to the first Tudors--a list containing five hundred names, shall we say?--and you can go to the histories, biographies, and cyclopedias and learn the particulars of the lives of every one of them. Every one of them except one--the most famous, the most renowned--by far the most illustrious of them all--Shakespeare! You can get the details of the lives of all the celebrated ecclesiastics in the list; all the celebrated tragedians, comedians, singers, dancers, orators, judges, lawyers, poets, dramatists, historians, biographers, editors, inventors, reformers, statesmen, generals, admirals, discoverers, prize-fighters, murderers, pirates, conspirators, horse-jockeys, bunco-steerers, misers, swindlers, explorers, adventurers by land and sea, bankers, financiers, astronomers, naturalists, claimants, impostors, chemists, biologists, geologists, philologists, college presidents and professors, architects, engineers, painters, sculptors, politicians, agitators, rebels, revolutionists, patriots, demagogues, clowns, cooks, freaks, philosophers, burglars, highwaymen, journalists, physicians, surgeons--you can get the life-histories of all of them but ONE. Just ONE--the most extraordinary and the most celebrated of them all-- Shakespeare!

You may add to the list the thousand celebrated persons furnished by the rest of Christendom in the past four centuries, and you can find out the life-histories of all those people, too. You will then have listed fifteen hundred celebrities, and you can trace the authentic life-histories of the whole of them. Save one--far and away the most colossal prodigy of the entire accumulation--Shakespeare! About him you can find out NOTHING. Nothing of even the slightest importance. Nothing worth the trouble of stowing away in your memory. Nothing that even remotely indicates that he was ever anything more than a distinctly commonplace person--a manager, an actor of inferior grade, a small trader in a small village that did not regard him as a person of any consequence, and had forgotten all about him before he was fairly cold in his grave. We can go to the records and find out the life-history of every renowned RACE-HORSE of modern times--but not Shakespeare's! There are many reasons why, and they have been furnished in cart-loads (of guess and conjecture) by those troglodytes; but there is one that is worth all the rest of the reasons put together, and is abundantly sufficient all by itself--HE HADN'T ANY HISTORY TO RECORD. There is no way of getting around that deadly fact. And no sane way has yet been discovered of getting around its formidable significance.

Its quite plain significance--to any but those thugs (I do not use the term unkindly) is, that Shakespeare had no prominence while he lived, and none until he had been dead two or three generations. The Plays enjoyed high fame from the beginning; and if he wrote them it seems a pity the world did not find it out. He ought to have explained that he was the author, and not merely a NOM DE PLUME for another man to hide behind. If he had been less intemperately solicitous about his bones, and more solicitous about his Works, it would have been better for his good name, and a kindness to us. The bones were not important. They will moulder away, they will turn to dust, but the Works will endure until the last sun goes down.

Mark Twain.

P.S. MARCH 25. About two months ago I was illuminating this Autobiography with some notions of mine concerning the Bacon-Shakespeare controversy, and I then took occasion to air the opinion that the Stratford Shakespeare was a person of no public consequence or celebrity during his lifetime, but was utterly obscure and unimportant. And not only in great London, but also in the little village where he was born, where he lived a quarter of a century, and where he died and was buried. I argued that if he had been a person of any note at all, aged villagers would have had much to tell about him many and many a year after his death, instead of being unable to furnish inquirers a single fact connected with him. I believed, and I still believe, that if he had been famous, his notoriety would have lasted as long as mine has lasted in my native village out in Missouri. It is a good argument, a prodigiously strong one, and most formidable one for even the most gifted and ingenious and plausible Stratfordolator to get around or explain away. Today a Hannibal COURIER-POST of recent date has reached me, with an article in it which reinforces my contention that a really celebrated person cannot be forgotten in his village in the short space of sixty years. I will make an extract from it:

Hannibal, as a city, may have many sins to answer for, but ingratitude is not one of them, or reverence for the great men she has produced, and as the years go by her greatest son, Mark Twain, or S. L. Clemens as a few of the unlettered call him, grows in the estimation and regard of the residents of the town he made famous and the town that made him famous. His name is associated with every old building that is torn down to make way for the modern structures demanded by a rapidly growing city, and with every hill or cave over or through which he might by any possibility have roamed, while the many points of interest which he wove into his stories, such as Holiday Hill, Jackson's Island, or Mark Twain Cave, are now monuments to his genius. Hannibal is glad of any opportunity to do him honor as he had honored her.

So it has happened that the "old timers" who went to school with Mark or were with him on some of his usual escapades have been honored with large audiences whenever they were in a reminiscent mood and condescended to tell of their intimacy with the ordinary boy who came to be a very extraordinary humorist and whose every boyish act is now seen to have been indicative of what was to come. Like Aunt Becky and Mrs. Clemens, they can now see that Mark was hardly appreciated when he lived here and that the things he did as a boy and was whipped for doing were not all bad, after all. So they have been in no hesitancy about drawing out the bad things he did as well as the good in their efforts to get a "Mark Twain" story, all incidents being viewed in the light of his present fame, until the volume of "Twainiana" is already considerable and growing in proportion as the "old timers" drop away and the stories are retold second and third hand by their descendants. With some seventy-three years and living in a villa instead of a house, he is a fair target, and let him incorporate, copyright, or patent himself as he will, there are some of his "works" that will go swooping up Hannibal chimneys as long as graybeards gather about the fires and begin with, "I've heard father tell," or possibly, "Once when I." The Mrs. Clemens referred to is my mother--WAS my mother.

And here is another extract from a Hannibal paper, of date twenty days ago:

Miss Becca Blankenship died at the home of William Dickason, 408 Rock Street, at 2.30 o'clock yesterday afternoon, aged 72 years. The deceased was a sister of "Huckleberry Finn," one of the famous characters in Mark Twain's TOM SAWYER. She had been a member of the Dickason family--the housekeeper--for nearly forty- five years, and was a highly respected lady. For the past eight years she had been an invalid, but was as well cared for by Mr. Dickason and his family as if she had been a near relative. She was a member of the Park Methodist Church and a Christian woman.

I remember her well. I have a picture of her in my mind which was graven there, clear and sharp and vivid, sixty-three years ago. She was at that time nine years old, and I was about eleven. I remember where she stood, and how she looked; and I can still see her bare feet, her bare head, her brown face, and her short tow-linen frock. She was crying. What it was about I have long ago forgotten. But it was the tears that preserved the picture for me, no doubt. She was a good child, I can say that for her. She knew me nearly seventy years ago. Did she forget me, in the course of time? I think not. If she had lived in Stratford in Shakespeare's time, would she have forgotten him? Yes. For he was never famous during his lifetime, he was utterly obscure in Stratford, and there wouldn't be any occasion to remember him after he had been dead a week.

"Injun Joe," "Jimmy Finn," and "General Gaines" were prominent and very intemperate ne'er-do-weels in Hannibal two generations ago. Plenty of grayheads there remember them to this day, and can tell you about them. Isn't it curious that two "town drunkards" and one half-breed loafer should leave behind them, in a remote Missourian village, a fame a hundred times greater and several hundred times more particularized in the matter of definite facts than Shakespeare left behind him in the village where he had lived the half of his lifetime?

THE WAR PRAYER

I T was a time of great and exalting excitement. The country was up in arms, the war was on, in every breast burned the holy fire of patriotism; the drums were beating, the bands playing, the toy pistols popping, the bunched firecrackers hissing and spluttering; on every hand and far down the receding and fading spread of roofs and balconies a fluttering wilderness of flags flashed in the sun; daily the young volunteers marched down the wide avenue gay and fine in their new uniforms, the proud fathers and mothers and sisters and sweethearts cheering them with voices choked with happy emotion as they swung by; nightly the packed mass meetings listened, panting, to patriot oratory which stirred the deepest deeps of their hearts, and which they interrupted at briefest intervals with cyclones of applause, the tears running down their cheeks the while; in the churches the pastors preached devotion to flag and country, and invoked the God of Battles beseeching His aid in our good cause in outpourings of fervid eloquence which moved every listener. It was indeed a glad and gracious time, and the half dozen rash spirits that ventured to disapprove of the war and cast a doubt upon its righteousness straightway got such a stern and angry warning that for their personal safety's sake they quickly shrank out of sight and offended no more in that way.

Sunday morning came--next day the battalions would leave for the front; the church was filled; the volunteers were there, their young faces alight with martial dreams--visions of the stern advance, the gathering momentum, the rushing charge, the flashing sabers, the flight of the foe, the tumult, the enveloping smoke, the fierce pursuit, the surrender! Then home from the war, bronzed heroes, welcomed, adored, submerged in golden seas of glory! With the volunteers sat their dear ones, proud, happy, and envied by the neighbors and friends who had no ᶊoᵘᵤ and brothers to send forth to the field of honor, there to win for the flag, or, failing, die the noblest of ᵘᵘᵇⱼₑ deaths. The service proceeded; a war chapter from the Old Testament was read; the first prayer was said; it was followed by an organ burst that shook the building, and with one impulse the house rose, with glowing eyes and beating hearts, and poured out that tremendous invocation

God the all-terrible! Thou who ordainest! Thunder thy clarion and lightning thy sword!

Then came the "long" prayer. None could remember the like of it for passionate pleading and moving and beautiful language. The burden of its supplication was, that an ever-merciful and benignant Father of us all would watch over our noble young soldiers, and aid, comfort, and encourage them in their patriotic work; bless them, shield them in the day of battle and the hour of peril, bear them in His mighty hand, make them strong and confident, invincible in the bloody onset; help them to crush the foe, grant to them and to their flag and country imperishable honor and glory--

An aged stranger entered and moved with slow and noiseless step up the main aisle, his eyes fixed upon the minister, his long body clothed in a robe that reached to his feet, his head bare, his white hair descending in a frothy cataract to his shoulders, his seamy face unnaturally pale, pale even to ghastliness. With all eyes following him and wondering, he made his silent way; without pausing, he ascended to the preacher's side and stood there waiting. With shut lids the preacher, unconscious of his presence, continued with his moving prayer, and at last finished it with the words, uttered in fervent appeal, "Bless our arms, grant us the victory, O Lord our God, Father and Protector of our land and flag!"

The stranger touched his arm, motioned him to step aside--
which the startled minister did--and took his place. During some
moments he surveyed the spellbound audience with solemn
eyes, in which burned an uncanny light; then in a deep voice he
said:

"I come from the Throne--bearing a message from Almighty
God!" The words smote the house with a shock; if the stranger
perceived it he gave no attention. "He has heard the prayer of
His servant your shepherd, and will grant it if such shall be your
desire after I, His messenger, shall have explained to you its
import--that is to say, its full import. For it is like unto many of
the prayers of men, in that it asks for more than he who utters
it is aware of--except he pause and think.

"God's servant and yours has prayed his prayer. Has he paused
and taken thought? Is it one prayer? No, it is two--one uttered,
the other not. Both have reached the ear of Him Who heareth
all supplications, the spoken and the unspoken. Ponder this--
keep it in mind. If you would beseech a blessing upon yourself,
beware! lest without intent you invoke a curse upon a neighbor
at the same time. If you pray for the blessing of rain upon your
crop which needs it, by that act you are possibly praying for a
curse upon some neighbor's crop which may not need rain and
can be injured by it.

"You have heard your servant's prayer--the uttered part of it. I
am commissioned of God to put into words the other part of it--
that part which the pastor--and also you in your hearts--
fervently prayed silently. And ignorantly and unthinkingly? God
grant that it was so! You heard these words: 'Grant us the
victory, O Lord our God!' That is sufficient. the whole of the
uttered prayer is compact into those pregnant words. Elabora-
tions were not necessary. When you have prayed for victory you
have prayed for many unmentioned results which follow

victory--must follow it, cannot help but follow it. Upon the listening spirit of God fell also the unspoken part of the prayer. He commandeth me to put it into words. Listen!

"O Lord our Father, our young patriots, idols of our hearts, go forth to battle--be Thou near them! With them--in spirit--we also go forth from the sweet peace of our beloved firesides to smite the foe. O Lord our God, help us to tear their soldiers to bloody shreds with our shells; help us to cover their smiling fields with the pale forms of their patriot dead; help us to drown the thunder of the guns with the shrieks of their wounded, writhing in pain; help us to lay waste their humble homes with a hurricane of fire; help us to wring the hearts of their unoffending widows with unavailing grief; help us to turn them out roofless with little children to wander unfriended the wastes of their desolated land in rags and hunger and thirst, sports of the sun flames of summer and the icy winds of winter, broken in spirit, worn with travail, imploring Thee for the refuge of the grave and denied it--for our sakes who adore Thee, Lord, blast their hopes, blight their lives, protract their bitter pilgrimage, make heavy their steps, water their way with their tears, stain the white snow with the blood of their wounded feet! We ask it, in the spirit of love, of Him Who is the Source of Love, and Who is the ever-faithful refuge and friend of all that are sore beset and seek His aid with humble and contrite hearts. Amen.

(After a pause.) "Ye have prayed it; if ye still desire it, speak! The messenger of the Most High waits!"

It was believed afterward that the man was a lunatic, because there was no sense in what he said.

THOU SHALT NOT KILL

THE TEN Commandments were made for man alone. We should think it strange if they had been made for all the animals.

We should say "Thou shalt not kill" is too general, too sweeping. It includes the field mouse and the butterfly. They can't kill. And it includes the tiger, which can't help it.

It is a case of Temperament and Circumstance again. You can arrange no circumstances that can move the field mouse and the butterfly to kill; their temperaments will ill keep them unaffected by temptations to kill, they can avoid that crime without an effort. But it isn't so with the tiger. Throw a lamb in his way when he is hungry, and his temperament will compel him to kill it.

Butterflies and field mice are common among men; they can't kill, their temperaments make it impossible. There are tigers among men, also. Their temperaments move them to violence, and when Circumstance furnishes the opportunity and the powerful motive, they kill. They can't help it.

No penal law can deal out justice; it must deal out injustice in every instance. Penal laws have a high value, in that they protect--in a considerable measure--the multitude of the gentle-natured from the violent minority.

For a penal law is a Circumstance. It is a warning which intrudes and stays a would-be murderer's hand--sometimes. Not always, but in many and many a case. It can't stop the real man-tiger; nothing can do that. Slade had 26 deliberate murders on his soul when he finally went to his death on the scaffold. He would kill a man for a trifle; or for nothing. He loved to kill. It was his temperament. He did not make his temperament, God gave it him at his birth. Gave it him and said Thou shalt not kill. It was like saying Thou shalt not eat. Both appetites were given him at birth. He could be obedient and starve both up to a certain point, but that was as far as he could go. Another man could go further; but not Slade.

Holmes, the Chicago monster, inveigled some dozens of men and women into his obscure quarters and privately butchered them. Holmes's inborn nature was such that whenever he had what seemed a reasonably safe opportunity to kill a stranger he couldn't successfully resist the temptation to do it.

Justice was finally meted out to Slade and to Holmes. That is what the newspapers said. It is a common phrase, and a very old one. But it probably isn't true. When a man is hanged for slaying one man that phrase comes into service and we learn that justice was meted out to the slayer. But Holmes slew sixty. There seems to be a discrepancy in this distribution of justice. If Holmes got justice, the other man got 59 times more than justice.

But the phrase is wrong, anyway. The word is the wrong word. Criminal courts do not dispense "justice"--they can't; they only dispense protections to the community. It is all they can do. (1905 or 1906)

Mine eyes have seen the orgy of the launching of the Sword;
He is searching out the hoardings where the stranger's wealth is stored;
He hath loosed his fateful lightnings, and with woe and death has scored;
His lust is marching on.

I have seen him in the watch-fires of a hundred circling camps;
They have builded him an altar in the Eastern dews and damps;
I have read his doomful mission by the dim and flaring lamps--
His night is marching on.

I have read his bandit gospel writ in burnished rows of steel:
"As ye deal with my pretensions, so with you my wrath shall deal;
Let the faithless son of Freedom crush the patriot with his heel;
Lo, Greed is marching on!"

We have legalized the strumpet and are guarding her retreat;*
Greed is seeking out commercial souls before his judgement seat;
O, be swift, ye clods, to answer him! be jubilant my feet!
Our god is marching on!

In a sordid slime harmonious Greed was born in yonder ditch,
With a longing in his bosom--and for others' goods an itch.
As Christ died to make men holy, let men die to make us rich--
Our god is marching on.

* NOTE: In Manila the Government has placed a certain industry under the protection of our flag. (M.T.)

THE FLY

HOW OFTEN we are moved to admit the intelligence exhibited in both the designing and the execution of some of His works. Take the fly, for instance. The planning of the fly was an application of pure intelligence, morals not being concerned. Not one of us could have planned the fly, not one of us could have constructed him; and no one would have considered it wise to try, except under an assumed name. It is believed by some that the fly was introduced to meet a long-felt want. In the course of ages, for some reason or other, there have been millions of these persons, but out of this vast multitude there has not been one who has been willing to explain what the want was. At least satisfactorily. A few have explained that there was need of a creature to remove disease-breeding garbage; but these being then asked to explain what long-felt want the disease-breeding garbage was introduced to supply, they have not been willing to undertake the contract.

There is much inconsistency concerning the fly. In all the ages he has not had a friend, there has never been a person in the earth who could have been persuaded to intervene between him and extermination; yet billions of persons have excused the Hand that made him--and this without a blush. Would they have excused a Man in the same circumstances, a man positively known to have invented the fly? On the contrary. For the credit of the race let us believe it would have been all day with that man. Would persons consider it just to reprobate in a child, with its undeveloped morals, a scandal which they would overlook in the Pope?

When we reflect that the fly was as not invented for pastime, but in the way of business; that he was not flung off in a heedless moment and with no object in view but to pass the time, but was the fruit of long and pains-taking labor and calculation, and with a definite and far-reaching, purpose in view; that his character and conduct were planned out with cold deliberation, that his career was foreseen and fore-ordered, and that there was no want which he could supply, we are hopeless-ly puzzled, we cannot understand the moral lapse that was able to render possible the conceiving and the consummation of this squalid and malevolent creature.

Let us try to think the unthinkable: let us try to imagine a Man of a sort willing to invent the fly; that is to say, a man destitute of feeling; a man willing to wantonly torture and harass and persecute myriads of creatures who had never done him any harm and could not if they wanted to, and--the majority of them--poor dumb things not even aware of his existence. In a word, let us try to imagine a man with so singular and so lumbering a code of morals as this: that it is fair and right to send afflictions upon the just--upon the unoffending as well as upon the offending, without discrimination.

If we can imagine such a man, that is the man that could invent the fly, and send him out on his mission and furnish him his orders: "Depart into the uttermost corners of the earth, and diligently do your appointed work. Persecute the sick child; settle upon its eyes, its face, its hands, and gnaw and pester and sting; worry and fret and madden the worn and tired mother who watches by the child, and who humbly prays for mercy and relief with the pathetic faith of the deceived and the unteacha-ble. Settle upon the soldier's festering wounds in field and hospital and drive him frantic while he also prays, and between-times curses, with none to listen but you, Fly, who get all the petting and all the protection, without even praying for it. Harry and persecute the forlorn and forsaken wretch who is perishing of the plague, and in his terror and despair praying; bite, sting, feed upon his ulcers, dabble your feet in his rotten blood, gum them thick with plague-germs--feet cunningly designed and perfected for this function ages ago in the beginning--carry this freight to a hundred tables, among the just and the unjust. the high and the low, and walk over the food and gaum it with filth and death. Visit all; allow no man peace till he get it in the grave; visit and afflict the hard-worked and unoffending horse, mule, ox, ass, pester the patient cow, and all the kindly animals that labor without fair reward here and perish without hope of it hereafter; spare no creature, wild or tame; but wheresoever you find one, make his life a misery, treat him as the innocent deserve; and so please Me and increase My glory Who made the fly.

We hear much about His patience and forbearance and long-suffering; we hear nothing about our own, which much exceeds it. We hear much about His mercy and kindness and goodness--in words--the words of His Book and of His pulpit--and the meek multitude is content with this evidence, such as it is, seeking no further; but whoso searcheth after a concreted sample of it will in time acquire fatigue. There being no instances of it. For what are gilded as mercies are not in any recorded case more than mere common justices, and due--due without thanks or compliment. To rescue without personal risk a cripple from a burning house is not a mercy, it is a mere commonplace duty; anybody would do it that could. And not by proxy, either--delegating the work but confiscating the credit for it. If men neglected "God's poor" and "God's stricken and helpless ones" as He does, what would become of them? The answer is to be found in those dark lands where man follows His example and turns his indifferent back upon them: they get no help at all; they cry, and plead and pray in vain, they linger and suffer, and miserably die. If you will look at the matter rationally and without prejudice, the proper place to hunt for the facts of His mercy, is not where man does the mercies and He collects the praise, but in those regions where He has the field to Himself.

It is plain that there is one moral law for heaven and another for the earth. The pulpit assures us that wherever we see suffering and sorrow which we can relieve and do not do it, we sin, heavily. There was never yet a case of suffering or sorrow which God could not relieve. Does He sin, then? If He is the Source of Morals He does--certainly nothing can be plainer than that, you will admit. Surely the Source of law cannot violate law and stand unsmirched; surely the judge upon the bench cannot forbid crime and then revel in it himself unreproached. Nevertheless we have this curious spectacle: daily the trained parrot in the pulpit gravely delivers himself of these ironies, which he has acquired at second-hand and adopted without examination, to a trained congregation which accepts them without examination, and neither the speaker nor the hearer laughs at himself. It does seem as if we ought to be humble when we are at a bench-show, and not put on airs of intellectual superiority there.

Religion had its share in the changes of civilization and national character, of course. What share? The lion's. In the history of the human race this has always been the case, will always be the case, to the end of time, no doubt; or at least until man by the slow processes of evolution shall develop into something really fine and high--some billions of years hence, say.

The Christian Bible is a drug store. Its contents remain the same; but the medical practice changes. For eighteen hundred years these changes were slight--scarcely noticeable. The practice was allopathic--allopathic in its rudest and crudest form. The dull and ignorant physician day and night, and all the days and all the nights, drenched his patient with vast and hideous doses of the most repulsive drugs to be found in the store's stock; he bled him, cupped him, purged him, puked him, salivated him, never gave his system a chance to rally, nor nature a chance to help. He kept him religion sick for eighteen centuries, and allowed him not a well day during all that time. The stock in the store was made up of about equal portions of baleful and debilitating poisons, and healing and comforting medicines; but the practice of the time confined the physician to the use of the former; by consequence, he could only damage his patient, and that is what he did.

Not until far within our century was any considerable change in the practice introduced; and then mainly, or in effect only, in Great Britain and the United States. In the other countries to-day, the patient either still takes the ancient treatment or does not call the physician at all. In the English-speaking countries the changes observable in our century were forced by that very thing just referred to--the revolt of the patient against the system; they were not projected by the physician. The patient fell to doctoring himself, and the physician's practice began to fall off. He modified his method to get back his trade. He did it gradually, reluctantly; and never yielded more at a time than the pressure compelled. At first he relinquished the daily dose of hell and damnation, and administered it every other day only; next he allowed another day to pass; then another and presently another; when he had restricted it at last to Sundays, and imagined that now there would surely be a truce, the homeopath arrived on the field and made him abandon hell and damnation altogether, and administered Christ's love, and comfort, and charity and compassion in its stead. These had been in the drug store all the time, gold labeled and conspicuous among the long shelfloads of repulsive purges and vomits and poisons, and so the practice was to blame that they had remained unused, not the pharmacy. To the ecclesiastical physician of fifty years ago, his predecessor for eighteen centuries was a quack; to the ecclesiastical physician of to-day, his predecessor of fifty years ago was a quack. To the every-man-his-own-ecclesiastical-doctor of--when?--what will the ecclesiastical physician of to-day be? Unless evolution, which has been a truth ever since the globes, suns, and planets of the solar system were but wandering films of meteor dust, shall reach a limit and become a lie, there is but one fate in store for him.

The methods of the priest and the parson have been very curious, their history is very entertaining. In all the ages the Roman Church has owned slaves, bought and sold slaves, authorized and encouraged her children to trade in them. Long after some Christian peoples had freed their slaves the Church still held on to hers. If any could know, to absolute certainty, that all this was right, and according to God's will and desire, surely it was she, since she was God's specially appointed representative in the earth and sole authorized and infallible expounder of his Bible. There were the texts; there was no mistaking their meaning; she was right, she was doing in this thing what the Bible had mapped out for her to do. So unassailable was her position that in all the centuries she had no word to say against human slavery. Yet now at last, in our immediate day, we hear a Pope saying slave trading is wrong, and we see him sending an expedition to Africa to stop it. The texts remain: it is the practice that has changed. Why? Because the world has corrected the Bible. The Church never corrects it; and also never fails to drop in at the tail of the procession--and take the credit of the correction. As she will presently do in this instance.

Christian England supported slavery and encouraged it for two hundred and fifty years, and her church's consecrated ministers looked on, sometimes taking an active hand, the rest of the time indifferent. England's interest in the business may be called a Christian interest, a Christian industry. She had her full share in its revival after a long period of inactivity, and his revival was a Christian monopoly; that is to say, it was in the hands of Christian countries exclusively. English parliaments aided the slave traffic and protected it; two English kings held stock in slave-catching companies. The first regular English slave hunter--John Hawkins, of still revered memory--made such successful havoc, on his second voyage, in the matter of surprising and burning villages, and maiming, slaughtering, capturing, and selling their unoffending inhabitants, that his delighted queen conferred the chivalric honor of knighthood on him--a rank which had acquired its chief esteem and distinction in other and earlier fields of Christian effort. The new knight, with characteristic English frankness and brusque simplicity, chose as his device the figure of a negro slave, kneeling and in chains. Sir John's work was the invention of Christians, was to remain a bloody and awful monopoly in the hands of Christians for a quarter of a millennium, was to destroy homes, separate families, enslave friendless men and women, and break a myriad of human hearts, to the end that Christian nations might be prosperous and comfortable, Christian churches be built, and the gospel of the meek and merciful Redeemer be spread abroad in the earth; and so in the name of his ship, unsuspected but eloquent and clear, lay hidden prophecy. She was called The Jesus.

But at last in England, an illegitimate Christian rose against slavery. It is curious that when a Christian rises against a rooted wrong at all, he is usually an illegitimate Christian, member of some despised and bastard sect. There was a bitter struggle, but in the end the slave trade had to go--and went. The Biblical authorization remained, but the practice changed.

Then--the usual thing happened; the visiting English critic among us began straightway to hold up his pious hands in horror at our slavery. His distress was unappeasable, his words full of bitterness and contempt. It is true we had not so many as fifteen hundred thousand slaves for him to worry about, while his England still owned twelve millions, in her foreign posses- sions; but that fact did not modify his wail any, or stay his tears, or soften his censure. The fact that every time we had tried to get rid of our slavery in previous generations, but had always been obstructed, balked, and defeated by England, was a matter of no consequence to him; it was ancient history, and not worth the telling.

Our own conversion came at last. We began to stir against slavery. Hearts grew soft, here, there, and yonder. There was no place in the land where the seeker could not find some small budding sign of pity for the slave. No place in all the land but one--the pulpit. It yielded at last; it always does. It fought a strong and stubborn fight, and then did what it always does, joined the procession--at the tail end. Slavery fell. The slavery text remained; the practice changed, that was all.

During many ages there were witches. The Bible said so. The Bible commanded that they should not be allowed to live. Therefore the Church, after doing its duty in but a lazy and indolent way for eight hundred years, gathered up its halters, thumbscrews, and firebrands, and set about its holy work in earnest. She worked hard at it night and day during nine centuries and imprisoned, tortured, hanged, and burned whole hordes and armies of witches, and washed the Christian world clean with their foul blood.

Then it was discovered that there was no such thing as witches, and never had been. One does not know whether to laugh or to cry. Who discovered that there was no such thing as a witch-- the priest, the parson? No, these never discover anything. At Salem, the parson clung pathetically to his witch text after the laity had abandoned it in remorse and tears for the crimes and cruelties it has persuaded them to do. The parson wanted more blood, more shame, more brutalities; it was the unconsecrated laity that stayed his hand. In Scotland the parson killed the witch after the magistrate had pronounced her innocent; and when the merciful legislature proposed to sweep the hideous laws against witches from the statute book, it was the parson who came imploring, with tears and imprecations, that they be suffered to stand.

There are no witches. The witch text remains; only the practice has changed. Hell fire is gone, but the text remains. Infant damnation is gone, but the text remains. More than two hundred death penalties are gone from the law books, but the texts that authorized them remain.

It is not well worthy of note that of all the multitude of texts through which man has driven his annihilating pen he has never once made the mistake of obliterating a good and useful one? It does certainly seem to suggest that if man continues in the direction of enlightenment, his religious practice may, in the end, attain some semblance of human decency.

LETTERS FROM THE EARTH

THE Creator sat upon the throne, thinking. Behind him stretched the illimitable continent of heaven, steeped in a glory of light and color; before him rose the black night of Space, like a wall. His mighty bulk towered rugged and mountain-like into the zenith, and His divine head blazed there like a distant sun. At His feet stood three colossal figures, diminished to extinction, almost, by contrast -- archangels -- their heads level with His ankle-bone.

When the Creator had finished thinking, He said, "I have thought. Behold!"

He lifted His hand, and from it burst a fountain-spray of fire, a million stupendous suns, which clove the blackness and soared, away and away and away, diminishing in magnitude and intensity as they pierced the far frontiers of Space, until at last they were but as diamond nailheads sparkling under the domed vast roof of the universe.

At the end of an hour the Grand Council was dismissed.

They left the Presence impressed and thoughtful, and retired to a private place, where they might talk with freedom. None of the three seemed to want to begin, though all wanted somebody to do it. Each was burning to discuss the great event, but would prefer not to commit himself till he should know how the others regarded it. So there was some aimless and halting conversation about matters of no consequence, and this dragged tediously along, arriving nowhere, until at last the archangel Satan gathered his courage together -- of which he had a very good supply -- and broke ground. He said: "We know what we are here to talk about, my lords, and we may as well put pretense aside, and begin. If this is the opinion of the Council -- "

"It is, it is!" said Gabriel and Michael, gratefully interrupting.

"Very well, then, let us proceed. We have witnessed a wonderful thing; as to that, we are necessarily agreed. As to the value of it -- if it has any -- that is a matter which does not personally concern us. We can have as many opinions about it as we like, and that is our limit. We have no vote. I think Space was well enough, just as it was, and useful, too. Cold and dark -- a restful place, now and then, after a season of the overdelicate climate and trying splendors of heaven. But these are details of no considerable moment; the new feature, the immense feature, is -- what, gentlemen?"

"The invention and introduction of automatic, unsupervised, self-regulating law for the government of those myriads of whirling and racing suns and worlds!"

"That is it!" said Satan. "You perceive that it is a stupendous idea. Nothing approaching it has been evolved from the Master Intellect before. Law -- Automatic Law -- exact and unvarying Law -- requiring no watching, no correcting, no readjusting while the eternities endure! He said those countless vast bodies would plunge through the wastes of Space ages and ages, at unimaginable speed, around stupendous orbits, yet never collide, and never lengthen nor shorten their orbital periods by so much as the hundredth part of a second in two thousand years! That is the new miracle, and the greatest of all -- Automatic Law! And He gave it a name -- the LAW OF NATURE -- and said Natural Law is the LAW OF GOD -- interchangeable names for one and the same thing."

"Yes," said Michael, "and He said He would establish Natural Law -- the Law of God -- throughout His dominions, and its authority should be supreme and inviolable."

"Also," said Gabriel, "He said He would by and by create animals, and place them, likewise, under the authority of that Law."

"Yes," said Satan, "I heard Him, but did not understand. What is animals, Gabriel?"

"Ah, how should I know? How should any of us know? It is a new word."

[Interval of three centuries, celestial time -- the equivalent of a hundred million years, earthly time. Enter a Messenger-Angel.]

"My lords, He is making animals. Will it please you to come and see?"

They went, they saw, and were perplexed. Deeply perplexed -- and the Creator noticed it, and said, "Ask. I will answer."

"Divine One," said Satan, making obeisance, "what are they for?"

"They are an experiment in Morals and Conduct. Observe them, and be instructed."

There were thousands of them. They were full of activities. Busy, all busy -- mainly in persecuting each other. Satan remarked -- after examining one of them through a powerful microscope: "This large beast is killing weaker animals, Divine One."

"The tiger -- yes. The law of his nature is ferocity. The law of his nature is the Law of God. He cannot disobey it."

"Then in obeying it he commits no offense, Divine One?"

"No, he is blameless."

"This other creature, here, is timid, Divine One, and suffers death without resisting."

"The rabbit -- yes. He is without courage. It is the law of his nature -- the Law of God. He must obey it."

"Then he cannot honorably be required to go counter to his nature and resist, Divine One?"

"No. No creature can be honorably required to go counter to the law of his nature -- the Law of God."

After a long time and many questions, Satan said, "The spider kills the fly, and eats it; the bird kills the spider and eats it; the wildcat kills the goose; the -- well, they all kill each other. It is murder all along the line. Here are countless multitudes of creatures, and they all kill, kill, kill, they are all murderers. And they are not to blame, Divine One?"

"They are not to blame. It is the law of their nature. And always the law of nature is the Law of God. Now -- observe -- behold! A new creature -- and the masterpiece -- Man!"

Men, women, children, they came swarming in flocks, in droves, in millions.

"What shall you do with them, Divine One?"

"Put into each individual, in differing shades and degrees, all the various Moral Qualities, in mass, that have been distributed, a single distinguishing characteristic at a time, among the nonspeaking animal world -- courage, cowardice, ferocity, gentleness, fairness, justice, cunning, treachery, magnanimity, cruelty, malice, malignity, lust, mercy, pity, purity, selfishness, sweetness, honor, love, hate, baseness, nobility, loyalty, falsity, veracity, untruthfulness -- each human being shall have all of these in him, and they will constitute his nature. In some, there will be high and fine characteristics which will submerge the evil ones, and those will be called good men; in others the evil characteristics will have dominion, and those will be called bad men. Observe -- behold -- they vanish!"

"Whither are they gone, Divine One?"

"To the earth -- they and all their fellow animals."

"What is the earth?"

"A small globe I made, a time, two times and a half ago. You saw it, but did not notice it in the explosion of worlds and suns that sprayed from my hand. Man is an experiment, the other animals are another experiment. Time will show whether they were worth the trouble. The exhibition is over; you may take your leave, my lords."

Several days passed by.

This stands for a long stretch of (our) time, since in heaven a day is as a thousand years.

Satan had been making admiring remarks about certain of the Creator's sparkling industries -- remarks which, being read between the lines, were sarcasms. He had made them confidentially to his safe friends the other archangels, but they had been overheard by some ordinary angels and reported at Headquarters.

He was ordered into banishment for a day -- the celestial day. It was a punishment he was used to, on account of his too flexible tongue. Formerly he had been deported into Space, there being nowhither else to send him, and had flapped tediously around there in the eternal night and the Arctic chill; but now it occurred to him to push on and hunt up the earth and see how the Human-Race experiment was coming along.

By and by he wrote home -- very privately -- to St. Michael and St. Gabriel about it.

Satan's Letter

This is a strange place, and extraordinary place, and interesting. There is nothing resembling it at home. The people are all insane, the other animals are all insane, the earth is insane, Nature itself is insane. Man is a marvelous curiosity. When he is at his very very best he is a sort of low grade nickel-plated angel; at is worst he is unspeakable, unimaginable; and first and last and all the time he is a sarcasm. Yet he blandly and in all sincerity calls himself the "noblest work of God." This is the truth I am telling you. And this is not a new idea with him, he has talked it through all the ages, and believed it. Believed it, and found nobody among all his race to laugh at it.

Moreover -- if I may put another strain upon you -- he thinks he is the Creator's pet. He believes the Creator is proud of him; he even believes the Creator loves him; has a passion for him; sits up nights to admire him; yes, and watch over him and keep him out of trouble. He prays to Him, and thinks He listens. Isn't it a quaint idea? Fills his prayers with crude and bald and florid flatteries of Him, and thinks He sits and purrs over these extravagancies and enjoys them. He prays for help, and favor, and protection, every day; and does it with hopefulness and confidence, too, although no prayer of his has ever been answered. The daily affront, the daily defeat, do not discourage him, he goes on praying just the same. There is something almost fine about this perseverance. I must put one more strain upon you: he thinks he is going to heaven!

He has salaried teachers who tell him that. They also tell him there is a hell, of everlasting fire, and that he will go to it if he doesn't keep the Commandments. What are Commandments? They are a curiosity. I will tell you about them by and by.

Letter II

"I have told you nothing about man that is not true." You must pardon me if I repeat that remark now and then in these letters; I want you to take seriously the things I am telling you, and I feel that if I were in your place and you in mine, I should need that reminder from time to time, to keep my credulity from flagging.

For there is nothing about man that is not strange to an immortal. He looks at nothing as we look at it, his sense of proportion is quite different from ours, and his sense of values is so widely divergent from ours, that with all our large intellectual powers it is not likely that even the most gifted among us would ever be quite able to understand it.

For instance, take this sample: he has imagined a heaven, and has left entirely out of it the supremest of all his delights, the one ecstasy that stands first and foremost in the heart of every individual of his race -- and of ours -- sexual intercourse!

It is as if a lost and perishing person in a roasting desert should be told by a rescuer he might choose and have all longed-for things but one, and he should elect to leave out water!

His heaven is like himself: strange, interesting, astonishing, grotesque. I give you my word, it has not a single feature in it that he actually values. It consists -- utterly and entirely -- of diversions which he cares next to nothing about, here in the earth, yet is quite sure he will like them in heaven. Isn't it curious? Isn't it interesting? You must not think I am exaggerating, for it is not so. I will give you details.

Most men do not sing, most men cannot sing, most men will not stay when others are singing if it be continued more than two hours. Note that.

Only about two men in a hundred can play upon a musical instrument, and not four in a hundred have any wish to learn how. Set that down.

Many men pray, not many of them like to do it. A few pray long, the others make a short cut.

More men go to church than want to.

To forty-nine men in fifty the Sabbath Day is a dreary, dreary bore.

Of all the men in a church on a Sunday, two-thirds are tired when the service is half over, and the rest before it is finished.

The gladdest moment for all of them is when the preacher uplifts his hands for the benediction. You can hear the soft rustle of relief that sweeps the house, and you recognize that it is eloquent with gratitude.

All nations look down upon all other nations.

All nations dislike all other nations.

All white nations despise all colored nations, of whatever hue, and oppress them when they can.

White men will not associate with "niggers," nor marry them.

They will not allow them in their schools and churches.

All the world hates the Jew, and will not endure him except when he is rich.

I ask you to note all those particulars.

Further. All sane people detest noise.

All people, sane or insane, like to have variety in their life. Monotony quickly wearies them.

Every man, according to the mental equipment that has fallen to his share, exercises his intellect constantly, ceaselessly, and this exercise makes up a vast and valued and essential part of his life. The lowest intellect, like the highest, possesses a skill of some kind and takes a keen pleasure in testing it, proving it, perfecting it. The urchin who is his comrade's superior in games is as diligent and as enthusiastic in his practice as are the sculptor, the painter, the pianist, the mathematician and the rest. Not one of them could be happy if his talent were put under an interdict.

Now then, you have the facts. You know what the human race enjoys, and what it doesn't enjoy. It has invented a heaven out of its own head, all by itself: guess what it is like! In fifteen hundred eternities you couldn't do it. The ablest mind known to you or me in fifty million aeons couldn't do it. Very well, I will tell you about it.

1. First of all, I recall to your attention the extraordinary fact with which I began. To wit, that the human being, like the immortals, naturally places sexual intercourse far and away above all other joys -- yet he has left it out of his heaven! The very thought of it excites him; opportunity sets him wild; in this state he will risk life, reputation, everything -- even his queer heaven itself -- to make good that opportunity and ride it to the overwhelming climax. From youth to middle age all men and all women prize copulation above all other pleasures combined, yet it is actually as I have said: it is not in their heaven; prayer takes its place.

They prize it thus highly; yet, like all their so-called "boons," it is a poor thing. At its very best and longest the act is brief beyond imagination -- the imagination of an immortal, I mean. In the matter of repetition the man is limited -- oh, quite beyond immortal conception. We who continue the act and its supremest ecstasies unbroken and without withdrawal for centuries, will never be able to understand or adequately pity the awful poverty of these people in that rich gift which, possessed as we possess it, makes all other possessions trivial and not worth the trouble of invoicing.

2. In man's heaven everybody sings! The man who did not sing on earth sings there; the man who could not sing on earth is

able to do it there. The universal singing is not casual, not occasional, not relieved by intervals of quiet; it goes on, all day long, and every day, during a stretch of twelve hours. And everybody stays; whereas in the earth the place would be empty in two hours. The singing is of hymns alone. Nay, it is of one hymn alone. The words are always the same, in number they are only about a dozen, there is no rhyme, there is no poetry: "Hosannah, hosannah, hosannah, Lord God of Sabaoth, 'rah! 'rah! 'rah! siss! -- boom! ... a-a-ah!"

3. Meantime, every person is playing on a harp -- those millions and millions! -- whereas not more than twenty in the thousand of them could play an instrument in the earth, or ever wanted to.

Consider the deafening hurricane of sound -- millions and millions of voices screaming at once and millions and millions of harps gritting their teeth at the same time! I ask you: is it hideous, is it odious, is it horrible?

Consider further: it is a praise service; a service of compliment, of flattery, of adulation! Do you ask who it is that is willing to endure this strange compliment, this insane compliment; and who not only endures it, but likes it, enjoys it, requires if, commands it? Hold your breath!

It is God! This race's god, I mean. He sits on his throne, attended by his four and twenty elders and some other dignitaries pertaining to his court, and looks out over his miles and miles of tempestuous worshipers, and smiles, and purrs, and nods his satisfaction northward, eastward, southward; as quaint and nave a spectacle as has yet been imagined in this universe, I take it.

It is easy to see that the inventor of the heavens did not originate the idea, but copied it from the show-ceremonies of some sorry little sovereign State up in the back settlements of the Orient somewhere.

All sane white people hate noise; yet they have tranquilly accepted this kind of heaven -- without thinking, without reflection, without examination -- and they actually want to go to it! Profoundly devout old gray-headed men put in a large part of their time dreaming of the happy day when they will lay down the cares of this life and enter into the joys of that place. Yet you can see how unreal it is to them, and how little it takes a grip upon them as being fact, for they make no practical preparation for the great change: you never see one of them with a harp, you never hear one of them sing.

As you have seen, that singular show is a service of praise: praise by hymn, praise by prostration. It takes the place of "church." Now then, in the earth these people cannot stand much church -- an hour and a quarter is the limit, and they draw the line at once a week. That is to say, Sunday. One day in seven; and even then they do not look forward to it with longing. And so -- consider what their heaven provides for them: "church" that lasts forever, and a Sabbath that has no end! They quickly weary of this brief hebdomadal Sabbath here, yet they long for that eternal one; they dream of it, they talk about it, they think they think they are going to enjoy it -- with all their simple hearts they think they think they are going to be happy in it!

It is because they do not think at all; they only think they think. Whereas they can't think; not two human beings in ten thousand have anything to think with. And as to imagination -- oh, well, look at their heaven! They accept it, they approve it, they admire it. That gives you their intellectual measure.

4. The inventor of their heaven empties into it all the nations of the earth, in one common jumble. All are on an equality absolute, no one of them ranking another; they have to be "brothers"; they have to mix together, pray together, harp together, hosannah together -- whites, niggers, Jews, everybody -- there's no distinction. Here in the earth all nations hate each other, and every one of them hates the Jew. Yet every pious person adores that heaven and wants to get into it. He really does. And when he is in a holy rapture he thinks he thinks that if he were only there he would take all the populace to his heart, and hug, and hug, and hug!

He is a marvel -- man is! I would I knew who invented him.

5. Every man in the earth possesses some share of intellect, large or small; and be it large or be it small he takes pride in it. Also his heart swells at mention of the names of the majestic intellectual chiefs of his race, and he loves the tale of their splendid achievements. For he is of their blood, and in honoring themselves they have honored him. Lo, what the mind of man can do! he cries, and calls the roll of the illustrious of all ages; and points to the imperishable literatures they have given to the world, and the mechanical wonders they have invented, and the glories wherewith they have clothed science and the arts; and to them he uncovers as to kings, and gives to them the profoundest homage, and the sincerest, his exultant heart can furnish -- thus exalting intellect above all things else in the world, and enthroning it there under the arching skies in a supremacy unapproachable. And then he contrived a heaven that hasn't a rag of intellectuality in it anywhere!

Is it odd, is it curious, is it puzzling? It is exactly as I have said, incredible as it may sound. This sincere adorer of intellect and prodigal rewarder of its mighty services here in the earth has invented a religion and a heaven which pay no compliments to intellect, offer it no distinctions, fling it no largess: in fact, never even mention it.

By this time you will have noticed that the human being's heaven has been thought out and constructed upon an absolute definite plan; and that this plan is, that it shall contain, in labored detail, each and every imaginable thing that is repulsive to a man, and not a single thing he likes!

Very well, the further we proceed the more will this curious fact be apparent.

Make a note of it: in man's heaven there are no exercises for the intellect, nothing for it to live upon. It would rot there in a year -- rot and stink. Rot and stink -- and at that stage become holy. A blessed thing: for only the holy can stand the joys of that bedlam.

Letter III

You have noticed that the human being is a curiosity. In times past he has had (and worn out and flung away) hundreds and hundreds of religions; today he has hundreds and hundreds of religions, and launches not fewer than three new ones every year. I could enlarge that number and still be within the facts.

One of his principle religions is called the Christian. A sketch of it will interest you. It sets forth in detail in a book containing two million words, called the Old and New Testaments. Also it has another name -- The Word of God. For the Christian thinks every word of it was dictated by God -- the one I have been speaking of.

It is full of interest. It has noble poetry in it; and some clever fables; and some blood-drenched history; and some good morals; and a wealth of obscenity; and upwards of a thousand lies.

This Bible is built mainly out of the fragments of older Bibles that had their day and crumbled to ruin. So it noticeably lacks in originality, necessarily. Its three or four most imposing and impressive events all happened in earlier Bibles; all its best precepts and rules of conduct came also from those Bibles; there are only two new things in it: hell, for one, and that singular heaven I have told you about.

What shall we do? If we believe, with these people, that their God invented these cruel things, we slander him; if we believe that these people invented them themselves, we slander them. It is an unpleasant dilemma in either case, for neither of these parties has done us any harm.

For the sake of tranquility, let us take a side. Let us join forces with the people and put the whole ungracious burden upon him -- heaven, hell, Bible and all. It does not seem right, it does not seem fair; and yet when you consider that heaven, and how crushingly charged it is with everything that is repulsive to a human being, how can we believe a human being invented it? And when I come to tell you about hell, the stain will be greater still, and you will be likely to say, No, a man would not provide that place, for either himself or anybody else; he simply couldn't.

That innocent Bible tells about the Creation. Of what -- the universe? Yes, the universe. In six days!

God did it. He did not call it the universe -- that name is modern. His whole attention was upon this world. He constructed it in five days -- and then? It took him only one day to make twenty million suns and eighty million planets!

What were they for -- according to this idea? To furnish light for this little toy-world. That was his whole purpose; he had no other. One of the twenty million suns (the smallest one) was to light it in the daytime, the rest were to help one of the universe's countless moons modify the darkness of its nights.

It is quite manifest that he believed his fresh-made skies were diamond-sown with those myriads of twinkling stars the moment his first-day's sun sank below the horizon; whereas, in fact, not a single star winked in that black vault until three years and a half after that memorable week's formidable industries had been completed.[**] then one star appeared, all solitary and alone, and began to blink. Three years later another one appeared. The two blinked together for more than four years before a third joined them. At the end of the first hundred years there were not yet twenty-five stars twinkling in the wide wastes of those gloomy skies. At the end of a thousand years not enough stars were yet visible to make a show. At the end of a million years only half of the present array had sent their light over the telescopic frontiers, and it took another million for the rest to follow suit, as the vulgar phrase goes. There being at that time no telescope, their advent was not observed.

For three hundred years, now, the Christian astronomer has known that his Deity didn't make the stars in those tremendous six days; but the Christian astronomer does not enlarge upon that detail. Neither does the priest.

In his Book, God is eloquent in his praises of his mighty works, and calls them by the largest names he can find -- thus indicating that he has a strong and just admiration of magnitudes; yet he made those millions of prodigious suns to light this wee little orb, instead of appointing this orb's little sun to dance attendance upon them. He mentions Arcturus in his book -- you remember Arcturus; we went there once. It is one of the earth's night lamps! -- that giant globe which is fifty thousand times as large as the earth's sun, and compares with it as a melon compares with a cathedral.

However, the Sunday school still teaches the child that Arcturus was created to help light this earth, and the child grows up and continues to believe it long after he has found out that the probabilities are against it being so.

According to the Book and its servants the universe is only six thousand years old. It is only within the last hundred years that studious, inquiring minds have found out that it is nearer a hundred million.

During the Six Days, God created man and the other animals.

He made a man and a woman and placed them in a pleasant garden, along with the other creatures. they all lived together there in harmony and contentment and blooming youth for some time; then trouble came. God had warned the man and the woman that they must not eat of the fruit of a certain tree. And he added a most strange remark: he said that if they ate of it they should surely die. Strange, for the reason that inasmuch as they had never seen a sample death they could not possibly know what he meant. Neither would he nor any other god have been able to make those ignorant children understand what was meant, without furnishing a sample. The mere word could have no meaning for them, any more than it would have for an infant of days.

Presently a serpent sought them out privately, and came to them walking upright, which was the way of serpents in those days. The serpent said the forbidden fruit would store their vacant minds with knowledge. So they ate it, which was quite natural, for man is so made that he eagerly wants to know; whereas the priest, like God, whose imitator and representative he is, has made it his business from the beginning to keep him from knowing any useful thing.

Adam and Eve ate the forbidden fruit, and at once a great light streamed into their dim heads. They had acquired knowledge. What knowledge -- useful knowledge? No -- merely knowledge that there was such a thing as good, and such a thing as evil, and how to do evil. they couldn't do it before. Therefore all their acts up to this time had been without stain, without blame, without offense.

But now they could do evil -- and suffer for it; now they had acquired what the Church calls an invaluable possession, the Moral Sense; that sense which differentiates man from the beast and sets him above the beast. Instead of below the beast -- where one would suppose his proper place would be, since he is always foul-minded and guilty and the beast always clean-minded and innocent. It is like valuing a watch that must go wrong, above a watch that can't.

The Church still prizes the Moral Sense as man's noblest asset today, although the Church knows God had a distinctly poor opinion of it and did what he could in his clumsy way to keep his happy Children of the Garden from acquiring it.

Very well, Adam and Eve now knew what evil was, and how to do it. They knew how to do various kinds of wrong things, and among them one principal one -- the one God had his mind on principally. That one was the art and mystery of sexual intercourse. To them it was a magnificent discovery, and they stopped idling around and turned their entire attention to it, poor exultant young things!

In the midst of one of these celebrations they heard God walking among the bushes, which was an afternoon custom of his, and they were smitten with fright. Why? Because they were naked. They had not known it before. They had not minded it before; neither had God.

In that memorable moment immodesty was born; and some people have valued it ever since, though it would certainly puzzle them to explain why.

Adam and Eve entered the world naked and unashamed -- naked and pure-minded; and no descendant of theirs has ever entered it otherwise. All have entered it naked, unashamed, and clean in mind. They have entered it modest. They had to acquire immodesty and the soiled mind; there was no other way to get it. A Christian mother's first duty is to soil her child's mind, and she does not neglect it. Her lad grows up to be a missionary, and goes to the innocent savage and to the civilized Japanese, and soils their minds. Whereupon they adopt immodesty, they conceal their bodies, they stop bathing naked together.

The convention miscalled modesty has no standard, and cannot have one, because it is opposed to nature and reason, and is therefore an artificiality and subject to anybody's whim, anybody's diseased caprice. And so, in India the refined lady covers her face and breasts and leaves her legs naked from the hips down, while the refined European lady covers her legs and exposes her face and her breasts. In lands inhabited by the innocent savage the refined European lady soon gets used to full-grown native stark-nakedness, and ceases to be offended by it. A highly cultivated French count and countess -- unrelated to each other -- who were marooned in their nightclothes, by shipwreck, upon an uninhabited island in the eighteenth century, were soon naked. Also ashamed -- for a week. After that their nakedness did not trouble them, and they soon ceased to think about it.

You have never seen a person with clothes on. Oh, well, you haven't lost anything.

To proceed with the Biblical curiosities. Naturally you will think the threat to punish Adam and Eve for disobeying was of course not carried out, since they did not create themselves, nor their natures nor their impulses nor their weaknesses, and hence were not properly subject to anyone's commands, and not responsible to anybody for their acts. It will surprise you to know that the threat was carried out. Adam and Eve were punished, and that crime finds apologists unto this day. The sentence of death was executed.

As you perceive, the only person responsible for the couple's offense escaped; and not only escaped but became the executioner of the innocent.

In your country and mine we should have the privilege of making fun of this kind of morality, but it would be unkind to do it here. Many of these people have the reasoning faculty, but no one uses it in religious matters.

The best minds will tell you that when a man has begotten a child he is morally bound to tenderly care for it, protect it from hurt, shield it from disease, clothe it, feed it, bear with its waywardness, lay no hand upon it save in kindness and for its own good, and never in any case inflict upon it a wanton cruelty. God's treatment of his earthly children, every day and every night, is the exact opposite of all that, yet those best minds warmly justify these crimes, condone them, excuse them, and indignantly refuse to regard them as crimes at all, when he commits them. Your country and mine is an interesting one, but there is nothing there that is half so interesting as the human mind.

Very well, God banished Adam and Eve from the Garden, and eventually assassinated them. All for disobeying a command which he had no right to utter. But he did not stop there, as you will see. He has one code of morals for himself, and quite another for his children. He requires his children to deal justly -- and gently -- with offenders, and forgive them seventy-and-seven times; whereas he deals neither justly nor gently with anyone, and he did not forgive the ignorant and thoughtless first pair of juveniles even their first small offense and say, "You may go free this time, and I will give you another chance."

On the contrary! He elected to punish their children, all through the ages to the end of time, for a trifling offense committed by others before they were born. He is punishing them yet. In mild ways? No, in atrocious ones.

You would not suppose that this kind of Being gets many compliments. Undeceive yourself: the world calls him the All-Just, the All-Righteous, the All-Good, the All-Merciful, the All-Forgiving, the All-Truthful, the All-Loving, the Source of All Morality. These sarcasms are uttered daily, all over the world. But not as conscious sarcasms. No, they are meant seriously: they are uttered without a smile.

Letter IV

So the First Pair went forth from the Garden under a curse -- a permanent one. They had lost every pleasure they had possessed before "The Fall"; and yet they were rich, for they had gained one worth all the rest: they knew the Supreme Art.

They practiced it diligently and were filled with contentment. The Deity ordered them to practice it. They obeyed, this time. But it was just as well it was not forbidden, for they would have practiced it anyhow, if a thousand Deities had forbidden it.

Results followed. By the name of Cain and Abel. And these had some sisters; and knew what to do with them. And so there were some more results: Cain and Abel begot some nephews and nieces. These, in their turn, begot some second cousins. At this point classification of relationships began to get difficult, and the attempt to keep it up was abandoned.

The pleasant labor of populating the world went on from age to age, and with prime efficiency; for in those happy days the sexes were still competent for the Supreme Art when by rights they ought to have been dead eight hundred years. The sweeter sex, the dearer sex, the lovelier sex was manifestly at its very best, then, for it was even able to attract gods. Real gods. They came down out of heaven and had wonderful times with those hot young blossoms. The Bible tells about it.

By help of those visiting foreigners the population grew and grew until it numbered several millions. But it was a disappointment to the Deity. He was dissatisfied with its morals; which in some respects were not any better than his own. Indeed they were an unflatteringly close imitation of his own. They were a very bad people, and as he knew of no way to reform them, he wisely concluded to abolish them. This is the only really enlightened and superior idea his Bible has credited him with, and it would have made his reputation for all time if he could only have kept to it and carried it out. But he was always unstable -- except in his advertisements -- and his good resolution broke down. He took a pride in man; man was his finest invention; man was his pet, after the housefly, and he could not bear to lose him wholly; so he finally decided to save a sample of him and drown the rest.

Nothing could be more characteristic of him. He created all those infamous people, and he alone was responsible for their conduct. Not one of them deserved death, yet it was certainly good policy to extinguish them; especially since in creating them the master crime had already been committed, and to allow them to go on procreating would be a distinct addition to the crime. But at the same time there could be no justice, no fairness, in any favoritism -- all should be drowned or none.

No, he would not have it so; he would save half a dozen and try the race over again. He was not able to foresee that it would go rotten again, for he is only the Far-Sighted One in his advertisements.

He saved out Noah and his family, and arranged to exterminate the rest. He planned an Ark, and Noah built it. Neither of them had ever built an Ark before, nor knew anything about Arks; and so something out of the common was to be expected. It happened. Noah was a farmer, and although he knew what was required of the Ark he was quite incompetent to say whether this one would be large enough to meet the requirements or not (which it wasn't), so he ventured no advice. The Deity did not know it wasn't large enough, but took the chances and made no adequate measurements. In the end the ship fell far short of the necessities, and to this day the world still suffers for it.

Noah built the Ark. He built it the best he could, but left out most of the essentials. It had no rudder, it had no sails, it had no compass, it had no pumps, it had no charts, no lead-lines, no anchors, no log, no light, no ventilation, and as for cargo room -- which was the main thing -- the less said about that the better. It was to be at sea eleven months, and would need fresh water enough to fill two Arks of its size -- yet the additional Ark was not provided. Water from outside could not be utilized: half of it would be salt water, and men and land animals could not drink it.

For not only was a sample of man to be saved, but business samples of the other animals, too. You must understand that when Adam ate the apple in the Garden and learned how to multiply and replenish, the other animals learned the Art, too, by watching Adam. It was cunning of them, it was neat; for they got all that was worth having out of the apple without tasting it and afflicting themselves with the disastrous Moral Sense, the parent of all immoralities.

Letter V

Noah began to collect animals. There was to be one couple of each and every sort of creature that walked or crawled, or swam or flew, in the world of animated nature. We have to guess at how long it took to collect the creatures and how much it cost, for there is no record of these details. When Symmachus made preparation to introduce his young son to grown-up life in imperial Rome, he sent men to Asia, Africa and everywhere to collect wild animals for the arena-fights. It took the men three years to accumulate the animals and fetch them to Rome. Merely quadrupeds and alligators, you understand -- no birds, no snakes, no frogs, no worms, no lice, no rats, no fleas, no ticks, no caterpillars, no spiders, no houseflies, no mosquitoes --

nothing but just plain simple quadrupeds and alligators: and no quadrupeds except fighting ones. Yet it was as I have said: it took three years to collect them, and the cost of animals and transportation and the men's wages footed up $4,500,000.

How many animals? We do not know. But it was under five thousand, for that was the largest number ever gathered for those Roman shows, and it was Titus, not Symmachus, who made that collection. Those were mere baby museums, compared to Noah's contract. Of birds and beasts and fresh-water creatures he had to collect 146,000 kinds; and of insects upwards of two million species.

Thousands and thousands of those things are very difficult to catch, and if Noah had not given up and resigned, he would be on the job yet, as Leviticus used to say. However, I do not mean that he withdrew. No, he did not do that. He gathered as many creatures as he had room for, and then stopped.

If he had known all the requirements in the beginning, he would have been aware that what was needed was a fleet of Arks. But he did not know how many kinds of creatures there were, neither did his Chief. So he had no Kangaroo, and no 'possom, and no Gila monster, and no ornithorhynchus, and lacked a multitude of other indispensable blessings which a loving Creator had provided for man and forgotten about, they having long ago wandered to a side of this world which he had never seen and with whose affairs he was not acquainted. And so everyone of them came within a hair of getting drowned.

They only escaped by an accident. There was not water enough to go around. Only enough was provided to flood one small corner of the globe -- the rest of the globe was not then known, and was supposed to be nonexistent.

However, the thing that really and finally and definitely determined Noah to stop with enough species for purely business purposes and let the rest become extinct, was an incident of the last days: an excited stranger arrived with some most alarming news. He said he had been camping among some mountains and valleys about six hundred miles away, and he had seen a wonderful thing there: he stood upon a precipice overlooking a wide valley, and up the valley he was a billowy black sea of strange animal life coming. Presently the creatures passed by, struggling, fighting, scrambling, screeching, snorting -- horrible vast masses of tumultuous flesh! Sloths as big as an elephant; frogs as big as a cow; a megatherium and his harem huge beyond belief; saurians and saurians and saurians, group after group, family after family, species after species -- a hundred feet long, thirty feet high, and twice as quarrelsome; one of them hit a perfectly blameless Durham bull a thump with its tail and sent it whizzing three hundred feet into the air and it fell at the man's feet with a sigh and was no more. The man said that these prodigious animals had heard about the Ark and were coming. Coming to get saved from the flood. And not coming in pairs, they were all coming: they did not know the passengers were restricted to pairs, the man said, and wouldn't care a rap for the regulations, anyway -- they would sail in that Ark or know the reason why. The man said the Ark would not hold the half of them; and moreover they were coming hungry, and would eat up everything there was, including the menagerie and the family.

All these facts were suppressed, in the Biblical account. You find not a hint of them there. The whole thing is hushed up. Not even the names of those vast creatures are mentioned. It shows you that when people have left a reproachful vacancy in a contract they can be as shady about it in Bibles as elsewhere. Those powerful animals would be of inestimable value to man now, when transportation is so hard pressed and expensive, but they are all lost to him. All lost, and by Noah's fault. They all got drowned. Some of them as much as eight million years ago.

Very well, the stranger told his tale, and Noah saw that he must get away before the monsters arrived. He would have sailed at once, but the upholsterers and decorators of the housefly's drawing room still had some finishing touches to put on, and that lost him a day. Another day was lost in getting the flies aboard, there being sixty-eight billions of them and the Deity still afraid there might not be enough. Another day was lost in stowing forty tons of selected filth for the flies' sustenance.

Then at last, Noah sailed; and none too soon, for the Ark was only just sinking out of sight on the horizon when the monsters arrived, and added their lamentations to those of the multitude of weeping fathers and mothers and frightened little children who were clinging to the wave-washed rocks in the pouring rain and lifting imploring prayers to an All-Just and All-Forgiving and All-Pitying Being who had never answered a prayer since those crags were builded, grain by grain, out of the sands, and would still not have answered one when the ages should have crumbled them to sand again.

Letter VI

On the third day, about noon, it was found that a fly and been left behind. The return voyage turned out to be long and difficult, on account of the lack of chart and compass, and because of the changed aspects of all coasts, the steadily rising water having submerged some of the lower landmarks and given to higher ones an unfamiliar look; but after sixteen days of earnest and faithful seeking, the fly was found at last, and received on board with hymns of praise and gratitude, the

Family standing meanwhile uncovered, our of reverence for its divine origin. It was weary and worn, and had suffered somewhat from the weather, but was otherwise in good estate. Men and their families had died of hunger on barren mountain tops, but it had not lacked for food, the multitudinous corpses furnishing it in rank and rotten richness. Thus was the sacred bird providentially preserved.

Providentially. That is the word. For the fly had not been left behind by accident. No, the hand of Providence was in it. There are no accidents. All things that happen, happen for a purpose. They are foreseen from the beginning of time, they are ordained from the beginning of time. From the dawn of Creation the Lord had foreseen that Noah, being alarmed and confused by the invasion of the prodigious brevet fossils, would prematurely fly to sea unprovided with a certain invaluable disease. He would have all the other diseases, and could distribute them among the new races of men as they appeared in the world, but he would lack one of the very best -- typhoid fever; a malady which, when the circumstances are especially favorable, is able to utterly wreck a patient without killing him; for it can restore him to his feet with a long life in him, and yet deaf, dumb, blind, crippled, and idiotic. The housefly is its main disseminator, and is more competent and more calamitously effective than all the other distributors of the dreaded scourge put together. And so, by foreordination from the beginning of time, this fly was left behind to seek out a typhoid corpse and feed upon its corruptions and gaum its legs with germs and transmit them to the re-peopled world for permanent business. From that one housefly, in the ages that have since elapsed, billions of sickbeds have been stocked, billions of wrecked bodies sent tottering about the earth, and billions of cemeteries recruited with the dead.

It is most difficult to understand the disposition of the Bible God, it is such a confusion of contradictions; of watery instabilities and iron firmness; of goody-goody abstract morals made out of words, and concreted hell-born ones made out of acts; of fleeting kindness repented of in permanent malignities.

However, when after much puzzling you get at the key to his disposition, you do at last arrive at a sort of understanding of it. With a most quaint and juvenile and astonishing frankness he has furnished that key himself. It is jealousy!

I expect that to take your breath away. You are aware -- for I have already told you in an earlier letter -- that among human beings jealousy ranks distinctly as a weakness; a trade-mark of small minds; a property of all small minds, yet a property which even the smallest is ashamed of; and when accused of its possession will lyingly deny it and resent the accusation as an insult.

Jealousy. Do not forget it, keep it in mind. It is the key. With it you will come to partly understand God as we go along; without it nobody can understand him. As I have said, he has openly held up this treasonous key himself, for all to see. He says, naïvely, outspokenly, and without suggestion of embarrassment: "I the Lord thy God am a jealous God."

You see, it is only another way of saying, "I the Lord thy God am a small God; a small God, and fretful about small things."

He was giving a warning: he could not bear the thought of any other God getting some of the Sunday compliments of this comical little human race -- he wanted all of them for himself. He valued them. To him they were riches; just as tin money is to a Zulu.

But wait -- I am not fair; I am misrepresenting him; prejudice is beguiling me into saying what is not true. He did not say he wanted all of the adulations; he said nothing about not being willing to share them with his fellow gods; what he said was, "Thou shalt have no other gods before me."

It is a quite different thing, and puts him in a much better light -- I confess it. There was an abundance of gods, the woods were full of them, as the saying is, and all he demanded was that he should be ranked as high as the others -- not above any of them, but not below any of them. He was willing that they should fertilize earthly virgins, but not on any better terms than he could have for himself in his turn. He wanted to be held their equal. This he insisted upon, in the clearest language: he would have no other gods before him. They could march abreast with him, but none of them could head the procession, and he did not claim the right to head it himself.

Do you think he was able to stick to that upright and creditable position? No. He could keep to a bad resolution forever, but he couldn't keep to a good one a month. By and by he threw aside and calmly claimed to be the only God in the entire universe.

As I was saying, jealousy is the key; all through his history it is present and prominent. It is the blood and bone of his disposition, it is the basis of his character. How small a thing can wreck his composure and disorder his judgement if it touches the raw of his jealousy! And nothing warms up this trait so quickly and so surely and so exaggeratedly as a suspicion that some competition with the god-Trust is impending. The fear that if Adam and Eve ate of the fruit of the Tree of Knowledge they would "be as gods" so fired his jealousy that his reason was affected, and he could not treat those poor creatures either fairly or charitably, or even refrain from dealing cruelly and criminally with their blameless posterity.

To this day his reason has never recovered from that shock; a wild nightmare of vengefulness has possessed him ever since, and he has almost bankrupted his native ingenuities in inventing pains and miseries and humiliations and heartbreaks wherewith to embitter the brief lives of Adam's descendants. Think of the diseases he has contrived for them! They are multitudinous; no book can name them all. And each one is a trap, set for an innocent victim.

The human being is a machine. An automatic machine. It is composed of thousands of complex and delicate mechanisms, which perform their functions harmoniously and perfectly, in accordance with laws devised for their governance, and over which the man himself has no authority, no mastership, no control. For each one of these thousands of mechanisms the Creator has planned an enemy, whose office is to harass it, pester it, persecute it, damage it, afflict it with pains, and miseries, and ultimate destruction. Not one has been overlooked.

From cradle to grave these enemies are always at work; they know no rest, night or day. They are an army: an organized army; a besieging army; an assaulting army; an army that is alert, watchful, eager, merciless; an army that never relents, never grants a truce.

It moves by squad, by company, by battalion, by regiment, by brigade, by division, by army corps; upon occasion it masses its parts and moves upon mankind with its whole strength. It is the Creator's Grand Army, and he is the Commander-in-Chief. Along its battlefront its grisly banners wave their legends in the face of the sun: Disaster, Disease, and the rest.

Disease! That is the main force, the diligent force, the devastating force! It attacks the infant the moment it is born; it furnishes it one malady after another: croup, measles, mumps, bowel troubles, teething pains, scarlet fever, and other childhood specialties. It chases the child into youth and furnishes it some specialties for that time of life. It chases the youth into maturity, maturity into age, age into the grave.

With these facts before you will you now try to guess man's chiefest pet name for this ferocious Commander-in-Chief? I will save you the trouble -- but you must not laugh. It is Our Father in Heaven!

It is curious -- the way the human mind works. The Christian begins with this straight proposition, this definite proposition, this inflexible and uncompromising proposition: God is all-knowing, and all-powerful.

This being the case, nothing can happen without his knowing beforehand that it is going to happen; nothing happens without his permission; nothing can happen that he chooses to prevent.

That is definite enough, isn't it? It makes the Creator distinctly responsible for everything that happens, doesn't it?

The Christian concedes it in that italicized sentence. Concedes it with feeling, with enthusiasm.

Then, having thus made the Creator responsible for all those pains and diseases and miseries above enumerated, and which he could have prevented, the gifted Christian blandly calls him Our Father!

It is as I tell you. He equips the Creator with every trait that goes to the making of a fiend, and then arrives at the conclusion that a fiend and a father are the same thing! Yet he would deny that a malevolent lunatic and a Sunday school superintendent are essentially the same. What do you think of the human mind? I mean, in case you think there is a human mind.

Letter VII

Noah and his family were saved -- if that could be called an advantage. I throw in the if for the reason that there has never been an intelligent person of the age of sixty who would consent to live his life over again. His or anyone else's. The Family were saved, yes, but they were not comfortable, for they were full of microbes. Full to the eyebrows; fat with them, obese with them, distended like balloons. It was a disagreeable condition, but it could not be helped, because enough microbes had to be saved to supply the future races of men with desolating diseases, and there were but eight persons on board to serve as hotels for them. The microbes were by far the most important part of the Ark's cargo, and the part the Creator was most anxious about and most infatuated with. They had to have good nourishment and pleasant accommodations. There were typhoid germs, and cholera germs, and hydrophobia germs, and lockjaw germs, and consumption germs, and black-plague germs, and some hundreds of other aristocrats, specially precious creations, golden bearers of God's love to man, blessed gifts of the infatuated Father to his children -- all of which had to be sumptuously housed and richly entertained; these were located in the choicest places the interiors of the Family could furnish: in the lungs, in the heart, in the brain, in the kidneys, in the blood, in the guts. In the guts particularly. The great intestine was the favorite resort. There they gathered, by countless billions, and worked, and fed, and squirmed, and sang hymns of praise and thanksgiving; and at night when it was quiet you could hear the soft murmur of it. The large intestine was in effect their heaven. They stuffed it solid; they made it as rigid as a coil of gaspipe. They took pride in this. Their principal hymn made gratified reference to it:

> Constipation, O Constipation,
> The Joyful sound proclaim
> Till man's remotest entrail
> Shall praise its Maker's name

The discomforts furnished by the Ark were many and various. The family had to live right in the presence of the multitudinous animals, and breathe the distressing stench they make and be deafened day and night with the thunder-crash of noise their roarings and screechings produced; and in additions to these intolerable discomforts it was a peculiarly trying place for the ladies, for they could look in no direction without seeing some thousands of the creatures engaged in multiplying and replenishing. And then, there were the flies. They swarmed everywhere, and persecuted the Family all day long. They were the first animals up, in the morning, and the last ones down, at night. But they must not be killed, they must not be injured, they were sacred, their origin was divine, they were the special pets of the Creator, his darlings.

By and by the other creatures would be distributed here and there about the earth -- scattered: the tigers to India, the lions and the elephants to the vacant desert and the secret places of the jungle, the birds to the boundless regions of empty space, the insects to one or another climate, according to nature and requirement; but the fly? He is of no nationality; all the climates are his home, all the globe is his province, all creatures that breathe are his prey, and unto them all he is a scourge and a hell.

To man he is a divine ambassador, a minister plenipotentiary, the Creator's special representative. He infests him in his cradle; clings in bunches to his gummy eyelids; buzzes and bites and harries him, robbing him of his sleep and his weary mother of her strength in those long vigils which she devotes to protecting her child from this pest's persecutions. The fly harries the sick man in his home, in the hospital, even on his deathbed at his last gasp. Pesters him at his meals; previously hunts up patients suffering from loathsome and deadly diseases; wades in their sores, gaums its legs with a million death-dealing germs; then comes to that healthy man's table and wipes these things off on the butter and discharges a bowel-load of typhoid germs and excrement on his batter-cakes. The housefly wrecks more human constitutions and destroys more human lives than all God's multitude of misery-messengers and death-agents put together.

Shem was full of hookworms. It is wonderful, the thorough and comprehensive study which the Creator devoted to the great work of making man miserable. I have said he devised a special affliction-agent for each and every detail of man's structure, overlooking not a single one, and I said the truth. Many poor people have to go barefoot, because they cannot afford shoes. The Creator saw his opportunity. I will remark, in passing, that he always has his eye on the poor. Nine-tenths of his disease-inventions were intended for the poor, and they get them. The well-to-do get only what is left over. Do not suspect me of speaking unheedfully, for it is not so: the vast bulk of the Creator's affliction-inventions are specially designed for the persecution of the poor. You could guess this by the fact that one of the pulpit's finest and commonest names for the Creator is "The Friend of the Poor." Under no circumstances does the pulpit ever pay the Creator a compliment that has a vestige of truth in it. The poor's most implacable and unwearying enemy is their Father in Heaven. The poor's only real friend is their fellow man. He is sorry for them, he pities them, and he shows it by his deeds. He does much to relieve their distresses; and in every case their Father in Heaven gets the credit of it.

Just so with diseases. If science exterminates a disease which has been working for God, it is God that gets the credit, and all the pulpits break into grateful advertising-raptures and call attention to how good he is! Yes, he has done it. Perhaps he has waited a thousand years before doing it. That is nothing; the pulpit says he was thinking about it all the time. When exasperated men rise up and sweep away an age-long tyranny and set a nation free, the first thing the delighted pulpit does is to advertise it as God's work, and invite the people to get down on their knees and pour out their thanks to him for it. And the pulpit says with admiring emotion, "Let tyrants understand that the Eye that never sleeps is upon them; and let them remember that the Lord our God will not always be patient, but will loose the whirlwinds of his wrath upon them in his appointed day."

They forget to mention that he is the slowest mover in the universe; that his Eye that never sleeps, might as well, since it takes it a century to see what any other eye would see in a week; that in all history there is not an instance where he thought of a noble deed first, but always thought of it just a little after somebody else had thought of it and done it. He arrives then, and annexes the dividend.

Very well, six thousand years ago Shem was full of hookworms. Microscopic in size, invisible to the unaided eye. All of the Creator's specially deadly disease-producers are invisible. It is an ingenious idea. For thousands of years it kept man from getting at the roots of his maladies, and defeated his attempts to master them. It is only very recently that science has succeeded in exposing some of these treacheries.

The very latest of these blessed triumphs of science is the discovery and identification of the ambuscaded assassin which goes by the name of the hookworm. Its special prey is the barefooted poor. It lies in wait in warm regions and sandy places and digs its way into their unprotected feet.

The hookworm was discovered two or three years ago by a physician, who had been patiently studying its victims for a long time. The disease induced by the hookworm had been doing its evil work here and there in the earth ever since Shem landed on Ararat, but it was never suspected to be a disease at all. The people who had it were merely supposed to be lazy, and were therefore despised and made fun of, when they should have been pitied. The hookworm is a peculiarly sneaking and underhanded invention, and has done its surreptitious work unmolested for ages; but that physician and his helpers will exterminate it now.

God is back of this. He has been thinking about it for six thousand years, and making up his mind. The idea of exterminating the hookworm was his. He came very near doing it before Dr. Charles Wardell Stiles did. But he is in time to get the credit of it. He always is.

It is going to cost a million dollars. He was probably just in the act of contributing that sum when a man pushed in ahead of him -- as usual. Mr. Rockefeller. He furnishes the million, but the credit will go elsewhere -- as usual. This morning's journal tells us something about the hookworm's operations:

The hookworm parasites often so lower the vitality of those who are affected as to retard their physical and mental development, render them more susceptible to other diseases, make labor less efficient, and in the sections where the malady is most prevalent greatly increase the death rate from consumption, pneumonia, typhoid fever and malaria. It has been shown that the lowered vitality of multitudes, long attributed to malaria and climate and seriously affecting economic development, is in fact due in some districts to this parasite. The disease is by no means confined to any one class; it takes its toll of suffering and death from the highly intelligent and well to do as well as from the less fortunate. It is a conservative estimate that two millions of our people are affected by this parasite. The disease is more common and more serious in children of school age than in other persons.

Widespread and serious as the infection is, there is still a most encouraging outlook. The disease can be easily recognized, readily and effectively treated and by simple and proper sanitary precautions successfully prevented [with God's help].

The poor children are under the Eye that never sleeps, you see. They have had that ill luck in all the ages. They and "the Lord's poor" -- as the sarcastic phrase goes -- have never been able to get away from that Eye's attentions.

Yes, the poor, the humble, the ignorant -- they are the ones that catch it. Take the "Sleeping Sickness," of Africa. This atrocious cruelty has for its victims a race of ignorant and unoffending blacks whom God placed in a remote wilderness, and bent his parental Eye upon them -- the one that never sleeps when there is a chance to breed sorrow for somebody. He arranged for these people before the Flood. The chosen agent was a fly, related to the tsetse; the tsetse is a fly which has command of the Zambezi country and stings cattle and horses to death, thus rendering that region uninhabitable by man. The tsetse's awful relative deposits a microbe which produces the Sleeping Sickness. Ham was full of these microbes, and when the voyage was over he discharged them in Africa and the havoc began, never to find amelioration until six thousand years should go by and science should pry into the mystery and hunt out the cause of the disease. The pious nations are now thanking God, and praising him for coming to the rescue of his poor blacks. The pulpit says the praise is due to him. He is surely a curious Being. He commits a fearful crime, continues that crime unbroken for six thousand years, and is then entitled to praise because he suggests to somebody else to modify its severities. He is called patient, and he certainly must be patient, or he would have sunk the pulpit in perdition ages ago for the ghastly compliments it pays him.

Science has this to say about the Sleeping Sickness, otherwise called the Negro Lethargy:

It is characterized by periods of sleep recurring at intervals. The disease lasts from four months to four years, and is always fatal. The victim appears at first languid, weak, pallid, and stupid. His eyelids become puffy, an eruption appears on his skin. He falls asleep while talking, eating, or working. As the disease progresses he is fed with difficulty and becomes much emaciated. The failure of nutrition and the appearance of bedsores are followed by convulsions and death. Some patients become insane.

It is he whom Church and people call Our Father in Heaven who has invented the fly and sent him to inflict this dreary long misery and melancholy and wretchedness, and decay of body and mind, upon a poor savage who has done that Great Criminal no harm. There isn't a man in the world who doesn't pity that poor black sufferer, and there isn't a man that wouldn't make him whole if he could. To find the one person who has no pity for him you must go to heaven; to find the one person who is able to heal him and couldn't be persuaded to do it, you must go to the same place. There is only one father cruel enough to afflict his child with that horrible disease -- only one. Not all the eternities can produce another one. Do you like reproachful poetical indignations warmly expressed? Here is one, hot from the heart of a slave:

> Man's inhumanity to man
> Makes countless thousands mourn!

I will tell you a pleasant tale which has in it a touch of pathos. A man got religion, and asked the priest what he must do to be worthy of his new estate. The priest said, "Imitate our Father in Heaven, learn to be like him." The man studied his Bible diligently and thoroughly and understandingly, and then with prayers for heavenly guidance instituted his imitations. He tricked his wife into falling downstairs, and she broke her back and became a paralytic for life; he betrayed his brother into the hands of a sharper, who robbed him of his all and landed him in the almshouse; he inoculated one son with hookworms, another with the sleeping sickness, another with gonorrhea; he furnished one daughter with scarlet fever and ushered her into her teens deaf, dumb, and blind for life; and after helping a rascal seduce the remaining one, he closed his doors against her and she died in a brothel cursing him. Then he reported to the priest, who said that that was no way to imitate his Father in Heaven. The convert asked wherein he had failed, but the priest changed the subject and inquired what kind of weather he was having, up his way.

Letter VIII

Man is without any doubt the most interesting fool there is. Also the most eccentric. He hasn't a single written law, in his Bible or out of it, which has any but just one purpose and intention -- to limit or defeat the law of God.

He can seldom take a plain fact and get any but a wrong meaning out of it. He cannot help this; it is the way the confusion he calls his mind is constructed. Consider the things he concedes, and the curious conclusions he draws from them.

For instance, he concedes that God made man. Made him without man's desire of privity.

This seems to plainly and indisputably make God, and God alone, responsible for man's acts. But man denies this.

He concedes that God has made the angels perfect, without blemish, and immune from pain and death, and that he could have been similarly kind to man if he had wanted to, but denies that he was under any moral obligation to do it.

He concedes that man has no moral right to visit the child of his begetting with wanton cruelties, painful diseases and death, but refuses to limit God's privileges in this sort with the children of his begetting.

The Bible and man's statutes forbid murder, adultery, fornication, lying, treachery, robbery, oppression and other crimes, but contend that God is free of these laws and has a right to break them when he will.

He concedes that God gives to each man his temperament, his disposition, at birth; he concedes that man cannot by any process change this temperament, but must remain always under its dominion. Yet if it be full of dreadful passions, in one man's case, and barren of them in another man's, it is right and rational to punish the one for his crimes, and reward the other for abstaining from crime.

There -- let us consider these curiosities.

Temperament (Disposition)

Take two extremes of temperament -- the goat and the tortoise.

Neither of these creatures makes its own temperament, but is born with it, like man, and can no more change it than can man.

Temperament is the law of God written in the heart of every creature by God's own hand, and must be obeyed, and will be obeyed in spite of all restricting or forbidding statutes, let them emanate whence they may.

Very well, lust is the dominant feature of the goat's tempera-ment, the law of God is in its heart, and it must obey it and will obey it the whole day long in the rutting season, without stopping to eat or drink. If the Bible said to the goat, "Thou shalt not fornicate, thou shalt not commit adultery," even Man -- sap-headed man -- would recognize the foolishness of the prohibi-tion, and would grant that the goat ought not to be punished for obeying the law of his Maker. Yet he thinks it right and just that man should be put under the prohibition. All men. All alike.

On its face this is stupid, for, by temperament, which is the real law of God, many men are goats and can't help committing adultery when they get a chance; whereas there are numbers of men who, by temperament, can keep their purity and let an opportunity go by if the woman lacks in attractiveness. But the Bible doesn't allow adultery at all, whether a person can help it or not. It allows no distinction between goat and tortoise -- the excitable goat, the emotional goat, that has to have some adultery every day or fade and die; and the tortoise, that cold calm puritan, that takes a treat only once in two years and then goes to sleep in the midst of it and doesn't wake up for sixty days. No lady goat is safe from criminal assault, even on the Sabbath Day, when there is a gentleman goat within three miles to leeward of her and nothing in the way but a fence fourteen feet high, whereas neither the gentleman tortoise nor the lady tortoise is ever hungry enough for solemn joys of fornication to be willing to break the Sabbath to get them. Now according to man's curious reasoning, the goat has earned punishment, and the tortoise praise.

"Thou shalt not commit adultery" is a command which makes no distinction between the following persons. They are all required to obey it:

Children at birth.

Children in the cradle.

School children.

Youths and maidens.

Fresh adults.

Older ones.

Men and women of 40.

Of 50.

Of 60.

Of 70.

Of 80.

Of 90.

Of 100.

The command does not distribute its burden equally, and cannot.

It is not hard upon the three sets of children.

It is hard -- harder -- still harder upon the next three sets -- cruelly hard.

It is blessedly softened to the next three sets.

It has now done all the damage it can, and might as well be put out of commission. Yet with comical imbecility it is continued, and the four remaining estates are put under its crushing ban. Poor old wrecks, they couldn't disobey if they tried. And think -- because they holily refrain from adulterating each other, they get praise for it! Which is nonsense; for even the Bible knows enough to know that if the oldest veteran there could get his lost heyday back again for an hour he would cast that commandment to the winds and ruin the first woman he came across, even though she were an entire stranger.

It is as I have said: every statute in the Bible and in the law-books is an attempt to defeat a law of God -- in other words an unalterable and indestructible law of nature. These people's God has shown them by a million acts that he respects none of the Bible's statutes. He breaks every one of the himself, adultery and all.

The law of God, as quite plainly expressed in woman's construction is this: There shall be no limit put upon your intercourse with the other sex sexually, at any time of life.

The law of God, as quite plainly expressed in man's construction is this: During your entire life you shall be under inflexible limits and restrictions, sexually.

During twenty-three days in every month (in absence of pregnancy) from the time a woman is seven years old till she dies of old age, she is ready for action, and competent. As competent as the candlestick is to receive the candle. Competent every day, competent every night. Also she wants that candle -- yearns for it, longs for it, hankers after it, as commanded by the law of God in her heart.

But man is only briefly competent; and only then in the moderate measure applicable to the word in his sex's case. He is competent from the age of sixteen or seventeen thenceforward for thirty-five years. After fifty his performance is of poor quality, the intervals between are wide, and its satisfactions of no great value to either party; whereas his greatgrandmother is as good as new. There is nothing the matter with her plant. Her candlestick is as firm as ever, whereas his candle is increasingly softened and weakened by the weather of age, as the years go by, until at last it can no longer stand, and is mournfully laid to rest in the hope of a blessed resurrection which is never to come.

By the woman's make, her plant has to be out of service three days in the month, and during a part of her pregnancy. These are times of discomfort, often of suffering. For fair and just compensation she has the high privilege of unlimited adultery all the other days of her life.

That is the law of God, as revealed in her make. What becomes of this high privilege? Does she live in free enjoyment of it? No. Nowhere in the whole world. She is robbed of it everywhere. Who does this? Man. Man's statutes -- if the Bible is the Word of God.

Now there you have a sample of man's "reasoning powers," as he calls them. He observes certain facts. For instance, that in all his life he never sees the day that he can satisfy one woman; also, that no woman ever sees the day that she can't overwork, and defeat, and put out of commission any ten masculine plants that can be put to bed to her.[**] He puts those strikingly suggestive and luminous facts together, and from them draws this astonishing conclusion: The Creator intended the woman to be restricted to one man.

So he concretes that singular conclusion into law, for good and all.

And he does it without consulting the woman, although she has a thousand times more at stake in the matter than he has. His procreative competency is limited to an average of a hundred exercises per year for fifty years, hers is good for three thousand a year for that whole time -- and as many years longer as she may live. Thus his life interest in the matter is five thousand refreshments, while hers is a hundred and fifty thousand; yet instead of fairly and honorably leaving the making of the law to the person who has an overwhelming interest at stake in it, this immeasurable hog, who has nothing at stake in it worth considering, makes it himself!

You have heretofore found out, by my teachings, that man is a fool; you are now aware that woman is a damned fool.

Now if you or any other really intelligent person were arranging the fairness and justices between man and woman, you would give the man one-fiftieth interest in one woman, and the woman a harem. Now wouldn't you? Necessarily. I give you my word, this creature with the decrepit candle has arranged it exactly the other way. Solomon, who was one of the Deity's favorites, had a copulation cabinet composed of seven hundred wives and three hundred concubines. To save his life he could not have kept two of these young creatures satisfactorily refreshed, even if he had had fifteen experts to help him. Necessarily almost the entire thousand had to go hungry years and years on a stretch. Conceive of a man hardhearted enough to look daily upon all that suffering and not be moved to mitigate it. He even wantonly added a sharp pang to that pathetic misery; for he kept within those women's sight, always, stalwart watchmen whose splendid masculine forms made the poor lassies' mouths water but who hadn't anything to solace a candlestick with, these gentry being eunuchs. A eunuch is a person whose candle has been put out. By art.[**]

From time to time, as I go along, I will take up a Biblical statute and show you that it always violates a law of God, and then is imported into the lawbooks of the nations, where it continues its violations. But those things will keep; there is no hurry.

Letter IX

The Ark continued its voyage, drifting around here and there and yonder, compassless and uncontrolled, the sport of the random winds and swirling currents. And the rain, the rain, the rain! It kept falling, pouring, drenching, flooding. No such rain had ever been seen before. Sixteen inches a day had been heard of, but that was nothing to this. This was a hundred and twenty inches a day -- ten feet! At this incredible rate it rained forty days and forty nights, and submerged every hill that was four hundred feet high. Then the heavens and even the angels went dry; no more water was to be had.

As a Universal flood it was a disappointment, but there had been heaps of Universal Floods before, as is witnessed by all the Bibles of all the nations, and this was as good as the best one.

At last the Ark soared aloft and came to rest on top of Mount Ararat, seventeen thousand feet above the valley, and its living freight got out and went down the mountain.

Noah planted a vineyard, and drank the wine and was overcome.

This person had been selected from all the populations because he was the best sample there was. He was to start the human race on a new basis. This was the new basis. The promise was bad. To go further with the experiment was to run a great and most unwise risk. Now was the time to do with these people what had been so judiciously done with the others -- drown them. Anybody but the Creator would have seen this. But he didn't see it. That is, maybe he didn't.

It is claimed that from the beginning of time he foresaw everything that would happen in the world. If that is true, he foresaw that Adam and Eve would eat the apple; that their posterity would be unendurable and have to be drowned; that Noah's posterity would in their turn be unendurable, and that by and by he would have to leave his throne in heaven and come down and be crucified to save that same tiresome human race again. The whole of it? No! A part of it? Yes. Now much of it? In each generation, for hundreds and hundreds of generations, a billion would die and all go to perdition except perhaps ten thousand out of the billion. The ten thousand would have to come from the little body of Christians, and only one in the hundred of that little body would stand any chance. None of them at all except such Roman Catholics as should have the luck to have a priest handy to sandpaper their souls at the last gasp, and here and there a presbyterian. No others savable. All the others damned. By the million.

Shall you grant that he foresaw all this? The pulpit grants it. It is the same as granting that in the matter of intellect the Deity is the Head Pauper of the Universe, and that in the matter of morals and character he is away down on the level of David.

Letter X

The two Testaments are interesting, each in its own way. The Old one gives us a picture of these people's Deity as he was before he got religion, the other one gives us a picture of him as he appeared afterward. The Old Testament is interested mainly in blood and sensuality. The New one in Salvation. Salvation by fire.

The first time the Deity came down to earth, he brought life and death; when he came the second time, he brought hell.

Life was not a valuable gift, but death was. Life was a fever-dream made up of joys embittered by sorrows, pleasure poisoned by pain, a dream that was a nightmare-confusion of spasmodic and fleeting delights, ecstasies, exultations, happinesses, interspersed with long-drawn miseries, griefs, perils, horrors, disappointments, defeats, humiliations, and despairs -- the heaviest curse devisable by divine ingenuity; but death was sweet, death was gentle, death was kind; death healed the bruised spirit and the broken heart, and gave them rest and forgetfulness; death was man's best friend; when man could endure life no longer, death came and set him free.

In time, the Deity perceived that death was a mistake; a mistake, in that it was insufficient; insufficient, for the reason that while it was an admirable agent for the inflicting of misery upon the survivor, it allowed the dead person himself to escape from all further persecution in the blessed refuge of the grave. This was not satisfactory. A way must be conceived to pursue the dead beyond the tomb.

The Deity pondered this matter during four thousand years unsuccessfully, but as soon as he came down to earth and became a Christian his mind cleared and he knew what to do. He invented hell, and proclaimed it.

Now here is a curious thing. It is believed by everybody that while he was in heaven he was stern, hard, resentful, jealous, and cruel; but that when he came down to earth and assumed the name Jesus Christ, he became the opposite of what he was before: that is to say, he became sweet, and gentle, merciful, forgiving, and all harshness disappeared from his nature and a deep and yearning love for his poor human children took its place. Whereas it was as Jesus Christ that he devised hell and proclaimed it!

Which is to say, that as the meek and gentle Savior he was a thousand billion times crueler than ever he was in the Old Testament -- oh, incomparably more atrocious than ever he was when he was at the very worst in those old days!

Meek and gentle? By and by we will examine this popular sarcasm by the light of the hell which he invented.

While it is true that the palm for malignity must be granted to Jesus, the inventor of hell, he was hard and ungentle enough for all godlike purposes even before he became a Christian. It does not appear that he ever stopped to reflect that he was to blame when a man went wrong, inasmuch as the man was merely acting in accordance with the disposition he had afflicted him with. No, he punished the man, instead of punishing himself. Moreover, the punishment usually oversized the offense. Often, too, it fell, not upon the doer of a misdeed, but upon somebody else -- a chief man, the head of a community, for instance.

And Israel abode in Shittim, and the people began to commit whoredom with the daughters of Moab.

And the Lord said unto Moses, Take all the heads of the people, and hang them up before the Lord against the Sun, that the fierce anger of the Lord may be turned away from Israel.

Does that look fair to you? It does not appear that the "heads of the people" got any of the adultery, yet it is they that are hanged, instead of "the people."

If it was fair and right in that day it would be fair and right today, for the pulpit maintains that God's justice is eternal and unchangeable; also that he is the Fountain of Morals, and that his morals are eternal and unchangeable. Very well, then, we must believe that if the people of New York should begin to commit whoredom with the daughters of New Jersey, it would be fair and right to set up a gallows in front of the city hall and hang the mayor and the sheriff and the judges and the archbishop on it, although they did not get any of it. It does not look right to me.

Moreover, you may be quite sure of one thing: it couldn't happen. These people would not allow it. They are better than their Bible. Nothing would happen here, except some lawsuits, for damages, if the incident couldn't be hushed up; and even down South they would not proceed against persons who did not get any of it; they would get a rope and hunt for the correspondents, and if they couldn't find them they would lynch a nigger.

Things have greatly improved since the Almighty's time, let the pulpit say what it may.

Will you examine the Deity's morals and disposition and conduct a little further? And will you remember that in the Sunday school the little children are urged to love the Almighty, and honor him, and praise him, and make him their model and try to be as like him as they can? Read:

1 And the Lord spake unto Moses, saying,
2 Avenge the children of Israel of the Midianites: afterward shalt thou be gathered unto thy people....
7 And they warred against the Midianites, as the Lord commanded Moses; and they slew all the males.
8 And they slew the kings of Midian, beside the rest of them that were slain; namely, Evi, and Rekem, and Zur, and Hur, and Reba, five kings of Midian: Balaam also the son of Beor they slew with the sword.
9 And the children of Israel took all the women of Midian captives, and their little ones, and took the spoil of all their cattle, and all their flocks, and all their goods.
10 And they burnt all their cities wherein they dwelt, and all their goodly castles, with fire.
11 And they took all the spoil, and all the prey, both of men and of beasts.

12 And they brought the captives, and the prey, and the spoil unto Moses, and Eleazar the priest, and unto the congregation of the children of Israel, unto the camp at the plains of Moab, which are by Jordan near Jericho.

13 And Moses, and Eleazar the priest, and all the princes of the congregation, went forth to meet them without the camp.

14 And Moses was wroth with the officers of the host, with the captains over thousands, and captains over hundreds, which came from the battle.

15 And Moses said unto them, Have ye saved all the women alive?

16 Behold, these caused the children of Israel, through the counsel of Balaam, to commit trespass against the Lord in the matter of Peor, and there was a plague among the congregation of the Lord.

17 Now therefore kill every male among the little ones, and kill every woman that hath known man by lying with him.

18 But all the women children, that have not known a man by lying with him, keep alive for yourselves.

19 And do ye abide without the camp seven days: whosoever hath killed any person, and whosoever hath touched any slain, purify both yourselves and your captives on the third day, and on the seventh day.

20 And purify all your raiment, and all that is made of skins, and all work of goats' hair, and all things made of wood.

21 And Eleazar the priest said unto the men of war which went to the battle, This is the ordinance of the law which the Lord commanded Moses....

25 And the Lord spake unto Moses, saying,

26 Take the sum of the prey that was taken, both of man and of beast, thou, and Eleazar the priest, and the chief fathers of the congregation:

27 And divide the prey into two parts; between them that took the war upon them, who went out to battle, and between all the congregation:

28 And levy a tribute unto the Lord of the men of war which went out to battle....

31 And Moses and Eleazar the priest did as the Lord commanded Moses.

32 And the booty, being the rest of the prey which the men of war had caught, was six hundred thousand and seventy thousand and five thousand sheep,

33 And threescore and twelve thousand beeves,

34 And threescore and one thousand asses,

35 And thirty and two thousand persons in all, of woman that had not known man by lying with him....

40 And the persons were sixteen thousand; of which the Lord's tribute was thirty and two persons.

41 And Moses gave the tribute, which was the Lord's heave offering, unto Eleazar the priest, as the Lord commanded Moses....

47 Even of the children of Israel's half, Moses took one portion of fifty, both of man and of beast, and gave them unto the Levites, which kept the charge of the tabernacle of the Lord; as the Lord commanded Moses.

10 When thou comest nigh unto a city to fight against it, then proclaim peace unto it....

13 And when the Lord thy God hath delivered it into thine hands, thou shalt smite every male thereof with the edge of the sword:

14 But the women, and the little ones, and the cattle, and all that is in the city, even all the spoil thereof, shalt thou take unto thyself; and thou shalt eat the spoil of thine enemies, which the Lord thy God hath given thee.

15 Thus shalt thou do unto all the cities which are very far off from thee, which are not of the cities of these nations.

16 But of the cities of these people, which the Lord thy God doth give thee for an inheritance, thou shalt save alive nothing that breatheth:

The Biblical law says: "Thou shalt not kill."

The law of God, planted in the heart of man at his birth, says: "Thou shalt kill."

The chapter I have quoted shows you that the book-statute is once more a failure. It cannot set aside the more powerful law of nature.

According to the belief of these people, it was God himself who said: "Thou shalt not kill."

Then it is plain that he cannot keep his own commandments.

He killed all those people -- every male.

They had offended the Deity in some way. We know what the offense was, without looking; that is to say, we know it was a trifle; some small thing that no one but a god would attach any importance to. It is more than likely that a Midianite had been duplicating the conduct of one Onan, who was commanded to "go into his brother's wife" -- which he did; but instead of finishing, "he spilled it on the ground." The Lord slew Onan for that, for the lord could never abide indelicacy. The Lord slew Onan, and to this day the Christian world cannot understand why he stopped with Onan, instead of slaying all the inhabitants for three hundred miles around -- they being innocent of offense, and therefore the very ones he would usually slay. For that had always been his idea of fair dealing. If he had had a motto, it would have read, "Let no innocent person escape."

You remember what he did in the time of the flood. There were multitudes and multitudes of tiny little children, and he knew they had never done him any harm; but their relations had, and that was enough for him: he saw the waters rise toward their screaming lips, he saw the wild terror in their eyes, he saw that agony of appeal in the mothers' faces which would have touched any heart but his, but he was after the guiltless particularly, than he drowned those poor little chaps.

And you will remember that in the case of Adam's posterity all the billions are innocent -- none of them had a share in his offense, but the Deity holds them guilty to this day. None gets off, except by acknowledging that guilt -- no cheaper lie will answer.

Some Midianite must have repeated Onan's act, and brought that dire disaster upon his nation. If that was not the indelicacy that outraged the feelings of the Deity, then I know what it was: some Midianite had been pissing against the wall. I am sure of it, for that was an impropriety which the Source of all Etiquette never could stand. A person could piss against a tree, he could piss on his mother, he could piss on his own breeches, and get off, but he must not piss against the wall -- that would be going quite too far. The origin of the divine prejudice against this humble crime is not stated; but we know that the prejudice was very strong -- so strong that nothing but a wholesale massacre of the people inhabiting the region where the wall was defiled could satisfy the Deity.

Take the case of Jeroboam. "I will cut off from Jeroboam him that pisseth against the wall." It was done. And not only was the man that did it cut off, but everybody else.

The same with the house of Baasha: everybody was exterminated, kinsfolks, friends, and all, leaving "not one that pisseth against a wall."

In the case of Jeroboam you have a striking instance of the Deity's custom of not limiting his punishments to the guilty; the innocent are included. Even the "remnant" of that unhappy house was removed, even "as a man taketh away dung, till it be all gone." That includes the women, the young maids, and the little girls. All innocent, for they couldn't piss against a wall. Nobody of that sex can. None but members of the other sex can achieve that feat.

A curious prejudice. And it still exists. Protestant parents still keep the Bible handy in the house, so that the children can study it, and one of the first things the little boys and girls learn is to be righteous and holy and not piss against the wall. They study those passages more than they study any others, except those which incite to masturbation. Those they hunt out and study in private. No Protestant child exists who does not masturbate. That art is the earliest accomplishment his religion confers upon him. Also the earliest her religion confers upon her.

The Bible has this advantage over all other books that teach refinement and good manners: that it goes to the child. It goes to the mind at its most impressible and receptive age -- the others have to wait.

"Thou shalt have a paddle upon thy weapon; and it shall be, when thou wilt ease thyself abroad, thou shalt dig therewith, and shalt turn back and cover that which cometh from thee."

That rule was made in the old days because "The Lord thy God walketh in the midst of thy camp."

It is probably not worthwhile to try to find out, for certain, why the Midianites were exterminated. We can only be sure that it was for no large offense; for the cases of Adam, and the Flood, and the defilers of the wall teach us that much. A Midianite may have left his paddle at home and thus brought on the trouble. However, it is no matter. The main thing is the trouble itself, and the morals of one kind and another that it offers for the instruction and elevation of the Christian of today.

God wrote upon the tables of stone: "Thou shalt not kill," Also: "Thou shalt not commit adultery."

Paul, speaking by the divine voice, advised against sexual intercourse altogether. A great change from the divine view as it existed at the time of the Midianite incident.

Letter XI

Human history in all ages is red with blood, and bitter with hate, and stained with cruelties; but not since Biblical times have these features been without a limit of some kind. Even the Church, which is credited with having spilt more innocent blood, since the beginning of its supremacy, than all the political wars put together have spilt, has observed a limit. A sort of limit. But you notice that when the Lord God of Heaven and Earth, adored Father of Man, goes to war, there is no limit. He is totally without mercy -- he, who is called the Fountain of Mercy. He slays, slays, slays! All the men, all the beasts, all the boys, all the babies; also all the women and all the girls, except those that have not been deflowered.

He makes no distinction between innocent and guilty. The babies were innocent, the beasts were innocent, many of the men, many of the women, many of the boys, many of the girls were innocent, yet they had to suffer with the guilty. What the insane Father required was blood and misery; he was indifferent as to who furnished it.

The heaviest punishment of all was meted out to persons who could not by any possibility have deserved so horrible a fate -- the 32,000 virgins. Their naked privacies were probed, to make sure that they still possessed the hymen unruptured; after this humiliation they were sent away from the land that had been their home, to be sold into slavery; the worst of slaveries and the shamefulest, the slavery of prostitution; bed-slavery, to excite lust, and satisfy it with their bodies; slavery to any buyer, be he gentleman or be he a coarse and filthy ruffian.

It was the Father that inflicted this ferocious and undeserved punishment upon those bereaved and friendless virgins, whose parents and kindred he had slaughtered before their eyes. And were they praying to him for pity and rescue, meantime? Without a doubt of it.

These virgins were "spoil" plunder, booty. He claimed his share and got it. What use had he for virgins? Examine his later history and you will know.

His priests got a share of the virgins, too. What use could priests make of virgins? The private history of the Roman Catholic confessional can answer that question for you. The confessional's chief amusement has been seduction -- in all the ages of the Church. Père Hyacinth testifies that of a hundred priests confessed by him, ninety-nine had used the confessional effectively for the seduction of married women and young girls.

One priest confessed that of nine hundred girls and women whom he had served as father and confessor in his time, none had escaped his lecherous embrace but he elderly and the homely. The official list of questions which the priest is required to ask will overmasteringly excite any woman who is not a paralytic.

There is nothing in either savage or civilized history that is more utterly complete, more remorselessly sweeping than the Father of Mercy's campaign among the Midianites. The official report does not furnish the incidents, episodes, and minor details, it deals only in information in masses: all the virgins, all the men, all the babies, all "creatures that breathe," all houses, all cities; it gives you just one vast picture, spread abroad here and there and yonder, as far as eye can reach, of charred ruin and storm-swept desolation; your imagination adds a brooding stillness, an awful hush -- the hush of death. But of course there were incidents. Where shall we get them?

Out of history of yesterday's date. Out of history made by the red Indian of America. He has duplicated God's work, and done it in the very spirit of God. In 1862 the Indians in Minnesota, having been deeply wronged and treacherously treated by the government of the United States, rose against the white settlers and massacred them; massacred all they could lay their hands upon, sparing neither age nor sex. Consider this incident:

Twelve Indians broke into a farmhouse at daybreak and captured the family. It consisted of the farmer and his wife and four daughters, the youngest aged fourteen and the eldest eighteen. They crucified the parents; that is to say, they stood them stark naked against the wall of the living room and nailed their hands to the wall. Then they stripped the daughters bare, stretched them upon the floor in front of their parents, and repeatedly ravished them. Finally they crucified the girls against the wall opposite this parents, and cut off their noses and their breasts. They also -- but I will not go into that. There is a limit. There are indignities so atrocious that the pen cannot write them. One member of that poor crucified family -- the father -- was still alive when help came two days later.

Now you have one incident of the Minnesota massacre. I could give you fifty. They would cover all the different kinds of cruelty the brutal human talent has ever invented.

And now you know, by these sure indications, what happened under the personal direction of the Father of Mercies in his Midianite campaign. The Minnesota campaign was merely a duplicate of the Midianite raid. Nothing happened in the one that didn't happen in the other.

No, that is not strictly true. The Indian was more merciful than was the Father of Mercies. He sold no virgins into slavery to minister to the lusts of the murderers of their kindred while their sad lives might last; he raped them, then charitably made their subsequent sufferings brief, ending them with the precious gift of death. He burned some of the houses, but not all of them. He carried out innocent dumb brutes, but he took the lives of none.

Would you expect this same conscienceless God, this moral bankrupt, to become a teacher of morals; of gentleness; of meekness; of righteousness; of purity? It looks impossible, extravagant; but listen to him. These are his own words:

Blessed are the poor in spirit, for theirs is the kingdom of heaven.
Blessed are they that mourn, for they shall be comforted.
Blessed are the meek, for they shall inherit the earth.

Blessed are they which do hunger and thirst after righteousness, for they shall be filled.

Blessed are the merciful, for they shall obtain mercy.

Blessed are the pure in heart, for they shall see God.

Blessed are the peacemakers, for they shall be called the children of God.

Blessed are they which are persecuted for righteousness' sake, for theirs is the kingdom of heaven.

Blessed are ye, when men shall revile you, and persecute you, and say all manner of evil against you falsely, for my sake.

The mouth that uttered these immense sarcasms, these giant hypocrisies, is the very same that ordered the wholesale massacre of the Midianitish men and babies and cattle; the wholesale destruction of house and city; the wholesale banishment of the virgins into a filthy and unspeakable slavery. This is the same person who brought upon the Midianites the fiendish cruelties which were repeated by the red Indians, detail by detail, in Minnesota eighteen centuries later. The Midianite episode filled him with joy. So did the Minnesota one, or he would have prevented it.

The Beatitudes and the quoted chapters from Numbers and Deuteronomy ought always to be read from the pulpit together; then the congregation would get an all-round view of Our Father in Heaven. Yet not in a single instance have I ever known a clergyman to do this.

Notes:

*NOTE: It takes the light of the nearest star (61 Cygni) three and a half years to come to the earth, traveling at the rate of 186,000 miles per second. Arcturus had been shining 200 years before it was visible from the earth. Remoter stars gradually became visible after thousands and thousands of years. -- The Editor [M. T.]

*NOTE: In the Sandwich Islands in 1866 a buxom royal princess died. Occupying a place of distinguished honor at her funeral were thirty-six splendidly built young native men. In a laudatory song which celebrated the various merits, achievements and accomplishments of the late princess those thirty-six stallions were called her harem, and the song said it had been her pride and boast that she kept the whole of them busy, and that several times it had happened that more than one of them had been able to charge overtime. [M.T.]

*NOTE: I purpose publishing these Letters here in the world before I return to you. Two editions. One, unedited, for Bible readers and their children; the other, expurgated, for persons of refinement. [M.T.]

Forgotten Books

Read these similar books for free at forgottenbooks.org:

Clarence Darrow on Religion

Read or order online at:

www.forgottenbooks.org
or
www.amazon.com

1217224R0

Printed in Germany by
Amazon Distribution
GmbH, Leipzig